Anywhere But Here

ANYWHERE

Black Intellectuals in the Atlantic World and Beyond

BUT HERE

Edited by

Kendahl Radcliffe, Jennifer Scott, and Anja Werner

University Press of Mississippi / Jackson

www.upress.state.ms.us

The University Press of Mississippi is a member
of the Association of American University Presses.

First printing 2015
∞
Library of Congress Cataloging-in-Publication Data

Anywhere but here : Black intellectuals in the Atlantic world and beyond /
edited by Kendahl Radcliffe, Jennifer Scott, and Anja Werner.
pages cm
Includes bibliographical references and index.
ISBN 978-1-62846-155-8 (cloth : alkaline paper) —ISBN 978-1-62846-156-5 (ebook)
1. Blacks—Intellectual life. 2. African Americans—Intellectual life. 3. African diaspora—
History. 4. America—Relations—Africa. 5. Africa—Relations—America. 6. Transnationalism—History. I. Radcliffe, Kendahl. II. Scott, Jennifer, 1967- III. Werner, Anja.
CB235.A59 2015
305.896'073—dc23   2014024118

British Library Cataloging-in-Publication Data available

Contents

I. REORDERING WORLDVIEWS: REBELLIOUS THINKERS, POETS, WRITERS, AND POLITICAL ARCHITECTS

II. CRAFTING CONNECTIONS: STRATEGIC AND IDEOLOGICAL ALLIANCES

Acknowledgments

The editors would like to thank the University Press of Mississippi, and particularly Craig Gill and Katie Keene, for their support and good spirits throughout the preparation and publication of this book. In addition, they would like to thank the following:

Loving thanks go to my parents, Kenneth and Shirley Radcliffe, who instilled in me a deep understanding of the phrase "sense of history, sense of self." To my sister Lisa Radcliffe—a great source of support as I edited this very manuscript while visiting her during the summer of 2013, the hottest I've ever experienced in New York City. To the University of California, Los Angeles, African American and Women Studies Departments, and California State University, Fullerton, Ethnic Studies Program, all of whom provided the opportunity over the years to design both graduate and undergraduate courses that explored many of the themes addressed in this book. Individual shout-outs go to my colleagues Alexandro Gradilla, chair of the African American Studies Department, California State University, Fullerton; Scot Brown, Department of History, University of California, Los Angeles; and all of my colleagues at El Camino College Compton Center, Social and Behavioral Sciences for their friendship and collegial support. A special thanks to my late friend Clyde Woods, University of California, Santa Barbara; my mentor Marc Primus of Atlanta, Georgia; and my son, Elijah Radcliffe Davis. Elijah—I dedicate this book to you.

Kendahl Radcliffe

I am deeply grateful to all of the people who have been crucial in my development as an intellectual. In particular, I want to thank my mentors from the University of California, Los Angeles in the Afro-American Studies and History Departments, namely Brenda Stevenson, Ruth Gilmore, and the late Clyde Woods, who first nurtured my graduate-level academic interests in black intellectualism. I am also appreciative of my colleagues and students at the New School for Public Engagement, New York, who allowed me, for over thirteen years, to develop historically inclusive courses within a thriving intellectual community. In my museum and public history work, I must acknowledge the historian friends and colleagues who have been wonderful advocates and partners in reclaiming "lost histories": Joan Geismar, Leslie Harris, Willard Jenkins, William Loren Katz, Chris Moore, Carla Peterson, Gunja Sengupta, Judith Wellman, and Deborah Willis. This includes the next generation of history intellectuals I had the pleasure of working with through Weeksville Heritage Center: Megan Goins-Diouf, Kaitlyn Greenidge, LaShaya Howie, Joyce LeeAnn Joseph, Alexsandra Mitchell, Kristina Nazimova, and Ardra Whitney. Last, I am forever indebted to my family in New Orleans and California, especially my parents, who taught me more than anyone else the importance of becoming a global citizen and student of the Diaspora.

Jennifer Scott

I am particularly thankful to Joel Dark and his students at Tennessee State University (TSU) in Nashville. Our conversations, especially in connection with 2008 and 2014 study tours to Germany, got me started thinking more intensely about black perspectives and histories in global contexts. It was furthermore particularly rewarding for me to make friends among TSU art students and professors and to meet them again during black art exhibits in Berlin years later. I am also deeply grateful to the Vanderbilt University Black Cultural Center, above all its director, Frank E. Dobson Jr., for including me during many mind-broadening events. My friends Sabine Schlunk, John R. Jones, and Archana Narasanna were my colorful "Nashville family" far away from home while this book project began taking shape. Their friendship continues to inspire me. Last but not least, this project could not have been finished without the love and support of my husband, fellow-historian Oliver Werner. He provided not just constructive professional feedback but, together with our daughter, Frieda, delightful distraction from serious study.

Anja Werner

Anywhere But Here

Introduction: The Black Atlantic Revisited

Methodological Considerations

Kendahl Radcliffe, Jennifer Scott, and Anja Werner

A Fresh Look at the Atlantic World

The year 2013 marked the twentieth anniversary of Paul Gilroy's landmark work, *The Black Atlantic: Modernity and Double Consciousness*.[1] Since Gilroy's groundbreaking 1993 publication, scholars have continued to refine their methodologies so as to deepen their understanding of the creation of knowledge across the African Diaspora.[2] Kim Butler makes the argument that "Diasporan study be defined not by the group itself but by the research question asked."[3] This enables us to understand a multitude of conditions and relationships, which have given rise to the Diaspora, allowing us to make new, interesting, and otherwise unseen connections across disparate groups or geographical boundaries. Existing research that reflects these newer and more expansive approaches reveals that the impact of the African Diaspora on the production and circulation of ideas has been far more extensive, unwavering, and fluid than initially perceived.

Although praised, Gilroy has also been critiqued, in particular for asserting narrow definitions of the Black Atlantic, including a limited selection of relevant historical figures. While these criticisms have some validity, they fall short in their perception that a hegemonic viewpoint is dictating the scholarship. Anna Lisa Oboe and Anna Scacchi reflect such a bias when, referencing Pierre Bourdieu and Loïc Wacquant, they argue that the concept of the "Black Atlantic that is circulating in the academic world is largely a product of American research and of its 'version' of Gilroy's proposition."[4] In their view, "the universalization of the (black) American experience appears as just another instance of U.S. imperialism and its drive to turn the globe into 'McWorld.'"[5] It is, however, highly simplistic to reduce the collective experiences within the

African Diaspora to merely an extension of U.S.-imposed hegemonic thinking that, in this instance, is supposedly carried by black Americans. This sim-
plification fails to acknowledge the diversity of experiences throughout the
African Diaspora and the range of empowered choices that people have made
and continue to make within, against, or in conjunction with their nonideal
circumstances.

Diaspora studies have repeatedly demonstrated that African Americans
are far from being homogenous.[6] A study of hybridity and of hybrids in relation to the African Diaspora reveals the range of intellectual approaches
employed by people of African descent, as they interacted with different cultures and traveled to various locations. Jan Nederveen Piertse defines hybridity as "the ways in which forms become separated from existing practices and
recombine with new forms and practices."[7] He suggests a "politics of hybridity" in relation to the ways in which differences may be encountered or val-
ued. Identifying a range of hybridities, Piertse includes those that reproduce
hegemonies (an "assimilationist hybridity") alongside those that reconfigure
them (a "destabilizing hybridity"), the latter containing the most potential by
the subject, when positioned in the "interstices," for enacting change and a
challenge to the existing order. Thus framing black identity as any kind of
a homogenous paradigm not only erases the various aspects that make up
hybridity, it also glosses over complicated power relationships.

The claim that American imperialism directs Black Diaspora studies illus-
trates some of the limited approaches in analyzing collective black experiences.
Various experiences are treated as isolated incidents in history—disconnected
from one another—and restricted to narrow geographies and time frames.
This is not to say that previous approaches stymied the study of the Black
Atlantic. Far to the contrary: they have uncovered the impact of the Middle
Passage on both sides of the Atlantic; they have de-emphasized Eurocentric
frameworks that might demean or ignore black agency and black diversity
altogether; they have identified possible cultural or ethnic retentions; and, last
but not least, they have explored cultural change, adaptations, and resistance.

Current scholarship, especially within the past ten years, embraces multifaceted interpretations of "the" black experience. For instance, in his essay
"Black Transnationalism, Africana Studies, and the 21st Century," Michael
George Hanchard places hybridity into a contemporary context of transnational networks that is rooted not only in the "increased immigration to
the United States from other parts of the Americas and Africa"[8] but also in
"the increased fluidity of movement of populations, technologies and information." As a result, "African, Afro-Caribbean and U.S. African Americans
(not to mention people of African descent in other parts of the world) have

increasingly engaged in dialogue concerning political, cultural, and economic cooperation that transcends the boundaries of national and regional distinctions while underscoring the tensions and differences between them."

For Hanchard, black American hybridity should be positioned not only within a historical continuum but also within an international context; given the transnational face of many black urban communities in the United States, Caribbean, South America, Europe, and Africa, hybridity is very much about situating knowledge within the relationships between the local and the global. The intertwined local and global dimensions of the Black Diaspora have had a profound impact on discourses within the academy in the United States and elsewhere; "viewed historically, Africana and African American studies provides an opportunity to connect contemporary globalization to its antecedents in global history." As a consequence, Hanchard points out, "The middle passage and racial slavery generated two distinct but deeply intertwined modes of globalization affecting African and African-derived populations: The circulation and dissemination of ideologies of race and racism and the scattering of various African peoples, technologies, cosmological systems and cultural practices throughout the world. The middle passage, symbol of the forced migration of peoples across the Atlantic and their enslaved labor in multiple colonial and imperial societies, constitutes a moment of globalization." Likewise, "The dissemination of racist ideologies justifying African enslavement, from the 16th century onward was also made transnational during this period." Both processes "were distinct from the slave trade across the Indian Ocean or connections between peoples from the African continent prior to the middle passage because they did not entail racialization processes that situated African descended subjects at or near the bottom of a hierarchy of humanity."

New and broader directions in the study of the African Diaspora in a globalized context, as articulated by Hanchard, can illuminate important and previously overlooked distinctions and interconnections between expanded areas—both geographical and topical: between Atlantic and Indian Ocean regions; between the movement of people versus the distribution of racial and racist ideologies. This is important, as the study of African Diasporan communities often forces one to choose between cultural retention and cultural assimilation, between the survival of heritage and its destruction, between agency and victimization. In other words, one must decide whether the history of enslavement primarily severed all evidence or ties to an African past (rather, pasts) or if, in spite of its brutality, it mainly facilitated a preservation of African identities and collective practices.

A focus on black intellectualism dissolves these binary oppositions—as Paul Gilroy, W. E. B. DuBois, and others have attempted to do in their explorations of "double consciousness" and other (intellectual) ways in which people of African descent have proactively negotiated their heritage, past, and present in the face of external conditions of hardship and change.[9] Studies on black intellectualism create a space for understanding self-determined conscious actions and creative choices, without ignoring historical and systemic obstacles of inequality, discrimination, violence, enslavement, misfortune, or other circumstances that may victimize. New literature focusing on the intellectualism of the Black Atlantic and beyond can now go further to make more connections across time and space and to show how these inventive connections and collaborations are an inherent part of the process of facing uncertainty, movement, and change. What, for example, connects the eighteenth-century Igbo author Olaudah Equiano with 1940s literary figure Richard Wright; nineteenth-century expatriate anthropologist Anténor Firmin with 1960s Haitian émigrés to the Congo; Japanese Pan-Asianists and Southern Hemisphere Aboriginal activists with Jamaican-born Marcus Garvey; and Angela Davis with artists of the British Black Arts Movement, Ingrid Pollard and Zarina Bhimji? They are all part of a mapping that reaches across and beyond geographical, historical, and ideological boundaries typically associated with the Black Atlantic. They reflect accounts of individuals and communities that are equally united in their will to seek out better realities, often, as our title suggests, "anywhere but here."

Anywhere But Here: Black Intellectuals in the Atlantic World and Beyond brings together scholarship on the cross-cultural experiences of intellectuals of African descent since the nineteenth century, while expanding traditional categories of both the Black Atlantic and the "intellectual." Our intent with this book is not to dismantle Gilroy's thesis, but to embrace and further it, like an octopus with many tentacles, as the volume's title indicates: to venture "beyond" the traditional organization and symbolism of the Black Atlantic.

From a review of existing literature, it becomes clear that the idea of an Atlantic World is defined, for the most part, in unambiguous terms: first, geographically synonymous with the economic triangle in which enslaved Africans figure as passive commodities; second, historically associated almost exclusively with (or overshadowed by) the period of the transatlantic slave trade—basically from Christopher Columbus's voyage to the abolition of slavery in all of the Americas; and third, ideologically emphasizing traditional ideas of intellectualism, given the constraints of enslavement.[10]

The goal of this volume is to look at the Black Atlantic World (and beyond), rather, as a space in which people of African descent—enslaved or free—were and continue to be active agents in processes of cultural, intellectual, and social transformation. Slavery, of course, cannot and should not be deleted from the discourse; neither should it serve as the defining element in comprehending experiences of black intellectualism. Black intellectualism and the idea of a Black Atlantic cannot be confined to a particular time frame. Historical as well as contemporary figures participate in these significant intercultural exchanges. Linking their experiences across time uncovers for us what is at the heart of black intellectualism—a self-determination that, at once, transcends time or space and unites a diversity of black experiences.

Hence this volume illustrates how, primarily, in the nineteenth and twentieth centuries, people of African descent have moved across space to broaden their minds, to seek inspiration and knowledge, to become autonomous, and to find allies in order to expose and fight against racial discrimination at home and abroad, proceeding as they saw necessary. *Anywhere But Here* represents the complex and omnipresent intellectual, spiritual, and physical exchanges by agents of the African Diaspora who did whatever necessary to improve their existing conditions. This often included crossing oceans, seas, and rivers to assert a level of autonomy, relief, alliance, and protest. In some instances, the Atlantic is the starting point; in others, it is not. The starting point may be the Amazon, the Congo, the Orinoco, the Mississippi, the Elbe, or the Yangtze.

Expanding the idea of the Black Atlantic beyond its traditional geographical boundaries to grasp black experiences more thoroughly allows us, furthermore, to include the Pacific and Indian Oceans, and, by extension, other lesser-known regions of the Southern Hemisphere and to include them in a self-determined context. How, for example, does the Pacific World figure into Black Atlantic discussions of anti-imperialism, civil rights movements, and histories of decolonization? The idea and meaning of a "Pacific World" appear to be older than the academic discussion of an Atlantic World and might well have inspired the latter.[11] The numerous peoples of the Pacific World have rich and long-standing cultural histories and interactions with the world that cannot be reduced to mere European interests, influences, and presence.[12]

This volume is an opportunity to explore the self-determining and autonomous views of lesser-known Black Diasporic experiences within and beyond the Atlantic, and to identify exchanges and connections across this nontraditional space. As we began acquiring contributions for this volume, we gained a glimpse of how closely the intellectual histories of black people are linked to those of Australian, Asian, South Asian, and South American peoples, to list just a few, in fighting against racial prejudices, naturally questioning, even subverting, the supposed superiority of European cultures. These essays reflect the local and the global, resistance and agency, and the ideological shifts that occur within time and space.

Broadening the Idea of the Black Intellectual

In this volume, the emphasis is not so much on the movement of ideas and culture as it is on the ways in which people have "shrewdly" facilitated that movement for their own designs. In our view, black intellectuals are characterized by an ability to reflect, engage, and assert a type of agency by which they have left an indelible mark. They were observant, deliberate, and articulate of their own experiences.[13] Their work gives us insight into the elaborate, and sometimes contradictory, processes of self-determination, identity formation, cultural preservation, and political consciousness. Our definition allows us to include individuals who may not have seen themselves as intellectuals but were eager to articulate new ways of seeing and understanding their current condition. It allows us to include accounts of individuals who may have traveled for escape, adventure, understanding, and personal fulfillment—that is to say, by choice or, most likely, as their best choice.

As black intellectuals engaged in an exchange of ideas with other African-rooted traditions and (non-African) communities elsewhere in the world, many began to reassess the cause-and-effect factors of the social, cultural, and technological challenges of their time. As a result of these exchanges, they formulated unique worldviews that reflected intellectual perspectives and challenged more Eurocentric worldviews. This volume brings together a number of specific experiences rather than makes broad assumptions about a collective experience.

A new, multilayered collective image of the Black Atlantic is bound to emerge from individual accounts if we look for connecting points that may be found in experiences of black intellectuals across the globe and at different moments in the past. Mere geographical and chronological analyses do not suffice to understand the interconnectedness of people moving within and outside the realm of Eurocentric knowledge. In his insightful essay on new ways of looking at the Black Atlantic by studying individual stories, Gunvor Simonson observes that there has been a shift from focusing on African survivals to concrete cultural transfers from Africa to the Americas. Such transfers can best be illustrated by looking at personal experiences rather than by jumping to broad conclusions about African identities in the "New World" based on descriptive evidence.[14] We do not claim that the individuals represented in this volume are exemplary of a collective experience, but we do suggest that their stories reflect, potentially, a diversity of experiences and perspectives that better contribute to an understanding of a broader picture. How did these individuals fashion an understanding of their place in the larger world and within a collective identity? In what ways do they diverge from a collective experience? The latter question does not pose a threat to an African Diasporic collective, but instead affirms the humanity and the diversity of the subjects we explore.

At the basis of the creation of their worldviews is the movement and transfer of ideas, a transmission that does not happen in isolation. No thinker appears "out of the blue"—that is, no individual episode in the history of ideas can stand on its own without being connected to earlier and later developments. This idea also implies that the Black Atlantic need not be forever described as an interaction in a simple black/white/European context; nor should it be simply observed from an East/West perspective. In fact, as mentioned above, the study of the Pacific World is vital, as well, to thoroughly comprehend the movement of ideas within the realm of the Atlantic—for example, the mutual admiration between Marcus Garvey and the Pan-Asianists in the early twentieth century.

The journeys of interest to this project are nonlinear—in fact, spiral (rather than circular): black people and their ideas moved back and forth between different continental spaces, but never quite returned to the place they had left behind, either physically or intellectually or both. Major events and general upheaval in both accessible and remote corners of the world left an imprint on the intensity and direction of journeys of black intellectuals in the Atlantic World and beyond.

As a result of broadening the category of the Black Atlantic intellectual, this collection of essays is not organized geographically or historically by era; instead, we have arranged the articles into three sections, which highlight the rationale, motivations, and characteristics that connect a certain set of "agents," thinkers, and intellectuals: Reordering Worldviews: Rebellious Thinkers, Poets, Writers, and Political Architects; Crafting Connections: Strategic and Ideological Alliances; and Cultural Mastery in Foreign Spaces: Evolving Visions of Home and Identity. For traditional African Diaspora scholars, our groupings may look odd at first glance. However, they are intentionally organized to expand categories and to suggest other patterns at play that have united individuals and communities across the African Diaspora. They highlight at times unlikely similarities in the self-determined stories of individuals, who from their often marginalized position challenged the status quo, created strategic (and unexpected) international alliances, cultivated expertise and cultural competency abroad in places that were unfamiliar to them, and crafted (physical and intellectual) spaces where their self-expression and dignity could thrive.

Reordering Worldviews: Rebellious Thinkers, Poets, Writers, and Political Architects

The first section is a reflection of individual challenges to the prevailing paradigms of Enlightenment, scientific racism, and imperialist rhetoric, which have often been cited as pillars of modernity. Douglas W. Leonard's essay, "Writing Against the Grain: Anténor Firmin and the Refutation of Nineteenth-Century European Race Science," places the Haitian expatriate and statesman in square opposition to the rising tide of the racism that was inherent in the widely accepted perspective of Arthur de Gobineau. Firmin challenged the notion of racial hierarchy perpetuated by such works as Gobineau's *Essai sur l'inégalité des races humaines* (1853),[15] which would thrive as one of the foundational bases for what would become the development of anthropological sciences in the academy.[16] Recognizing it for what it was—that is, a treatise for the justification of slavery and imperialism under the guise of science—Firmin took on Gobineau's pseudoscience in his own work *De l'égalité des races humaines* and boldly challenged the latter's presumptive assessment and scientific authority.[17]

A similarly subversive nineteenth-century black intellectual was José da Natividade Saldanha, the Afro-Brazilian lawyer, poet, and, in 1824, secretary of the revolutionary government during the confederation of the Quator, who was viewed by some as a "black Jacobin." A man of contradictions whose call for reconciliation, according to Amy Caldwell de Farias, emphasized "the virtuous characteristics of the Brazilian 'mestizos,'" his very existence and rise to political prominence as an intellectual challenged the predominant racial order. His own writings were influenced by his travels to North and South America, which also had a profound impact on his attempts to create a poetic art form that would defy, according to Caldwell de Farias, the "hegemonic power of the new Brazilian monarchy." Or did it? In "Activist in Exile: José da Natividade Saldanha, Free Man of Color in the Tropical Atlantic," Caldwell de Farias examines the fascinating polemics of racial consciousness in the life of a politician and poet struggling to confront conventional relationships of power.

In the last essay in this section, "Developmentalism, Tanzania, and the Arusha Declaration: Perspectives of an Observing Participant," Ikaweba Bunting questions existing structures of power through an in-depth exploration of the Arusha Declaration of 1967, a turning point in the history of Tanzania and indeed for Africa as a whole. The Arusha Declaration, brainchild of the late Tanzanian leader Julius Nyerere, was an Africa-centered response to the model of developmentalism that Western governments were pushing onto poor and newly independent non-European nations. A son of the Diaspora and *Mrejajiji* (returnee), as well as an active participant in and organizer of national development programs, Bunting offers an eyewitness account of the tension between these two approaches: one reflects an indigenous cultural framework and—according to the author—a human-centered sociocultural approach; the other is imposed from outside and rooted in the classical development paradigm reliant on the dictates of the International Monetary Fund (IMF) and World Bank fostering a continued cyle of interventionism and dependence.

Crafting Connections: Strategic and Ideological Alliances

The second section explores connections between people of African descent who fit our broad definition of black intellectuals and what appear to be allies, either because of geographical separation or because of underlying ideologies that seem contradictory to black objectives. Alliances between Garveyites and Australian Aboriginal nationalists, between Pan-Africanists and Japanese Pan-Asianists, and between African American civil rights leaders and East German Communists were nonetheless pursued or explored. To what extent were these exchanges or relationships mutually beneficial or reciprocal? In which ways were they strategic?

The spread of Marcus Garvey's ideas has already been thoroughly explored as it relates to peoples of African descent on both sides of the Atlantic. From as far north as Canada to as far as South Africa, the message was carried by merchant seamen into ports and small villages throughout the Diaspora and beyond. Marcus Garvey and his charismatic message in life and in death spread like wildfire. However, in this section we have two groundbreaking essays that focus on Garvey, his movement, and his profound influence on efforts for self-determination far beyond the Atlantic Ocean.

Both essays explore aspects of Garveyism in the Pacific World. In the first, "Garvey in Oz: The International Black Influence on Australian Aboriginal Political Activism," John Maynard brings to light the power of a historic exchange between West Indian merchant marines and the politically radical Aboriginal communities they engaged with in regard to Garvey's philosophy. A universal recognition of their desire to "shake the yoke" set the powerful stage for the establishment of a Universal Negro Improvement Association

(UNIA) headquarters in Sydney. A precondition for this exchange was the fact that Aboriginal leaders such as Fred Maynard, who worked on the waterfront during the 1920s, acquired a knowledge of the writings of African American intellectuals. Alongside correspondence with black leaders, such knowledge formed a powerful basis of future Aboriginal political activism and organizations such as the Australian Aboriginal Progressive Association (AAPA).

The second essay, Keiko Araki's "Africa for Africans and Asia for Asians: Japanese Pan-Asianism and Its Impact in the Post–World War I Era," explores the history of Japanese nationalists, who, in the process of forging a Pan-Asianist movement, looked at Pan-Africanism as a model in their mutual struggle against Eurocentric racism. Garvey, in turn, observed Japan as a model for black people. He viewed Japan as a non-European power seeking to secure its presence on the world stage. Pan-Asianists appreciated Garvey's rhetoric as a useful tool in challenging the position of racial inferiority to which European powers had relegated them. But their idea of self-determination had a problematic flip side in that it formed the root of Japan's own imperialist designs in the region, at which point Garvey's Pan-Africanism and Japanese Pan-Asianism part ways.

In "Convenient Partnerships?: African American Civil Rights Leaders and the East German Dictatorship," Anja Werner discusses another unlikely ideological alliance, this time between civil rights and Black Power activists in the United States, on the one hand, and East German political leaders, on the other. Since the 1980s there has been vivid scholarly interest in the subject of black Germany and connecting points between the civil rights activism of African Americans and both West and East Germans.[18] However, we still know little about African American activists' interaction with the Communist East German dictatorship. This essay traces W. E. B. DuBois, Paul and Eslanda Robeson, Angela Davis, and Martin Luther King Jr. during visits to the Communist German Democratic Republic (GDR) mainly between 1959 and 1981. It juxtaposes a close reading of the black leaders' motives with the goals and expectations of the East German dictatorship, revealing that both sides used the media attention that their contacts garnered to further their respective agendas. For African Americans, rather than allowing themselves to be used by the Communist cause, it was meant to draw international attention to the American race problem and thus to pressure the U.S. government during the Cold War. For the East German Communists, it was meant to boost their standing in the Western world at a time when the GDR was striving for international recognition beyond the Eastern Bloc. However, while the GDR dictatorship attempted to control African Americans' perception among the East German population, they ultimately failed on account of the force of the black freedom fight, revealing deeply rooted underlying racism and thus belying the claim that the Communist bloc had been more successful in uprooting it.

Cultural Mastery in Foreign Spaces:
Evolving Visions of Home and Identity

As people move across space and time, their expressed articulation of identity and place comes in many forms. One may draw upon memories from the recent or distant and, in some instances, imagined pasts. As Kim Butler eloquently points out, visions of Diaspora need not be contingent upon a single homeland—there can be many.[19] Homelands can be physical and even a state of mind. They can be articulated in ways that force us to look into a mirror for deeper understanding of who we are in relationship to our past and present circumstances. Inherent in this exercise is a readjustment of the lens. The following four essays are prime examples of redefining home and identity.

Kimberly Cleveland's "Abdias Nascimento: Afro-Brazilian Painting Connections Across the Diaspora," an essay on Abdias Nascimento, who passed away on May 23, 2011, is a timely reflection of his work on many levels. Born in 1914, Nascimento was politically active in Brazil and became the first Afro-Brazilian congressman (1983–1986) and senator (1991, 1997, 1999). However, his lesser-known life's work as a visual artist was about guiding this political-cultural lens to a deeper understanding of the African influences in Brazilian art. Between 1968 and 1981, Nascimento lived in a self-imposed exile in the United States taking on the role of cultural ambassador between Black Brazilians and African Americans. He intellectually embraced the ideas of Negritude, Pan-Africanism, and the politics of Diaspora, which, as a cultural exchange, enriched his perspective and work as a painter.

"'Of Remarkable Omens in My Favour': Olaudah Equiano, Two Identities, and the Cultivation of a Literary Economic Exchange," by Edward L. Robinson Jr., explores *The Interesting Narrative of the Life of Olaudah Equiano, or, Gustavus Vassa, the African, Written by Himself* (1789)[20] as a work that seeks to "ingeniously" cultivate a relationship between two identities and two audiences—African and European. "For Equiano," Robinson writes in his essay, "the narrative stands as a careful negotiation of the complexities that are critical in cultivating sociopolitical and economic capital in the commercial Atlantic." Again, the past, real or imaginary, plays an important role in seeking legitimacy with multiple audiences. As a way to connect with his European audiences, Equiano scripted an African past, adopted the European name Gustavus Vassa in reference to Swedish King Gustav I, and succeeded in combining both narratives. Imbued with the values and ideals representative of both communities in the Atlantic World, his narrative becomes a voice against racial injustice and slavery.

Kimberli Gant's essay, "Ruptures and Disrupters: The Photographic Landscapes of Ingrid Pollard and Zarina Bhimji as Revisionist History of Great Britain," underscores the importance of the emergence of two artists whose work reflects the racially charged climate of the United Kingdom in the 1980s. By focusing on the work of Pollard's *Pastoral Interludes* and Bhimji's series *Cleaning the Garden*, Gant explores how their depictions of the iconic English garden, a symbol of "white Englishness" and the "purity of heritage," challenge the concept of English and British cultural identity. Both artists appropriate the idyllic country garden as the backdrop to the invisibility of black people who made these very gardens possible as a result of the "enterprise of Empire." Black English activists and artists drew inspiration from the African American Black Arts and Black Power movements to formulate and cultivate what would become Britain's Black Arts Movement. Through their appropriation of the traditional English garden, the artists make the seemingly invisible visible.

In the last and final essay in the collection, "From Port-au-Prince and Kinshasa: A Haitian Journey from the Americas to Africa," Danielle Legros Georges addresses the little-known history of the movement of hundreds of young Haitian professionals and their families to the Congo (Zaire, later to become the Democratic Republic of the Congo) between 1960 and 1975. Facing few economic opportunities and possible persecution under the regime of François Duvalier, these engineers, doctors, teachers, and lawyers saw the invitation by the United Nations Educational, Scientific, and Cultural Organization (UNESCO) and the Congolese government as a way to start their lives anew. Georges, herself a child at the time her parents went to the Congo in the late 1960s, reconstructs this journey through interviews, letters, and other historical sources. Her story includes reflections and analyses during a time of cross-cultural optimism and cooperation within the Francophone African Diaspora.

Final Reflections on Significance:
Hybridity, the Cosmopolitan, and Beyond

The essays in this volume are a valuable contribution to current and future topics that touch on the Black Atlantic and Black Diaspora, such as discussions on "hybridity" and also the "cosmopolitan," which is not typically associated with Black Diasporans. However, many of the protagonists in this volume became true "cosmopolitans." While cosmopolitans have traditionally been considered those who simply move around frequently in the world across spaces and over time, Ulf Hannerz regards true cosmopolitans as those who, in their traversing, also "alter structures of meaning more than marginally," rather than merely reproducing old meanings and structures.[21] Hannerz's cosmopolitans tend to mingle with others cross-culturally and with a certain degree of competence; they maintain a plurality of relationships. The cosmopolitan is able to traffic between peripheries and "centers" of (mainstream) culture as a knowledge broker and translocal mediator.

Although Hannerz mainly refers to privileged actors, elite travelers who can always go "home," as epitomized in the expatriate, people of African descent, alongside other representatives of marginalized communities, have also strategically and historically positioned themselves as intercultural actors. Despite their often-disadvantaged social or economic positions, they acquired a cross-cultural participation and sophistication equal to that of Hannerz's expatriates. An intercultural person does not simply bring two cultures together or simply participate in a new cultural experience, such as one would in trying out a foreign restaurant or learning a different language. Rather, as Hannerz puts it, an intercultural person's power lies in "mediating possibilities. . . . One can use the mobility connected with them to make contact with the meanings of other rounds of life."[22] Cosmopolitans and hybrids occupy a special, potentially powerful, position between traditional spaces of culture. This has never been truer for people of African descent throughout the Diaspora, who have found and placed themselves, historically, in nontraditional spaces, quite often to subvert or improve their own—as well as their surrounding—realities.

We are better able to see and study the range of intellectual perspectives and approaches by following individual accounts of the African Diasporan cosmopolitan. Many writings within the context of Atlantic, transnational, or Diaspora studies tend to utilize the single voice to define or interpret collective memory and traditions, rather than focus on the individual to observe nuances, departures, or even contradictions *within* the collective—differences that might tell us even more about the collective—its diversity *and* its commonality. Several of these essays are reflective, autobiographical, biographical, and personal in many ways. We allow room for more fluid interpretations by leaving the reader free to decide for herself or himself the context in which these essays speak to a greater understanding of collective and individual experiences.

From an academic standpoint, while the articulation of a collective experience has been the mainstay of African and African American studies in the interpretation of slavery, imperialism, the "black experience," and so forth, the individual and the collective renderings of memory often overlap. How the individual in her or his hybrid position and her or his ideas interact with the collective and the wider world (and in the process becomes cosmopolitan) is an inquiry that, potentially, provides us with a fresher and broader understanding of the production of black intellectualism, the methods of self-determination, and the complexities and sophistication of intercultural engagement over time and throughout the African Diaspora. By moving beyond traditional and formerly limiting geographical, historical, and conceptual categories of the Black Atlantic, we expand and liberate this discourse to make possible the study of how movement to "anywhere but here" helped individuals to arrive at where they needed to be spiritually, socially, politically, and culturally.

Notes

1. Gilroy, *Black Atlantic*.

2. See, for example, Butler, "From Black History to Diasporan History," 125–139. Following quote in ibid.

3. Butler, "From Black History," 127.

4. See Oboe and Scacchi, *Recharting the Black Atlantic*, 4.

5. See ibid.

6. See, for instance, Gordon and Anderson, "African Diaspora," 282–296.

7. Piertse "Globalization as Hybridization," 49.

8. Hanchard, "Black Transnationalism," 151. Following quotes in ibid.

9. DuBois, *Souls of Black Folk*.

10. See Blackburn, *Making of New World Slavery*; Apter and Derby, *Activating the Past*; Dubois and Scott, *Origins of the Black Atlantic*; Egerton, "Slaves to the Marketplace," 617–639.

11. See, for instance, Keesing, *Native Peoples of the Pacific World*, and also Gasteyger, *Japan and the Atlantic World*.

12. Some recent works on Afro-Asian connections (overlapping diasporas), both historical and within the context of aesthetics and popular culture, are part of a growing interest in long-standing transnational exchange and include Raphael-Hernandez and Steen, *Afro Asian Encounters*; Steen, *Racial Geometries*; Prashad, *Everybody Was Kung Fu Fighting*.

13. See the preface in Banks, *Black Intellectuals*, xv–xvi. In his own effort to define the meaning of "intellectual," he too did not want to restrict himself "to definitions based on a list of professions or occupations." He goes on to state, "my conception was the distinction Richard Hofstadter drew between intellect and intelligence," quoting Hofstadter, "'intellect is the critical, contemplative side of mind. Whereas intelligence seeks to grasp, manipulate,

re-order, adjust, intellect examines, ponders, wonders, theorizes imagines. Intelligence will seize the immediate meaning in a situation and evaluate it. Intellect evaluates, and looks for the meaning of situations as a whole.'"

14. Simonsen, *Moving in Circles.*

15. Gobineau, *Essai sur l'inégalité des races humaines.* A contemporary English-language edition is Gobineau, *Inequality of Human Races.*

16. The biographical accounts published in the first half of the nineteenth century are too numerous to be included here. Critical English-language assessments of Gobineau's work appeared in the 1960s and 1970s.

17. Firmin, *De l'égalité des races humaines.* A contemporary English edition is Firmin, *Equality of the Human Races.*

18. See Höhn and Klimke, *Breath of Freedom.*

19. Butler, "From Black History to Diasporan History," 125–139.

20. A recent edition is Equiano and Eversley, *Interesting Narrative of the Life of Olaudah Equiano.*

21. Hannerz, "Cosmopolitans and Locals."

22. Hannerz, "Transnational Connections," 245.

Bibliography

Adebajo, Adekeye, and Kaye Whiteman. *The EU and Africa: From Eurafrique to Afro-Europa.* New York: Columbia University Press, 2012.

Aljoe, Nicole N. *Creole Testimonies: Slave Narratives from the British West Indies, 1709–1838.* New York: Palgrave Macmillan, 2012.

Apter, Andrew H., and Lauren Hutchinson Derby. *Activating the Past: History and Memory in the Black Atlantic World.* Newcastle upon Tyne: Cambridge Scholars, 2010.

Atkins, Keletso E. "The 'Black Atlantic Communication Network': African American Sailors and the Cape of Good Hope Connection." *Issue: A Journal of Opinion* 24.2 (1996): 23–25.

Bandele, Ramla M. *Black Star: African American Activism in the International Political Economy.* Urbana: University of Illinois Press, 2008.

Banks, William M. *Black Intellectuals: Race and Responsibility in American Life.* New York: Norton and Co., 1998.

Barnes, Natasha. "Black Atlantic–Black America." *Research in African Literatures* 27.4 (1996): 106–107.

Barson, Tanya, Peter Gorschlüter, Petrine Archer, and Tate Gallery Liverpool. *Afro Modern: Journeys through the Black Atlantic.* Liverpool: Tate Liverpool, 2010; in association with Tate Pub. Distributed in the United States by Harry N. Abrams.

Benjamin, Thomas. *The Atlantic World: European, Africans, Indians and Their Shared History, 1400–1900.* Cambridge: Cambridge University Press, 2009.

Bennett, Herman L. "The Subject in the Plot: National Boundaries and the 'History' of the Black Atlantic." *African Studies Review* 43.1 (2000): 101–124.

Bermúdez, Silvia. "Rocking the Boat: The Black Atlantic in Spanish Pop Music from the 1980s and the '90s." *Arizona Journal of Hispanic Cultural Studies* 5 (2001): 177–193.

Blackburn, Robin. *The Making of New World Slavery: From Boroque Tradition to the Modern 1492–1800*. London: Verso, 2010.

Boelhower, William. "The Rise of the New Atlantic Studies Matrix." *American Literary History* 20.1/2 (2008): 83–101.

Bolster, W. Jeffrey. "Putting the Ocean in Atlantic History: Maritime Communities and Marine Ecology in the Northwest Atlantic, 1500–1800." *American Historical Review* 113.1 (2008): 19–47.

Boulukos, George. *The Grateful Slave: The Emergence of Race in Eighteenth-Century British and American Culture*. Cambridge: Cambridge University Press, 2008.

Braddock, Jeremy. *Paris, Modern Fiction, and the Black Atlantic*. Baltimore: Johns Hopkins University Press, 2013.

Braziel, Jana Evans. *Duvalier's Ghosts: Race, Diaspora, and U.S. Imperialism in Haitian Literatures*. Gainesville: University Press of Florida, 2010.

Brooks, Joanna, and John Saillant. *"Face Zion Forward": First Writers of the Black Atlantic, 1785–1798*. Boston: Northeastern University Press, 2002.

Bryant, Kelly Duke. "Black but Not African: Francophone Black Diaspora and the 'Revue des Colonies,' 1834–1842." *International Journal of African Historical Studies* 40.2 (2007): 251–282.

Butler, Kim D. "From Black History to Diasporan History: Brazilian Abolition in Afro-Atlantic Context." *African Studies Review* 43.1 (2000): 125–139.

Campbell, Kofi Omoniyi Sylvanus. *Literature and Culture in the Black Atlantic: From Pre- to Postcolonial*. New York: Palgrave Macmillan, 2006.

Castronovo, Russ, and Susan Kay Gillman. *States of Emergency: The Object of American Studies*. Chapel Hill: University of North Carolina Press, 2009.

Catterall, Douglas, and Jodi Campbell. *Women in Port: Gendering Communities, Economies, and Social Networks in Atlantic Port Cities, 1500–1800*. Leiden: Brill, 2012.

Clarke, George Elliott. *Odysseys Home: Mapping African-Canadian Literature*. Toronto: University of Toronto Press, 2002.

Cobley, Alan. "Black West Indian Seamen in the British Merchant Marine in the Mid Nineteenth Century." *History Workshop Journal* 58 (2004): 259–274.

Coclanis, Peter A. "Drang Nach Osten: Bernard Bailyn, the World-Island, and the Idea of Atlantic History." *Journal of World History* 13.1 (2002): 169–182.

Coclanis, Peter A., and J. C. Marlow. "Inland Rice Production in the South Atlantic States: A Picture in Black and White." *Agricultural History* 72.2 (1998): 197–212.

Conyers, James L. *African American Consciousness: Past and Present*. New Brunswick, N.J.: Transaction, 2012.

Cooper, Carolyn. "Race and the Cultural Politics of Self-Representation: A View from the University of the West Indies." *Research in African Literatures* 27.4 (1996): 97–105.

Curtis, Edward E. *Muslims in America: A Short History*. Oxford: Oxford University Press, 2009.

David, Marlo. "Afrofuturism and Post-Soul Possibility in Black Popular Music." *African American Review* 41.4 (2007): 695–707.

Dayan, Joan. "Paul Gilroy's Slaves, Ships, and Routes: The Middle Passage as Metaphor." *Research in African Literatures* 27.4 (1996): 7–14.

Desai, Gaurav. "Gendered Self-Fashioning: Adelaide Casely Hayford's Black Atlantic." *Research in African Literatures* 35.3 (2004): 141–160.

Dillon, Elizabeth. "Atlantic Practices: Minding the Gap between Literature and History." *Early American Literature* 43.1 (2008): 205–210.

———. "Atlantic Practices: Minding the Gap between Literature and History." *William and Mary Quarterly* 65.1 (2008): 181–186.

Donnell, Alison. *Twentieth-Century Caribbean Literature: Critical Moments in Anglophone Literary History*. Oxford: Routledge, 2006.

Dorsey, Peter A. *Common Bondage: Slavery as Metaphor in Revolutionary America*. Knoxville: University of Tennessee Press, 2009.

Dresser, Madge. *Slavery Obscured: The Social History of the Slave Trade in an English Provincial Port*. New York: Continuum, 2001.

Dubin, Lois. "Introduction: Port Jews in the Atlantic World 'Jewish History.'" *Jewish History* 20.2 (2006): 117–127.

Dubois, Laurent, and Julius Sherrard Scott. *Origins of the Black Atlantic*. New York: Routledge, 2010.

DuBois, W. E. B. *The Souls of Black Folk*. New York: Dover, 1903.

Egerton, Douglas R. "Slaves to the Marketplace: Economic Liberty and Black Rebelliousness in the Atlantic World." *Journal of the Early Republic* 26.4 (2006): 617–639.

Elmer, Jonathan. "The Black Atlantic Archive." *American Literary History* 17.1 (2005): 160–170.

Equiano, Olaudah, and Shelly Eversley. *The Interesting Narrative of the Life of Olaudah Equiano, or, Gustavus Vassa, the African, Written by Himself*. New York: Modern Library, 2004.

Farred, Grant. "You Can Go Home Again, You Just Can't Stay: Stuart Hall and the Caribbean Diaspora." *Research in African Literatures* 27.4 (1996): 28–48.

Feldstein, Ruth. "'I Don't Trust You Anymore': Nina Simone, Culture, and Black Activism in the 1960s." *Journal of American History* 91.4 (2005): 1349–1379.

Firmin, Joseph-Anténor. *The Equality of the Human Races*. Urbana: University of Illinois Press, 2000.

Games, Alison. "Atlantic History: Definitions, Challenges, and Opportunities." *American Historical Review* 111.3 (2006): 741–757.

Gasteyger, Curt Walter. *Japan and the Atlantic World*. Farnborough: Saxon House, 1972.

Gates, Henry Louis, Jr. *Tradition and the Black Atlantic: Critical Theory in the African Diaspora*. New York: BasicCivitas, 2010.

Gates, Henry Louis, Jr., and William L. Andrews. *Pioneers of the Black Atlantic: Five Slave Narratives from the Enlightenment, 1772–1815*. Washington, D.C.: Civitas, 1998.

Gilroy, Paul. *The Black Atlantic: Modernity and Double Consciousness*. Cambridge, Mass.: Harvard University Press, 1993.

———. "Black Fascism." *Transition* 81/82 (2000): 70–91.

———. "Nationalism, History and Ethnic Absolutism." *History Workshop* 30 (1990): 114–120.

———. "Sounds Authentic: Black Music, Ethnicity, and the Challenge of a 'Changing' Same." *Black Music Research Journal* 11.2 (1991): 111–136.

Gobineau, Arthur. *Essai sur l'inégalité des races humaines*. Paris: Librairie de Firmin Didot, 1853.

———. *The Inequality of Human Races*. New York: H. Fertig, 2009.

Goebel, Walter, and Saskia Schabio. *Beyond the Black Atlantic: Relocating Modernization and Technology*. New York: Routledge, 2006.

Gordon, Edmund T., and Mark Anderson. "The African Diaspora: Toward an Ethnography of Diasporic Identification." *Journal of American Folklore* 112.445 (Summer 1999): 282–296.

Gould, Eliga H. "Atlantic History and the Literary Turn." *Early American Literature* 43.1 (2008): 197–203.

Gould, Philip. "Free Carpenter, Venture Capitalist: Reading the Lives of the Early Black Atlantic." *American Literary History* 12.4 (2000): 659–684.

Greene, Larry A., and Anke Ortlepp. *Germans and African Americans: Two Centuries of Exchange*. Jackson: University Press of Mississippi, 2011.

Gruesser, John Cullen. *Confluences: Postcolonialism, African American Literary Studies, and the Black Atlantic*. Athens: University of Georgia Press, 2005.

Gunvor, Simonsen. "Moving in Circles: African and Black History in the Atlantic World." *Nuevo Mundo Mundos Nuevos*, Coloquios, 2008. http://nuevomundo.revues.org/42303.

Hanchard, Michael George. "Black Transnationalism, Africana Studies, and the 21st Century." *Journal of Black Studies* 35.2 (2004): 139–153.

Hannerz, Ulf. "Cosmopolitans and Locals in World Culture." In *Transnational Connections: People, Culture, Places*. New York: Routledge, 1996.

Harris, Daryl B. "Postmodernist Diversions in African American Thought." *Journal of Black Studies* 36.2 (2005): 209–228.

Hawthorne, Walter. "From 'Black Rice' to 'Brown': Rethinking the History of Risiculture in the Seventeenth- and Eighteenth-Century Atlantic." *American Historical Review* 115.1 (2010): 151–163.

Jackson, Maurice, and Jacqueline Bacon. *African Americans and the Haitian Revolution: Selected Essays and Historical Documents*. New York: Routledge, 2010.

Jakubiak, Katarzyna. "Between a Failure and a New Creation: (Re)reading Yusef Komunyakaa's 'The Beast & Burden' in the Light of Paul Gilroy's 'Black Atlantic.'" *Callaloo* 28.3 (2005): 864–881.

Kaba, Lansiné. "The Atlantic Slave Trade Was Not a 'Black-on-Black Holocaust.'" *African Studies Review* 44.1 (2001): 1–20.

Keesing, Felix Maxwell. *Native Peoples of the Pacific World*. New York: Macmillan, 1946.

Keizer, Arlene R. *Black Subjects: Identity Formation in the Contemporary Narrative of Slavery*. Ithaca, N.Y.: Cornell University Press, 2004.

Kerr-Ritchie, Jeffrey R. *Rites of August First: Emancipation Day in the Black Atlantic World*. Baton Rouge: Louisiana State University Press, 2007.

Killingray, David. "The Black Atlantic Missionary Movement and Africa, 1780s–1920s." *Journal of Religion in Africa* 33.1 (2003): 3–31.

Kiron, Arthur. "An Atlantic Jewish Republic of Letters?" *Jewish History* 20.2 (2006): 171–211.

Kortenaar, Neil ten. "Where the Atlantic Meets the Caribbean: Kamau Brathwaite's 'The Arrivants' and T. S. Eliot's 'The Waste Land.'" *Research in African Literatures* 27.4 (1996): 15–27.

Ledent, Bénédicte, and Pilar Cuder Domínguez. *New Perspectives on the Black Atlantic: Definitions, Readings, Practices, Dialogues.* Bern: Peter Lang, 2012.

Lockpez, Inverna, Judith McWillie, and INTAR Latin American Gallery. *Another Face of the Diamond: Pathways through the Black Atlantic South, January 23–March 3, 1989.* New York: INTAR, Hispanic Arts Center, 1988.

Lovejoy, Paul E. *Identity in the Shadow of Slavery: The Black Atlantic.* London: Continuum, 2000.

Lovejoy, Paul E., and David Vincent Trotman. *Trans-Atlantic Dimensions of Ethnicity in the African Diaspora.* London: Continuum, 2003.

Lowney, John. "Haiti and Black Transnationalism: Remapping the Migrant Geography of Home to Harlem." *African American Review* 34.3 (2000): 413–429.

Luis-Brown, David. "An 1848 for the Americas: The Black Atlantic, 'El negro mártir,' and Cuban Exile Anticolonialism in New York City." *American Literary History* 21.3 (2009): 431–463.

Mackenthun, Gesa. *Fictions of the Black Atlantic in American Foundational Literature.* London: Routledge, 2004.

Mamigonian, Beatriz G., and Karen Racine. *The Human Tradition in the Black Atlantic, 1500–2000.* Lanham, Md.: Rowman & Littlefield, 2010.

Mancall, Peter Cooper. *The Atlantic World and Virginia, 1550–1624.* Chapel Hill: Published for the Omohundro Institute of Early American History and Culture, Williamsburg, Virginia, by the University of North Carolina Press, 2007.

Mardorossian, Carine M. *Reclaiming Difference: Caribbean Women Rewrite Postcolonialism.* Charlottesville: University of Virginia Press, 2005.

Masilela, Ntongela. "The 'Black Atlantic' and African Modernity in South Africa." *Research in African Literatures* 27.4 (1996): 88–96.

May, Cedrick. *Evangelism and Resistance in the Black Atlantic, 1760–1835.* Athens: University of Georgia Press, 2008.

McKay, George. *Circular Breathing: The Cultural Politics of Jazz in Britain.* Durham, N.C.: Duke University Press, 2005.

McNeil, D. R. *Sex and Race in the Black Atlantic: Mulatto Devils and Multiracial Messiahs.* New York: Routledge, 2010.

Meadows, R. Darrell. "Engineering Exile: Social Networks and the French Atlantic Community, 1789–1809." *French Historical Studies* 23.1 (2000): 67–102.

Miller, Monica L. "W. E. B. DuBois and the Dandy as Diasporic Race Man." *Callaloo* 26.3 (2003): 738–765.

Moore, David Chioni. "Local Color, Global 'Color': Langston Hughes, the Black Atlantic, and Soviet Central Asia, 1932." *Research in African Literatures* 27.4 (1996): 49–70.

Mosley, Albert. "The Moral Significance of the Music of the Black Atlantic." *Philosophy East and West* 57.3 (2007): 345–356.

Nair, Supriya. "Expressive Countercultures and Postmodern Utopia: A Caribbean Context." *Research in African Literatures* 27.4 (1996): 71–87.

Naro, Nancy Priscilla, Roger Sansi-Roca, and Dave Treece. *Cultures of the Lusophone Black Atlantic.* New York: Palgrave Macmillan, 2007.

Northrup, David. *Crosscurrents in the Black Atlantic, 1770–1965: A Brief History with Documents.* Boston: Bedford/St. Martins, 2008.

Oboe, Annalisa, and Anna Scacchi. *Recharting the Black Atlantic: Modern Cultures, Local Communities, Global Connections.* New York: Routledge, 2008.

Okpewho, Isidore. "Walcott, Homer, and the 'Black Atlantic.'" *Research in African Literatures* 33.1 (2002): 27–44.

O'Neill, Peter D., and David Lloyd. *The Black and Green Atlantic: Cross-Currents of the African and Irish Diasporas.* Basingstoke, England: Palgrave Macmillan, 2009.

Parés, Luis Nicolau, and Roger Sansi. *Sorcery in the Black Atlantic.* Chicago: University of Chicago Press, 2011.

Pearce, Marsha. "Transnational Transcultural Identities: The Black Atlantic and Pythagoras's Theorem." *Callaloo* 30.2 (2007): 547–554.

Pettinger, Alasdair. *Always Elsewhere: Travels of the Black Atlantic.* London: Cassell, 1998.

Piertse, Jan Nederveen. "Globalization as Hybridization." In *Global Modernities*, ed. M. Featherstone, S. Lash, and R. Robertson. London: Sage, 1995.

———. *White on Black: Images of Africa and Blacks in Western Popular Culture.* New Haven, Conn.: Yale University Press, 1992.

Pinho, Patricia de Santana. *Mama Africa: Reinventing Blackness in Bahia.* Durham, N.C.: Duke University Press, 2010.

Pirker, Eva Ulrike. *Narrative Projections of a Black British History, Routledge Approaches to History.* New York: Routledge, 2011.

Prashad, Vijay. *Everybody Was Kung Fu Fighting: Afro-Asian Connections and the Myth of Cultural Purity.* Boston: Beacon Press, 2001.

Quilley, Geoff. *Empire to Nation: Art, History and the Visualization of Maritime Britain, 1768–1829.* New Haven, Conn.: Published for the Paul Mellon Centre for Studies in British Art by Yale University Press, 2011.

Rael, Patrick. "Free Black Activism in the Antebellum North." *History Teacher* 39.2 (2006): 215–253.

Raphael-Hernandez, Heike, and Shannon Steen, eds. *AfroAsian Encounters: Culture, History, Politics.* New York: New York University Press, 2006.

Reid-Salmon, Delroy A. *Home Away from Home: The Caribbean Diasporan Church in the Black Atlantic Tradition, Cross Cultural Theologies.* London: Equinox, 2008.

Reiland Rabaka. "The Souls of Black Radical Folk: W. E. B. DuBois, Critical Social Theory, and the State of Africana Studies." *Journal of Black Studies* 36.5 (2006): 732–763.

Rice, Alan J. *Radical Narratives of the Black Atlantic: The Black Atlantic.* London: Continuum, 2003.

———. "'Who's Eating Whom': The Discourse of Cannibalism in the Literature of the Black Atlantic from Equiano's 'Travels' to Toni Morrison's 'Beloved.'" *Research in African Literatures* 29.4 (1998): 107–121.

Saillant, John. "Antiguan Methodism and Antislavery Activity: Anne and Elizabeth Hart in the Eighteenth-Century Black Atlantic." *Church History* 69.1 (2000): 86–115.

Sandberg, Brian. "Beyond Encounters: Religion, Ethnicity, and Violence in the Early Modern Atlantic World, 1492–1700." *Journal of World History* 17.1 (2006): 1–25.

Schmidt-Nowara, Chris. "Big Questions and Answers: Three Histories of Slavery, the Slave Trade and the Atlantic World." *Social History* 27.2 (2002): 210–217.

———. "'This Rotting Corpse': Spain between the Black Atlantic and the Black Legend." *Arizona Journal of Hispanic Cultural Studies* 5 (2001): 149–160.

Sensbach, Jon F. *Rebecca's Revival: Creating Black Christianity in the Atlantic World*. Cambridge, Mass.: Harvard University Press, 2005.

Sharpley, Richard, and Philip R. Stone. *The Darker Side of Travel: The Theory and Practice of Dark Tourism, Aspects of Tourism*. Bristol, U.K.: Channel View Publications, 2009.

Shelby, Tommie, and Paul Gilroy. "Cosmopolitanism, Blackness, and Utopia." *Transition* 98 (2008): 116–135.

Shiach, Morag. *The Cambridge Companion to the Modernist Novel*. Cambridge: Cambridge University Press, 2007.

Sparks, Randy J. "Two Princes of Calabar: An Atlantic Odyssey from Slavery to Freedom." *William and Mary Quarterly* 59.3 (2002): 555–584.

Steen, Shannon. *Racial Geometries of the Black Atlantic, Asian Pacific and American Theatre*. Basingstoke, England: Palgrave Macmillan, 2010.

Tamarkin, Elisa. "Black Anglophilia; or, The Sociability of Antislavery." *American Literary History* 14.3 (2002): 444–478.

Thaler, Ingrid. *Black Atlantic Speculative Fictions: Octavia E. Butler, Jewelle Gomez, and Nalo Hopkinson*. New York: Routledge, 2010.

Thornton, John K. *Africa and Africans in the Making of the Atlantic World, 1400–1680*. 2nd exp. ed. Cambridge: Cambridge University Press, 2008.

———. *A Cultural History of the Atlantic World, 1250–1820*. Cambridge: Cambridge University Press, 2012.

Vambe, Maurice Taonezvi. "Orality in the Black Zimbabwean Novel in English." *Journal of Southern African Studies* 30.2 (2004): 235–249.

Veney, Cassandra Rachel, and Paul Tiyambe Zeleza. *Women in African Studies Scholarly Publishing*. Trenton, N.J.: Africa World Press, 2001.

Vieira, Vinícius Guilherme Rodrigues, and Jacquelyn Johnson. *Pictures and Mirrors: Race and Ethnicity in Brazil and the United States*. Sao Paulo: FEAUSP, 2009.

Wade, Bruce H. "How Does Racial Identity Affect Historically Black Colleges and Universities' Student Perceptions of September 11, 2001?" *Journal of Black Studies* 33.1 (2002): 25–43.

Walvin, James. *An African's Life: The Life and Times of Olaudah Equiano, 1745–1797*. London: Cassell, 1998.

———. *Making the Black Atlantic: Britain and the African Diaspora*. London: Cassell, 2000.

White, Bob W. *Music and Globalization: Critical Encounters*. Bloomington: Indiana University Press, 2012.

Wilson, Ivy G., and Ayo A. Coly. "Black Is the Color of the Cosmos or 'Callaloo' and the Cultures of the Diaspora Now." *Callaloo* 30.2 (2007): 415–419.

Zeleza, Paul Tiyambe. "Rewriting the African Diaspora: Beyond the Black Atlantic." *African Affairs* 104.414 (2005): 35–68.

I. REORDERING WORLDVIEWS

Rebellious Thinkers, Poets, Writers, and Political Architects

Writing Against the Grain

Anténor Firmin and the Refutation of
Nineteenth-Century European Race Science

Douglas W. Leonard

January 1911. As the steamer *Montréal* entered the port of Cap-Haïtien, Anténor Firmin (1850–1911) could see "the troops massed in front of the wharf with arms and weapons of war. The city was calm and dreary like a necropolis." The plenipotentiary minister of Haiti to London had been accused of "deserting his post" and was now being prevented from landing in Haiti, his *terre natale*.[1] Despite his long efforts to defend and represent Haiti, from France to England and the United States, he had fallen victim to one final political intrigue, forced into exile as a threat to the regime. Firmin would make one more futile attempt to gain entry later in the year before permanently retreating to his new home on the Danish island of St. Thomas, where he died a broken man on September 19, 1911, the heart-wrenching culmination of a lifelong journey.

Anténor Firmin's life as an itinerant intellectual, politician, and diplomat began in the 1880s, when he first traveled to France. His efforts to elevate Haiti in the eyes of the Western world would subsequently take him from Paris to Washington, D.C. Firmin's remarkable journeys mark him as both a "New World traveler" and an example of "performative cosmopolitanism," not defined by territorial, racial, or cultural boundaries.[2] While his role in the tumultuous political history of Haiti remains relatively well known,[3] his intellectual battle with the racialized theories of French anthropology in the 1880s and 1890s has returned to view only in the last decade. Firmin was disappointed by the discussion upon his 1884 entrance to the Société d'Anthropologie de Paris. In his mind, the voiced presuppositions were in many ways descended from the polemical racial tone set by Arthur de Gobineau's *Essai sur l'inégalité des races humaines* (1853–1855) thirty years earlier. As a counter to these notions of racial hierarchy and inferiority, Firmin penned his seminal *De l'égalité des races humaines.* The creative process that surrounded Firmin's work was anchored in his travels across the Atlantic in several dimensions: physical, temporal, and intertextual.

The Haitian lawyer's combat with Gobineau (1816–1882) occurred primarily in the pages of his work, where he fought to counter the pseudoscience offered by the famed French polemicist as proof of white superiority. While Gobineau looked to the past for perfection, Firmin gazed to the future for progress in the march of civilization. An examination of Firmin's response to Gobineau and other anthropological proponents of racial hierarchy reveals not only Firmin's intellectual journey but also his place in the continuum of black intellectuals in the nineteenth century and of French anthropology in general. In the eyes of one scholar, Firmin's combat, regardless of the environment, remained centered on "racial-national pride."[4] Some of these ideas stemmed, at least in part, from his interactions with Dr. Louis-Joseph Janvier (1855–1911), a Haitian physician in Paris who once remarked, perhaps of Firmin, that "Haitian youth is aware of all the scientific and literary movements of old Europe."[5] Firmin's views were anchored not only in the present but also in the rich legacy of Haitian intellectual history. At the same time, Firmin laid the foundation for the Négritude and Pan-African movements to follow, as evidenced by the homage paid him by Ghanaian leader Kwame Nkrumah in a 1964 speech: "Let us not forget the important contributions of others in the New World, for example, the sons of Africa in Haiti such as Anténor Firmin and Dr. Jean Price-Mars."[6]

Firmin in Paris: Setting the Stage

The story of Firmin's early life remains cloudy despite the best efforts of his biographer, famed Haitian social critic Jean Price-Mars. Born somewhere in Cap-Haïtien in 1850, Firmin was originally christened Joseph, but later took the name Anténor as part of an obscure family tradition.[7] His belief in the fluidity of identity and disregard for traditional boundaries may have begun with this tradition. Moreover, according to Firmin's friend and perhaps classmate Démétrius André, Firmin showed an early interest in race, particularly in the history of African peoples, their "role in the great work of civilization," and above all in "proving ... [their] equality with the other races of the earth."[8] In developing these ideas, Firmin gained from both a broad and sophisticated liberal arts education and self-study. André further related that Firmin had no interest in specializing in any particular branch of human knowledge—all was open and important to him.[9]

In 1885 Firmin put a few such ideas to paper, opining that anthropology was among the most complex fields of study, requiring one to "explore thoroughly all possible areas of knowledge" while remaining "wary of exclusive specialization, for it narrows the mind's horizons and renders the intellect incapable of considering every facet of a given reality."[10] Firmin cautioned that "the discipline is founded on no general principle and has no superior methodology"; scholars must use a wide range of techniques to analyze data, from mythology to history and sociology.[11] By that time, Firmin had moved on to France. Haiti's colonial overlord until the slave revolts of the late eighteenth and early nineteenth centuries, France nonetheless beckoned as a land of opportunity for foreign Francophonic elites. Searching for a way to prove that Haitians had intellectual capabilities on par with those of Europeans, Firmin sought to enter the French academy. From that place he could hope to have a greater voice and political impact.

Firmin arrived in France sometime in 1883 or 1884 and remained until 1887. His initial departure from Haiti was caused, at least in part, by electoral defeat in 1879 and the suppression of his liberal party by the newly elected National Party. He chose exile in France over the potential for political persecution in his homeland.[12] In France, he quickly came into contact with Dr. Louis-Joseph Janvier, a fellow black Haitian whom he apparently had not known previously. Firmin likely read Janvier's *L'Égalité des Races*, published first in 1883 in *Revue de la Jeune France* as "M. Renan et l'Egalité des Races: Bretons et Nègres."[13] The young exile may have gained inspiration from Janvier's method of direct response to the work of a white intellectual (in this case, Ernest Renan's *Dialogues Philosophiques*), either from the title or from the subject matter directly. Janvier described his work as "both a strategic step and a first light" in countering the argument that neither men nor races were equal, a position held by Renan (and reflected in the work of other white intellectuals of the era).[14] Janvier compared these racial ideas to the decadent system of nobility in ancien régime France.

Presaging the sentiments in Firmin's book of a year later, Janvier concluded that the inequities of the U.S. slave system (and its subsequent collapse) served as "decisive proof of the danger of a priori affirmations in matters of ethnography."[15] He did not trust the easy conclusions of anthropological measurement even when put forth by eminent scholars. Firmin also distrusted such notions. He saw himself as the only person able to stretch science to its limits by challenging racial hierarchies. "Time was of the essence," he later remembered, "and I was not sure that any of my Black colleagues had both the good will and the patience one needs in order to construct, combine, and present the arguments and the research materials in the way I strive to do."[16] He cast himself as sufficiently impartial and methodical to do the work, traits that, when combined with his prodigious learning, could not but lead to success.

Despite his classical education in Haiti, Firmin did not have a true grasp on the foundations of European racism until his induction into the Société d'anthropologie de Paris, which had been founded by the anatomist Paul Broca in 1859. At some point after his arrival in France, Firmin met Ernest Aubertin, a physician and member of the society. Aubertin introduced Firmin to Gabriel de Mortillet, another prominent member, and the aforementioned Louis-Joseph Janvier.[17] On July 17, 1884, these three men sponsored Firmin's application for induction into the society—he was elected that same day.[18] Entrance into this exclusive scientific club, the world's most prestigious physical anthropology society, did more than just introduce Firmin to European racial science of the nineteenth century; it also brought him into direct contact with the shadow of Arthur de Gobineau, a previous correspondent of the Société ethnologique de Paris, which was a forerunner and competitor of Broca's organization. Gobineau had also interacted professionally and personally with Armand de Quatrefages, the prominent monogenist anthropologist and member of the Paris anthropological society who would also factor significantly in Firmin's introduction to the discipline. This same scientist, among the most prominent of the day, presided over discussions at the society in which European speakers depicted blacks as inferior. Despite the presence of Firmin, Quatrefages and his peers refused to acknowledge the possibility of black intellectual equality. More than just a scientist, though, Quatrefages shared views with Gobineau and may have inspired the latter's pseudoscientific polemic. After all, Quatrefages—titular chair at the Musée d'ethnographie du Trocadero, a part of the prestigious Muséum national d'histoire naturelle—reportedly had sent a copy of his *L'Espèce Humaine* for placement in Gobineau's personal library.[19]

Firmin witnessed a wide-ranging debate on racial division on his first day, one driven in part by Quatrefages himself. The prominent anthropologist differed with another correspondent, André Sanson, a professor of zoology, on the plasticity of races. While Quatrefages believed that environment could shape inherited characteristics, Sanson thought that the races were in essence distinct species without overlap.[20] While the actual dynamic in the room is unclear, Janvier is reported as following Quatrefages. Again putting forth ideas that would later appear in Firmin's book, Janvier reported that Haitian public education "has wrought notable changes in the general physiognomy of the population."[21] He used the language of physical anthropology to tear at the notion of inherent racial inferiority while pointing to the importance of education, key evidence for Firmin. Janvier continued by discussing race mixing in Haiti: "under completely black skin circulates Indian blood, Spanish blood, English blood or French blood." He argued that creolization in Haiti had occasioned an "original human group" in a physical sense, but, in terms of intellectual development, Haiti "rapidly approached those nations that make up what philosopher Pierre Lafitte calls 'the Occidental group.'"[22] He thus attacked notions of intellectual difference as visible in physical appearance; such ideas, in his mind, could not cover the full extent of the mixing of blood underneath the surface.

Firmin, a young lawyer and budding scientist, was deeply affected by these debates. Janvier's comments drew no response from his opponents, who likely saw him as an exception that proved the rule. During this same period, Gobineau's ideas had found a new currency in France (he had been largely disregarded earlier) due to a re-publication of his work in 1884. While some scholars have depicted Firmin's focus on the title of Gobineau's volume as an "accident of timing," they have also acknowledged that Gobineau "was certainly read."[23] Firmin made several direct references to Gobineau in his 1885 publication, first calling the French author "a man blinded by passion."[24] Firmin nonetheless respected Gobineau's intellectual capability—he doubted only his ideas. The Haitian scholar wrote, "It suffices that a very talented scientist . . . adopts one of these attractive but ephemeral ideas and clothes it in the respectable garb of specific formulae and methods, and a school emerges, blocking all progress in this particular branch of science."[25] Decrying not only Gobineau's ideas but also the pervasiveness of his influence, Firmin strove to counter each notion with facts.

Firmin first considered offering direct resistance to the ideas during one of the society's gatherings. "At the opening of our meeting at the end of last year," he recalled, "I could have requested a debate about the issue within the society in order to elucidate the scientific reasons why most of my fellow scientists divide the human species into superior and inferior races."[26] But he rejected this course of action. The final meeting of 1884, held on December 18, appears to have been quite short according to the surviving transcript. The agenda featured little controversial material, although the final topic (with no discussion) was entitled *Liste des mots appartenant au langage des Aborigines de Haiti* (List of words pertaining to the language of the Haitian aborigines). The presenter, J. B. Dehoux, wanted to publish a vocabulary primer with the help of the society.[27]

Rather than ask for a debate on the intellectual capabilities of blacks, Firmin wrote *De l'égalité des races humaines* for presentation to the society, hoping to change minds with a compendium of data countering the reigning paradigm.[28] The organization acknowledged Firmin's book on October 1, 1885, although whether Firmin himself attended remains unknown. His work was one of nine presented on the day; none of the works featured commentary from the authors, a relatively common state of affairs.[29] While it is not clear whether Firmin inscribed the book "Homage respective à la Société d'anthropologie de Paris, A. Firmin," as one historian has noted,[30] he respected his peers as a group, for in *Egalité* he declared, "I hereby pay homage to each of its [the society] members, my honorable colleagues." However, he also openly stated his contempt for the racist conversations of the era: "Does it make sense to have seating as equals within the same society with men whom the science which one is supposed to represent seems to declare unequal?"[31] Firmin was now prepared to enter into combat, both with his peers and their intellectual antecedent, Arthur de Gobineau. At stake, in his mind, was his worldview of progress, movement, and the mutability of boundaries.

Combat Across Texts and Time

"If the three great types had remained strictly separate," Gobineau claimed in his work, "the supremacy would no doubt have always been in the hands of the finest of the white race, and the yellow and black varieties would have crawled forever at the feet of the lowest of the whites."[32] Gobineau's fundamental assertion, one of racial inequality, served as the unstated foundation for not only anthropology but also the rising tide of colonial expansion in his day. For Firmin, by contrast, "The anti-philosophical and anti-scientific doctrine of the inequality of the races rests on nothing more than the notion of man's exploitation of man."[33] The two opposing views on the relative status of the races and the resulting hierarchy are emblematic of the debate that shaped French anthropology in the period. In Firmin's eyes, Gobineau embodied all sentiments of racial supremacy; his text was a klaxon call of the openness to conquest of all nonwhites. Gobineau gave a voice to the troubling European need to justify the supremacy of one civilization over another by providing pseudohistorical and philosophical rationalizations.[34]

For Gobineau, race—and, more specifically, the inequality of races—stood at the center of all discourse on civilization, on progress, on the nature of man and his interactions. "The racial question overshadows all other problems of history. . . . It holds the key to them all, and . . . the inequality of the races from whose fusion a people is formed is enough to explain the whole course of its destiny," he declared.[35] These final words of Gobineau's original preface shed significant light on his purpose in penning the book, which he envisioned as part of an eleven-to-twelve-volume work on civilizations as he saw them.

In Gobineau's mind, race was foundational, at the heart of all discussion of human nature. Indeed, he could trace the history of humankind, the rise and fall of civilizations, through the intermixing of bloodlines between the "three great types." While Gobineau had little direct influence on the French anthropological community of the mid-nineteenth century, he, along with fellow racial theorist Houston Stewart Chamberlain, found purchase for his ideas in Germany and the circle of composer Richard Wagner. More than a musical savant, Wagner, from his position as purveyor of German high culture, supported ideas of European white racial supremacy. Firmin, for his part, believed that Gobineau's hierarchy served as "a bright light source" for the ideas of French physical anthropologists such as Paul Broca and Paul Topinard.[36] In the end, Firmin's choice of book title owes much to Gobineau, as he used the inflammatory title of the latter's work to strike a note for positivism and progress.

At the bottom of his imagined racial ladder Gobineau placed the "negroid variety," which he viewed as having poor intellect, being governed by desire and sensation. He proposed that a black "kills willingly for the sake of killing"; ironically, as only humans are generally credited with the ability to take part in aimless destruction, Gobineau saw blacks as of "animal character."[37] He portrayed blacks as visceral beings without true intellect: "The very strength of his sensations is the most striking proof of his inferiority."[38] Put differently, most blacks were not capable of sophisticated social interaction, although Gobineau acknowledged some individuals might find a low position in white society: "I have no doubt that a fair number of negro chiefs are superior ... to the level usually reached by our peasants, or even by the average specimens of our half-educated middle class."[39] Gobineau, of middle-class origins despite his claims to aristocracy, nonetheless favored the return to prominence of a chosen upper class by virtue of their breeding and education. The middle and lower classes, threats to this established order since the French Revolution, had to be kept under strict social and political control. Blacks would reside at the very bottom of this traditional French estates system, incapable even of entering the realm of the bourgeoisie in their challenge to aristocracy. For Gobineau, reflecting the views of many European nobles in a period of rapid, significant social leveling and the loss of traditional privileges, social order required the elevation of European nobles at the expense of other economic or racial classes.

Gobineau placed the "yellow race" on the middle rung of his three-tiered racial hierarchy. "Every founder of a civilization would wish the backbone of his society, his middle class, to consist of such ['yellow'] men," he argued, as they tended toward "mediocrity," were "feeble," and lacked energy.[40] In

Gobineau's model, the "backbone" was not necessarily strong, but a structure populated by large numbers of people good only for labor. These people, notionally of Asian descent, remained "clearly superior to the black," with each individual demonstrating that "his whole desire is to live in the easiest and most comfortable way possible."[41] In an effort to buttress his idealized class structure, Gobineau needed a middle class that would work harder than the lower class, but not so hard as to challenge the supremacy of "white peoples" who possessed "energetic intelligence," an "instinct for order," and a greater consciousness of life.[42] In Gobineau's view, such a social order had existed since time immemorial, for he viewed the races as constant—and unchanging in capability—unless, of course, they intermixed.

Firmin dismissed the idea of hierarchy as an "absurd ranking of the races," seeing no scientific basis for the discussion.[43] Inequity was tied to the inescapable logic of colonialism, which required subjugation and categorization of colonized peoples. Without such distinction, the paternalism accompanying the objectification of the colonial project could not stand. Racism was inevitable, he thought, but not all-powerful. Firmin saw the incredible value of education, postulating that social problems and the intellectual disparity of races and colonized peoples would disappear simply with exposure to the great ideas of the day: "Cerebral power often remains dormant . . . they could have set the world ablaze if only they had been touched by a single spark. In this case, the spark is education."[44] Gobineau, in turn, was more pessimistic about education, which he thought could not assist in the development of man, at least not in ameliorating the condition of a race. In refuting the idea of correction of racial deficiency by education, Gobineau referred once again to the fixed nature of the races: "There has been no real progress in the intellectual conquests of man."[45] Man knew exactly what he had known in the primordial era of his creation, at least insofar as his race would allow him to understand.

Without question, Charles Darwin had greatly altered the intellectual landscape of the nineteenth century and beyond, as his ideas sparked new and different interpretations of animal and human development and interaction. Gobineau wrote in the period immediately preceding *On the Origin of Species* (1859), and his ideas reflect that sequence. Firmin, on the other hand, made use of some of Darwin's ideas combined with the positivism of Auguste Comte, which he considered his greatest influence. He saw black evolution as on par with the rest of humanity, with blacks clearly capable of "intellectual and moral achievements."[46] As mankind progressed, so too would blacks, creating as many great works of philosophy and science as those of other races, assuming the same access to educational resources. Firmin did not go so far as to claim real equality of the races, only their equality in terms of potential. He attributed the success of whites to "favorable evolutionary circumstances," as "social evolution alone is responsible for the differences in the moral and intellectual constitution of the different segments of humanity."[47] Intellectual and academic development would necessarily assist in moral advancement, as the "lower" races would be better capable of comprehending more complex social interaction.

Firmin continued his use of evolutionary models in specifically addressing the conflation of blacks and animals. He proposed, "Just as the climate confers to native plants the means to struggle successfully against alien species and chase them away from their own natural habitat, human beings too are naturally protected."[48] Much as plants and animals adapted to (and changed) their environments, so too did humans alter their surroundings to survive and thrive. He pointed to the white "conviction . . . of their ethnic superiority" as proof of their ultimate downfall, for they would cease to seek ways to improve. Instead, whites would "settle in certain places only [to] die out or to blend with the native race."[49]

Gobineau agreed, in spirit, with this idea, although for a very different reason. He understood the human races to be slowly merging, ceasing to exist as distinct entities. At the same time, the extant races were not and could never be equal. "The existing races constitute separate branches of one or many primitive stocks," he wrote, "this permanence of racial qualities is quite sufficient to generate the radical unlikeness and inequality that exists [*sic*] between the different branches."[50] While Firmin interpreted the advancement of the lower races perhaps at the expense of the white race, Gobineau pointed to a sullying of the white race as the reason for the advancement of the others, a transfer of civilizational capability via the crossing of bloodlines. While the races were inherently distinct and separate, history had caused a slow intermixing of the different types and subtypes. Whites should not intermix with blacks in Gobineau's opinion, and vice versa, but such mixing had already occurred sufficiently so as to blur the distinctions and eliminate the pure races from the planet.

Gobineau had therefore developed a sense of resignation: while vital to civilizational advancement, racial hybrids weakened the individual strains.[51] As useful products of racial mixing, art and literature were more than offset by the loss of the pure white race to civilization: "The small have been raised. Unfortunately, the great have been lowered by the same process; and this is an evil that nothing can balance or repair."[52] The great civilizations founded by the white race were disappearing as they became "degenerate" due to a crossing of stocks with lower forms.[53]

Social order was the only possible remedy to the rise of inferior, hybrid races, thought Gobineau. Many French aristocrats concurred: all peoples were not equally capable of governance. Gobineau believed himself, like others of his time, a defender of the old order against the rising scourge of the poor or the foreign. He tried to justify his and his family's position atop the social ladder of a nation constructed, he believed, on the greatness of the white race. In his mind, only "heterogeneous" peoples, the products of racial mixing, could possibly "assert that the most different powers are, or can be, possessed in the same measure by every faction of the human race."[54] Gobineau, however, added that not only were the races inherently unequal, but the same inequity existed between the components of each national society. Racial hierarchy became more than simply a comparative civilizational tool in his hands; it propped up the social and political order of traditional Europe. Such reactionary ideas certainly played to the privileged backgrounds of some French scientists and politicians of the nineteenth century.

Firmin, in turn, countered that privilege was easily struck down by equality in education and position within a national structure. "Recognition of the equality of the races entails a definitive recognition of the quality of all social classes in every nation in the world. . . . Wherever the struggle for democracy is being waged, wherever social inequality is still a cause of conflict, the doctrine of the equality of the races will be a salutary remedy," he argued.[55] Firmin saw Gobineau's hierarchy and the resultant inequality of perception and political action as at the heart of all problems of colonized peoples across the world. In Firmin's model, races became social organizations struggling against barriers erected by the upper classes to prevent movement. Such inequality, he thought, "leads to an oligarchic or despotic system."[56] Racial hierarchy and political inequality were thus inextricably intertwined, mutually sustaining entities. Blacks could not hope to escape their position at the bottom of the civilizational pyramid without recognition of their equality by whites on racial and social grounds. Democracy stood as the goal of such subaltern groups, as they needed a forum to be heard and appreciated. Racial justice could not come without political freedom.

Interestingly, Gobineau did not entirely discount the idea of some representative government, as his enlightened white upper classes embraced political liberty. In his description, the white race has "a remarkable, and even extreme, love of liberty, and [is] openly hostile to the formalism under which the Chinese are glad to vegetate, as well as to the strict despotism which is the only way of governing the negro."[57] Gobineau thus echoed the political current of the day, which found primitive blacks unable to govern themselves without a Hobbesian Leviathan in the form of a European government. By contrast, the white race—the upper classes in this conception—had moved away from absolutism to embrace more parliamentary forms of government.

Taking the view from the top, Gobineau found these white elites deeply resentful of encroachments on their personal rights, hence his emphasis on the love of liberty. Firmin, on the other hand, viewed the world from the bottom up, seeing lower classes deprived of liberty by an aristocratic and sometimes tyrannical white order. The Western concept of the individual existed only at the elite level for Gobineau, as he was unwilling to accede to the real existence of individuals among the lower races and classes. Firmin took the opposite stance, preferring to extol individual achievement among these lower races.

Gobineau's conception of racial divides thus led him to deal instead in generalities. He hypothesized French origins among large tribes such as the Normans, Celts, Aryans, and Vandals to validate his view of the white race as superior and grounded in primordial space. The deliberate omission of specific evidence of these links insulated his argument from direct critique: "I will not discuss . . . the moral and intellectual standing of individuals taken one by one."[58] After all, "the peoples who are not of white blood approach beauty, but do not attain it."[59] Gobineau approached much of his essay in the same way—he presented a wide, sweeping history in the classical tradition without many specific, verifiable facts and lacking much in the way of footnotes.

Firmin, in a stylistic as much as intellectual counterpoint, provided evidence directly to refute Gobineau's vague assertions. He presented a very specific analysis of human civilizations, including Egyptians, Hindus/Aryans, and, of course, the black race, particularly in Haiti. In providing those examples, he wove a rich tapestry (again focused on Haiti) of intellectual growth and discourse largely unknown outside of the Caribbean at that time, pointing, for instance, to the "brilliant" writer Ducas Hippolyte, whose poetry and passion rivaled any found in Europe. In this superior mind Firmin saw "an example of the superior moral and intellectual personality found in that Black race."[60] Firmin depicted Hippolyte and others like him as a "constellation of young poets, whose Black brows the Muse caresses with the same solicitous grace as she does those of Caucasian poets."[61] While he praised French Revolutionary forces as worthy of "universal admiration," he believed that black Haitian military leaders such as Henri Christophe or Jean-Jacques Dessalines, as well as the troops they led, were equally praiseworthy for their "extraordinary morality" as seen through both the eyes of the "historian" and those of the "philosopher."[62] The truth of black equality was obvious through objective evidence or considerations of comparative morality.

Despite the admittedly hasty nature of his research, Firmin managed to provide significant specific details to counter Gobineau's broad thesis of racial inequality. By providing these examples, though, Firmin did not necessarily reduce the power of Gobineau's more general concepts. Consequently, he continued his combat against the French writer and the notions of racial inequality with more transatlantic travel between the Caribbean and France.

Denouement and Exile

Firmin returned to Haiti in 1887, gaining a prominent voice in politics as Florvil Hyppolite gained the presidency after a bloody struggle. Following the completion of a new constitution, Firmin assumed the post of minister of finance and foreign affairs.[63] He at first dedicated himself to correcting years of neglect in the financial system; however, his most famous intervention would come against the rising power of the United States. The Americans, represented by Frederick Douglass, attempted to gain control of a small corner of Haiti called the Môle Saint-Nicolas. When rebuffed, they sent out a naval squadron as a show of force, one that ultimately returned to the United States in defeat. Allegations of backroom dealings sealed the fate of both Douglass and Firmin, both of whom were out of office by 1891.[64] Marked by scandal, Firmin spent the six years from 1891 to 1897 working as a lawyer in Cap-Haïtien and, apparently, combating the racist dogma he still perceived in anthropological circles.[65] Records show him as present at two meetings of the Paris anthropological society in 1892, each time responding to discussions he thought headed toward the separatist ideals of Gobineau.

The first of these meetings, on April 7, 1892, featured a discussion of "weaker" races inhabiting mountainous areas, groups that appeared inadequate when compared to the "stronger" races across the plains. Clémence Royer, among the most prominent members of the society and the original translator of Darwin into French, claimed ownership of this "evolutionary" law, which she had previously presented to the society.[66] At this point, Firmin joined the discussion, presenting many of the same ideas found in his book. He argued that the members settled far too easily on "the irrevocable inferiority of certain races without taking into account the external conditions in which they find themselves." These groups could easily raise themselves to a level commensurate with the "other civilized races." He cited specifically the example of Haiti, where sufficient time since independence had permitted an unbroken string of intellectual development. His comments, perhaps out of place in the discussion, received no reply in the record from Royer or any other member of the society.[67] Despite his best efforts over the previous eight years, he had still not managed to destroy the vestiges of Gobineau.

Firmin's fight did not end there, however. Only two weeks later he again rose in the society, this time to participate in a discussion of "negro" skulls and cephalic index ratings led by Gabriel de Mortillet and Léon Manouvrier, another well-published physical anthropologist. This time focusing on Africa, Firmin thought that Africans could not "show the great qualities they possess" due to "inferior conditions." While perhaps a repetitive argument, Firmin this time managed to elicit a response. Arthur Bordier, the society's president for 1892 and a professor at the École d'anthropologie de Paris (founded by Paul Broca), rose in response. He asked Firmin "if, among his ancestors, there weren't any whites."[68] Bordier thought that any trace of "white blood" could have modified Firmin's skull shape, making it more Occidental and less "negroid" in appearance. Firmin countered that a white ancestry was possible, but he did not believe lineage affected his intelligence in any manner. Manouvrier capped the discussion by calling for all blacks in Paris to submit to skull measurements.[69] While Firmin had countered these ideas through specifics in both his work and verbal comments, his colleagues continued to see him as the exception to the rule, the proof of Gobineau's assertion that the mixing of races served to elevate the "lower" classes ever closer to the "superior" classes.

This discussion is the last record of Firmin's direct participation in the Paris anthropological society. Though his verbal sparring with the anthropologists seems to have made little direct mark, his ideas did draw the attention of one of the great French minds of the late nineteenth century, Frédéric Passy, an economist, politician, and future Nobel Peace Prize laureate, in 1892. In that year Passy took the rare step of seeking out Firmin to acquire a copy of *Egalité* for review and presentation, as opposed to the routine procedure of authors requesting an audience. He discussed the work in the Académie des sciences morales et politiques, the premier state-sponsored institution for the study of the human condition and part of the Institut de France. Passy told the assembled academics: "Mr. Firmin's book eloquently pleads the case for the equality of the races. . . . Anthropology, history or linguistics, cerebral characteristics or abilities . . . nothing escapes his patient and detailed investigation. . . . Firmin demonstrates a truly extraordinary erudition; there are few works that so powerfully destroy the supposed inferiority of the negro brain."[70] While Passy's remarks did little to change the immediate views of his colleagues, he presented Firmin's work to an audience to which the Haitian scholar could never have hoped to gain access, testament to the power of the racial equality argument to at least some contemporary minds.

Despite this success in academia, Firmin's fortunes soon took a turn for the worse in Haiti. With the death of Florvil Hyppolite in 1897, General Tirésias Sam took control of the Haitian government; in the early days of that regime,

Firmin briefly resumed his post as foreign minister. Once again caught up in scandal, this time in the Chamber of Deputies, Firmin retired late in 1897, only to be recalled by Sam in 1900 to serve as the plenipotentiary minister to Paris, a post he held until 1902. Few records survive attesting to his activities in that period.[71] He remained on the registers of the Paris anthropological society throughout this period, up to and beyond his death, at least until 1938. By that time he was the oldest tenured member on the rolls, which listed him accurately as having entered in 1884.[72] He attended the 1900 Pan-African Conference with the ex-president of Haiti, François-Denis Légitime. This illustrious gathering brought together representatives from Africa, Canada, and the United States, including W. E. B. DuBois. Participating black intellectuals drafted pleas to the colonizing powers calling for reform in Africa, but they had little direct impact.[73]

The departure of General Sam in 1902 brought Nord Alexis to the presidency; no friend of Firmin, Alexis sent his political rival into exile. During this time, spent largely in St. Thomas, Firmin often used natural metaphors to illustrate his positivist philosophy. At one point he described a "vast and majestic horizon, awakening the idea of infinity like liberation of the human soul."[74] Firmin envisaged a time without racial and national distinctions. Avoiding the traditional depictions of black and white mixing, Firmin instead turned toward Europe: "Far be it for me ... to consider myself qualified to proclaim the inferiority of the English vis-à-vis the French. Each has strengths and weaknesses that one cannot deny.... Perhaps they could gain from completing, from modifying each other."[75] He thus espoused a radical recombination of notionally disparate types to find greater strength. Like Gobineau, he saw much strength in the mixing of groups. Unlike his foe, however, he was convinced that such a march was necessary, important, perhaps inevitable, and leading toward progress. For Haiti, his erstwhile homeland, he advocated a similar recombination, this time with France. Haitians had "nothing to lose and everything to gain from following the French method" both in terms of education and republican method of governance. The resultant human group would lead, in his eyes, to "the most beautiful flowering of urbane Roman civilization, which one finds only in the beautiful country of France."[76] Firmin, so sophisticated in his critique of racialized thought, did not expect all positive progress to emanate strictly from black achievements. Rather, he saw French intellectual and political methods as useful and interesting; after all, he had descended largely from those traditions himself. In his mind, the continued circulation of people and ideas from all sides, both black and white, could destroy the barriers erected by Gobineau and by anthropological science.

Firmin's Final Act

As with many forward-thinking intellectuals, Firmin's influence did not end with his death in 1911. His devotion to progress forced him to believe in the continued relevance of his works after his death; as early as 1885 he wrote of a "shiningly obvious truth. . . . These small traces which I have indicated will be sufficient for a sagacious mind."[77] The anthropologist intended to leave bread crumbs for future scientists to consider and follow as they moved toward objective truth. He had hoped that his colleagues in the Société d'anthropologie de Paris would continue his work eliminating racial boundaries; unfortunately, few, if any, took him up on his proposition in his lifetime. Instead, he found another way to continue the fight against racist dogma even after death and across time. His legacy motivated and informed future Pan-African and négritude scholars, foremost among them Jean Price-Mars.

Just as Firmin railed against the inequities of European colonialism and the use of Gobineau's doctrine as its justification, so too did Price-Mars work to "decolonize knowledge."[78] Wisdom and understanding, in his view, were the province of all peoples, not just those with military or political power. This passing of the torch did not occur exclusively via text; Price-Mars knew Firmin from some shared time in Europe. The younger man reported a dinner he had in Paris with Firmin, the esteemed diplomat's wife, and Firmin's daughter Anna in 1901. He unabashedly recounted his admiration of the young woman, but was saddened by her death the following year.[79] Even in 1906 Price-Mars gave lectures declaring the absolute equality of the races, talks so close in tone and substance to those of Firmin that Haitian president Nord Alexis condemned him as "Firminist" and "seditious" (Firmin was then in exile in St. Thomas).[80]

In some ways Firmin was among the first of the "postcolonial" theorists, as he wrote roughly four generations after Haitian independence.[81] Firmin's critique of Gobineau and other racial theorists pointed to the fundamental paradox of the French method of colonization. The Haitian theorist struggled to conceive of why France, in his mind the torchbearer for the idea of a "universal brotherhood of man," did not produce laws "proclaiming their [the human races] equality."[82] Even Gobineau had added a similarly hopeful note in his analysis, finding that "if the human races were equal, the course of history would form an affecting, glorious, and magnificent picture."[83] Firmin believed that if anthropologists could move past the fundamental conception of racial distinction and inherent inferiority, they could then contribute to a worldwide effort to level the playing field.

While some scholars have suggested that Firmin was a martyr, deserving of a place next to Toussaint L'Ouverture and Dessalines in the pantheon of Haitian heroes,[84] he was perhaps more important for his example and his belief in the permeability of human-created barriers. His ideas prefigured the development of modern French ethnology and anthropology, a process that would move through Durkheimian sociology to the concepts developed by Claude Lévi-Strauss and Pierre Bourdieu. Intellectual and physical movement enabled Firmin's continued relevance into the twenty-first century, ironically tied to his great foil Gobineau. Démétrius André, one of Firmin's admirers, believed the scholar's work would live on after his death: "No, Firmin, you aren't completely dead! You left this earth, but the next instant you woke up to eternal life."[85] Firmin's voyage to demonstrate the equality of the races had led him across the Atlantic, across time, across death, delivering his message to contemporaries and successors alike.

Notes

I must thank Laurent Dubois for pointing me toward Firmin as an important but little-known figure in French anthropology. As always, I owe much to Kathryn Leonard for her copyediting and honest commentary. The views expressed in this article are those of the author and do not reflect the official policy or position of the U.S. Air Force, Department of Defense, or U.S. government. Any errors that remain are my own.

1. Firmin, *L'Effort dans le mal*, 24–25.

2. Dash, "Nineteenth-Century Haiti," 46, 50.

3. Not surprisingly, much of this writing has come from Haiti, where his political legacy continues to resonate. See, for example, Benjamin, *Diplomatie d'Anténor Firmin*; Péan, *L'échec du Firminisme*; and Jean, *La pensée politique haïtienne*.

4. Benjamin, *Diplomatie d'Anténor Firmin*, 21.

5. Janvier, *L'Egalité des Races*, 25.

6. Nkrumah, "Speech at the Opening Session of the First Meeting of the Editorial Board of the Encyclopaedia Africana." Also quoted in Fluehr-Lobban, "Anténor Firmin," 94. Jean Price-Mars (1876–1969) was an important social critic and writer, particularly during and subsequent to the 1915–1935 American occupation of Haiti. He described the localized origins of Haitian culture as distinct and unique when compared to others in the region. For more on Price-Mars, see Shannon, *Jean Price-Mars*.

7. Price-Mars, *Joseph-Anténor Firmin*, 14.

8. André, *L'anniversaire ou éloge de Joseph-Anténor Firmin*, 7; also cited in Moise, "Anténor Firmin," 14.

9. André, *L'anniversaire ou éloge de Joseph-Anténor Firmin*, 9; also quoted in Moise, "Anténor Firmin," 16. See also the discussion of these lines in Magloire-Danton, "Anténor Firmin and Jean Price-Mars," 150–170.

10. Firmin, *Equality of the Human Races*, 4. The original appeared as *De l'égalite des races humaines (anthropologie positive)*. I have chosen to use the English translations of both Firmin and Gobineau to assist in references for the nonspecialist. For direct comparison of the translation and original of Firmin's work, see Bernasconi, "Haitian in Paris," 365–383.

11. Ibid., 334.

12. André, *Anniversaire*, 11–14; Price-Mars, *Joseph-Anténor Firmin*, 146, 162. Although Carolyn Fluehr-Lobban, in "Anténor Firmin," 449–466, refers to Firmin as a "diplomat" during this period in Paris, the best available information indicates he left Haiti as an exile in 1884 after a brief visit to Venezuela (where André indicates he attended the "Caracas parties"). See also Benjamin, *Diplomatie d'Anténor Firmin*, for more on this movement as an exile, not a diplomatic mission.

13. Janvier, *L'Egalité des Races*, 5.

14. Ibid., 13, 19.

15. Ibid., 22–23.

16. Firmin, *Equality*, liv.

17. Price-Mars, *Joseph-Anténor Firmin*, 148.

18. "394eme Séance, 17 Jul 1884," *Bulletins et Mémoires de la Société d'Anthropologie de Paris*, IIIe Série, Tome 7 (1884), 571.

19. Smith, *Gobineau et l'histoire naturelle*, 67–68, 71.

20. "394eme Séance"; see 585 for Quatrefages's summation of the overall debate.

21. Ibid., 583.

22. Ibid., 583–584.

23. Bernasconi, "Haitian in Paris," 372–373.

24. Firmin, *Equality*, lviii

25. Ibid., 145.

26. Ibid., liv.

27. "400eme Séance, 18 December 1884," *Bulletins et Mémoires de la Société d'Anthropologie de Paris*, IIIe Série, Tome 7 (1884), 835. Dehoux also authored *Du sacrifice humain et de l'anthropophagie dans le vaudou.*

28. For a full consideration of the notion of paradigm construction and shift in scientific society, see Kuhn, *Structure of Scientific Revolutions*.

29. "416eme Séance, 1 October 1885," *Bulletins et Mémoires de la Société d'anthropologie de Paris*, IIIe Série, Tome 8 (1885), 599.

30. Fluehr-Lobban, "Legacy and Continuing Relevance," 88. Fluehr-Lobban gives no citation for this inscription, which is not present in the extant society bulletin.

31. Firmin, *Equality*, liv–lv.

32. Gobineau, *Inequality of the Human Races*, 208.

33. Firmin, *Equality*, 140.

34. Buenzod, *Formation de la pensée de Gobineau*, 327.

35. Gobineau, *Inequality*, xiv.

36. Firmin, *Equality*, 145. Topinard was, in many respects, Broca's successor as the general leader of French physical anthropology following the latter's death in 1880.

37. Gobineau, *Inequality*, 205–206.

38. Ibid., 205.

39. Ibid., 180.

40. Ibid., 206.

41. Ibid.

42. Ibid., 207.

43. Firmin, *Equality*, 384–385.

44. Ibid., 150.

45. Gobineau, *Inequality*, 157.

46. Firmin, *Equality*, 377.

47. Ibid., 444.

48. Ibid., 440.

49. Ibid.

50. Gobineau, *Inequality*, 133.

51. Ibid., 170.

52. Ibid., 209.

53. Ibid., 25.

54. Ibid., 37.

55. Firmin, *Equality*, 438.

56. Ibid.

57. Gobineau, *Inequality*, 207.

58. Ibid., 179.

59. Ibid., 151.

60. Firmin, *Equality*, 297–300. Firmin devotes all of chapter 12 (295–322) to similar examples. Most of his examples come from the literary realm, such as his discussions of Emmanuel Edouard and Tertulien Guilbaud.

61. Ibid., 305.

62. Ibid., 367–368.

63. André, *Anniversaire*, 17.

64. Ibid., 19. See also the discussion in Price-Mars, *Joseph-Anténor Firmin*; and, in great detail, in Benjamin, *Diplomatie d'Anténor Firmin*.

65. Price-Mars, *Joseph-Anténor Firmin*, 300.

66. "556eme Séance, 7 April 1892," *Bulletins et Mémoires de la Société d'anthropologie de Paris*, IVe Série, Tome 3 (1892), 235.

67. Ibid., 236.

68. "557eme Séance, 21 April 1892," *Bulletins et Mémoires de la Société d'anthropologie de Paris*, IVe Série, Tome 3 (1892), 329–330. Robert Bernasconi attributes this remark to Bordier, while Carolyn Fluehr-Lobban attributes it to Clémence Royer, perhaps confusing the April 7 and April 21 meetings.

69. Ibid., 330.

70. Passy, "De l'Egalité des Races Humaines," 726–727. André also comments on the reso- nance of Firmin's work in Paris, particularly on "l'enseignement officiel" (*Anniversaire*, 15).

71. André, *Anniversaire*, 22–25. See also Benjamin's account in *Diplomatie d'Anténor Firmin*.

72. "Vie de la Société," *Bulletins et Mémoires de la Société d'anthropologie de Paris*, VIIIe Série, Tome 9 (1938), 1–16.

73. Fluehr-Lobban, "Pioneer of Anthropology," 463.

74. Firmin, *Lettres de Saint-Thomas*, ii.

75. Ibid., 383.

76. Ibid., 386.

77. Firmin, *Equality*, lv. The second part of this line is rendered in Firmin's original as "Verum animo satis hoc [sic] vestigia parva sagaci sunt," a reference to Lucretius's *De rerum natura* (On the Nature of Things), an exposition of Epicurean philosophy. Translation from Rev. John Selby Watson, 1851. Thanks to John Martin for this reference.

78. Magloire-Danton, "Revolution, Memory, Humanism," 170.

79. Price-Mars, *Joseph-Anténor Firmin*, 328–329.

80. Fluehr-Lobban, "Legacy and Continuing Relevance," 90.

81. Ibid., 98.

82. Firmin, *Equality*, 404.

83. Gobineau, *Inequality*, 168.

84. Moise, "Firmin," 86.

85. André, *Anniversaire*, 34.

Bibliography

André, Démétrius. *L'anniversaire ou éloge de Joseph-Anténor Firmin*. Port-au-Prince: J. Verrollot, 1912.

Benjamin, Georges. *La Diplomatie d'Anténor Firmin: Ses péripéties, ses aspects*. Paris: A. Pedone, 1960.

Bernasconi, Robert. "A Haitian in Paris: Anténor Firmin as a Philosopher against Racism." *Patterns of Prejudice* 42.4–5 (2008): 365–383.

Buenzod, Janine. *La formation de la pensée de Gobineau et l'essai sur l'inégalité des races humaines*. Paris: A. G. Nizet, 1967.

Bulletins et Mémoires de la Société d'Anthropologie de Paris.

Dash, J. Michael. "Nineteenth-Century Haiti and the Archipelago of the Americas: Antenor Firmin's Letters from St. Thomas." *Research in African Literatures* 35.2 (Summer 2004): 44–53.

Firmin, Anténor. *L'Effort dans le mal*. Port-au-Prince: Editions Panorama, 1962.

———. *De l'égalité des races humaines (anthropologie positive)*. Paris: F. Pichon, 1885.

———. *The Equality of the Human Races*. Trans. Asselin Charles. New York: Garland, 2000.

———. *Lettres de Saint-Thomas: Etudes sociologiques, historiques et litteraires*. 2nd ed. Port-au-Prince: Editions Fardin, 1986.

Fluehr-Lobban, Carolyn. "Anténor Firmin: Haitian Pioneer of Anthropology." *American Anthropologist* New Series 102.3 (September 2000): 449–466.

———. "Anténor Firmin: His Legacy and Continuing Relevance." In *Reinterpreting the Haitian Revolution and Its Cultural Aftershocks*, ed. Martin Munro and Elizabeth Walcott-Hackshaw, 86–101. Kingston: University of the West Indies Press, 2006.

Gobineau, Arthur de. *Essai sur l'inégalité des races humaines*. Paris: Didot, 1853–1855.

———. *The Inequality of the Human Races*. Trans. Adrian Collins. New York: William Heinemann, 1915.

Janvier, Louis-Joseph. *L'Egalité des Races*. Paris: Imprimerie G. Bougier et cie, 1885.

Jean, Eddy Arnold. *La pensée politique haïtienne*. Port-au-Prince: Editions Haiti-Demain, 2001.

Magloire-Danton, Gérarde. "Anténor Firmin and Jean Price-Mars: Revolution, Memory, Humanism." *Small Axe* 18 (September 2005): 150–170.

Moise, Claude. "Anténor Firmin." *Conjonction: Bulletin de l'Institut français d'Haïti* 117 (1971): 8–86.

Nkrumah, Kwame. "Speech at the Opening Session of the First Meeting of the Editorial Board of the Encyclopaedia Africana." September 24, 1964. University of Ghana. http://www.africawithin.com/nkrumah/encyclopedia.htm.

Passy, Frédéric. "De l'Egalité des Races Humaines." *Séances et Travaux de l'Académie des Sciences Morales et Politiques* 52.138 (1892): 726–727.

Péan, Marc. *L'échec du Firminisme*. Port-au-Prince: H. Deschamps, 1985.

Price-Mars, Jean. *Joseph-Anténor Firmin: L'indomptable lutteur, mal aimé et martyr. Une grande partie de l'histoire d'Haiti à travers la formation et le destin d'un homme*. Port-au-Prince: Imprimerie Séminaire Adventiste, 1964.

Shannon, Magdaline W. *Jean Price-Mars, the Haitian Elite, and the American Occupation, 1915–1935*. New York: St. Martin's Press, 1996.

Smith, Annette. *Gobineau et l'histoire naturelle*. Geneva: Droz, 1984.

Activist in Exile

José da Natividade Saldanha, Free Man of Color in the Tropical Atlantic

Amy Caldwell de Farias

> I do not find conformity
>
> In dragging vile chains,
>
> Suppressing free ideas,
>
> Without liberty or a patria:
>
> To have one's reason and will
>
> Always subject to force.
>
> —José da Natividade Saldanha

José da Natividade Saldanha, the illegitimate son of a white priest and a poor black laundress, is an unfamiliar name to most historians and literary scholars of Brazil. Poet, lawyer, and secretary of the revolutionary government during the 1824 republican revolt in the port city of Recife, Pernambuco—known as the Confederation of the Equator (Confederação do Equador)[1]—he is a salient example of a Black Atlantic rebel in the early nineteenth century. After the defeat of the movement, Saldanha traveled to Philadelphia, New York, Paris, Liverpool, Caracas, and Bogotá. During his travels, he attempted to garner support to revive the revolt in northeastern Brazil. Accused of being a "black Jacobin" during his stay in France, and viewed as a dangerous republican in Colombia, he was murdered in 1831. This essay traces the multifarious and fascinating intellectual influences—both European and American—that informed Saldanha's anticolonial political project. It also illustrates how the poet's glorification of the virtuous characteristics of the Brazilian "mestizos" forged a new moral and racial identity for his compatriots. Finally, this article discusses why a man like Saldanha would represent such a formidable challenge to the racist and oppressive hegemonic power of the new Brazilian monarchy and, later, other powers.[2]

The difficulties of studying Saldanha, a free man of color who was not a member of the economic elite, are numerous. As a Brazilian historian recently lamented, there is still no space in the historiography on the independence of Brazil (1822) dedicated to the "negro," the "brown" (*pardo*), and the "mulattos" battles to achieve equal rights and to forge a new type of justice.[3] Moreover, as Herman Bennett recently argued, "the study of people of African descent remains mired in slavery's institutional prism," reminding us that scholars need to analyze the creation of black identities in the Americas from a different methodological perspective, one that does not center the black experience on the institution of slavery.[4] Paul Gilroy highlighted this poverty of the methodological practices employed to study the Black Atlantic in 1993. He noted that we still "struggle to have blacks perceived as agents, as people with cognitive capacities and even with an intellectual history."[5]

Saldanha was an intellectual who was actively involved in the transatlantic exchange of ideas. The politics of his poetry and his avid adherence to and dialogue with the Enlightenment and classical republicanism allowed for the possibility of a new cultural-ideological sphere to emerge, one that included black, brown, and "mulatto" intellectuals. The republican ideology that he professed during the Confederation of the Equator helped him during his painfully long period of exile to cling tenaciously to his dream of one day witnessing the implantation of an "American" system of government in Brazil, one based on republican values and a rejection of a monarch in the New World. This plan would alarm the members of the Holy Alliance, and Saldanha, who was viewed as one of the most arduous proponents of republicanism in Brazil, found his return to his beloved country permanently blocked. Living the life of a black intellectual in exile was fraught with hardships. He becomes this exiled and, afterward, oppositional intellectual.[6]

Who Was José da Natividade Saldanha?

Despite his racial and social background,[7] both obstacles in a hierarchical, racist society such as that of Pernambuco in the early nineteenth century, Saldanha managed to acquire the education characteristic of the wealthy elite classes. In 1817 an anticolonial revolt erupted in Recife, the capital city of the northeastern state of Pernambuco. It is unclear whether Saldanha participated. We do know, however, that after the triumph of the imperial forces, the police invaded his home to search for a poem that Saldanha wrote during the revolt. The poet had, luckily, already escaped and remained in hiding for several weeks. Local legend has it that many people copied and memorized the poem.[8]

After graduating from the Seminary of Olinda in 1819, Saldanha decided against a religious career, preferring to apply his talents toward the study of law, which, at the time, was a common academic choice for many of Latin America's most influential intellectuals. Saldanha managed to obtain a scholarship to study in Coimbra, Portugal. According to his school records, he was an exemplary student. During his first year of study in Coimbra, he won a prize based solely on academic merit. Due to his precarious financial situation in Portugal, he was forced to convert the prize into a cash scholarship. Overcome by nostalgia for his country and friends, in 1822 the law student published his first book of poetry, *Poemas Offerecidos aos Amantes do Brasil* (Poems Offered to the Lovers of Brazil).

Saldanha triumphantly returned to Brazil with a law degree from Coimbra University and a euphoric sense of pride in his newly independent country. He opened his law office in Recife and became active in an organization known as the Forum Recifense. According to a local historian, the organization's spirit was cemented by laws and gilded by poetry.[9] The promise of a successful future was thus slowly becoming a plausible reality for Saldanha: the illegitimate son of a Catholic priest and a poor black laundress had, it seemed, at least partially succeeded in overcoming the prejudices of nineteenth-century Brazilian society.[10]

Saldanha was an archetype of Latin American intellectuals of the time, cosmopolitan young writers who lived through the pulsating years of the independence process and, due to their adherence to the "new enlightened ideas," were, in a sense, "strangers nowhere in the world."[11] Instead, they considered themselves inheritors and interpreters of the so-called Radical Enlightenment, a movement that expanded far beyond Europe's borders, such as, for example, the Haitian Revolution and other revolts and movements during the independence epoch of the Americas. And, as Nick Nesbitt so eloquently argues, the Radical Enlightenment was a "transnational, world-systemic historical process."[12] Through their philosophical treatises, political speeches, and literary works, proponents of the movement hoped to contribute toward the construction of a new historical model for their nations.

In 1823, when news of the dissolution of the Constituent Assembly arrived in Pernambuco, followed by the subsequent imposition of a hastily and undemocratically written constitution, the lawyer Saldanha explained to his fellow citizens why they would have to reject the newly promulgated constitution. However, after the merciless defeat of the Confederation of the Equator,

Saldanha, then also the editor of a periodical, *Argos Pernambucano*, and the popularly elected secretary of the new rebellious provincial government, feared for his life. Having escaped from the fury of the imperial government's reaction to his above-mentioned patriotic sonnet, which he had hastily written during the earlier revolt (1817), he was now forced to succumb to the torrential force of the newly enthroned emperor of Brazil, Pedro I.

Saldanha fled the country in 1824, one year after his joyful return, and spent the next eight years in exile.[13] With the help of the U.S. consul stationed in Recife, Saldanha was able to escape to Philadelphia. One can only imagine, then, Saldanha's disappointment upon arriving in the city of liberty when, due to his race, he was barred from eating in the dining room with his fellow exiles.[14] Perhaps it is due to the racism he suffered in Philadelphia that he moved on to New York City shortly thereafter. In a letter to a friend dated December 1824, Saldanha observed that there was religious tolerance in New York, and women were seen in public places both day and night. However, the great deal of luxury he noted alarmed him. He ended the letter reminding his friend of a prophesy the French philosopher Gabriel Bonnot de Mably had made—that is, that luxury would be the downfall of republican states.[15]

It is unclear why Saldanha left New York, or even exactly when, but it appears that his next stop was France. Already a few days after his arrival Saldanha was summoned by the police in Paris and given forty-eight hours to leave. Why was he expelled when several of his compatriots were allowed to remain? I believe it was not only due to his ardent defense of republicanism but because he was an educated black man. The Atlantic World—and France in particular—was still haunted by the "spectre of Haiti," and Saldanha, labeled one of the most "brazen revolutionaries in the world," was considered a tangible threat to white society. His "extensive knowledge" and European education were mentioned in a French document. Saldanha was accused of not only professing the "most unbridled principle of demagoguery" but, even more serious a charge, of "propagating anarchy in Brazil and provoking the destruction of the white population in the country."[16] While in France, Saldanha's mail from Pernambuco and Coimbra was intercepted and his manuscripts confiscated. The papers have never resurfaced.[17]

The exiled poet, enraptured by Símon Bolívar's dream of creating a republican South America, decided, after a brief stay in Liverpool, England, to travel to Gran Colombia.[18] Bolívar's spectacular feats, which have "no equal in anticolonial history," must have captured the imagination of the poet, as well as of the revolutionary leaders of the 1824 revolt, as is evident in their adoption of the Colombian constitution.[19]

Antonio Joaquim de Mello's biography of his childhood friend Saldanha provides only vague and cryptic information concerning the generous reception that Simón Bolívar offered to Saldanha. We do know, however, that Saldanha arrived first in Caracas. In the 1980s Vamireh Chacon, a Brazilian diplomat, managed to locate two juridical discourses written and published by Saldanha while living in Venezuela, the first on religious tolerance and the other on the dissolution of marriage. One can imagine the scandal caused by such polemical writings thanks to another important find: a newspaper clipping prohibiting Saldanha from practicing law in Caracas.[20]

Poor and unemployed, Saldanha moved to Bogotá, where he survived by giving private lessons in Latin and rhetoric. Two of his favorite students, João and José Ortiz, grew up to be relatively successful writers in nineteenth-century Colombia. It is thanks to the publication of their memoirs that the mystery of their young Brazilian teacher's death is partially revealed. It appears that after a stormy night, Saldanha's dead body was found in a gutter overrun with water from the previous evening's heavy rainfall. Whether Saldanha's death was accidental or whether he was murdered, the truth remains uncertain to this day.[21] What is clear, however, is that throughout his tumultuous life and despite the suffering and hardships, Saldanha, unlike so many of his Brazilian contemporaries, never betrayed his principles.[22] His philosophical assumptions (equality, liberty, and virtue) are the transparent waters that flow through his discourses—both political and poetical.

The Political Importance of Saldanha's Poetry

The historical sources on Saldanha—and on this revolt in general—are sparse.[23] Scholars tend to classify the literature produced from the two decades preceding Brazilian independence up until 1836 as "subliterature."[24] Publishing in the 1820s, Saldanha's works would fall into this rather derogatory category.[25] The omission of Saldanha from the panorama of Brazilian national literature can be seen as an absence of a lack of historical sensibility on the part of the critics. There has been a tendency to de-emphasize the historical and focus on the theoretical and conceptual structure of his work.[26] One needs to read the poems as historical discourses and allow the vivid images of the local heroes to emerge with more clarity. Saldanha the revolutionary used the universalism of the Enlightenment to challenge the hegemonic political culture and colonial discourse emanating from Rio de Janeiro, the capital of the new Brazilian empire. In his poetry, however, localism infuses his work as ideological fervor. His narrativization of local life alongside his defense of "nativism" helped him to create a local historical idiom and, in doing so, transform himself into a respected leader of the revolt.

Although Saldanha employs an archaic poetical form—the Pindaric ode, named after the ancient Greek poet Pindar—he actually expanded the rigid and rhythmic meter of the stanzas in order to lodge some of Pernambuco's main historical protagonists, providing them, thus, with a new existence. Consciously adopting the poetical form used by the Greek poet and educator, Saldanha aestheticized his native city of Recife, ornamenting it not with monuments but with the virtuous and audaciously brave acts of its heroes such as Henrique Dias, the leader of the black troops, and the Indian leader Felipe Camarão.

Saldanha's "Pindar odes" retold the history of the seventeenth-century Dutch invasion of Pernambuco. His version, a Brazilian (or, more specifically, a Pernambucano) one, captivated Recife's urban lettered population.[27] For perhaps the first time, Pernambucanos appeared as the principal actors in their neglected history, and, more important, in the poet's odes they participated not as Portuguese subjects in a colonized land but as Brazilians defending their homes. Hence, while the form of Saldanha's verses relied upon traditional practices, their content and ideological intent were innovative.

Recognizing the pliable nature of historical figures, the poet manipulated them in order to undergird and forge a new model of moral virtue. Saldanha implored his fellow citizens to follow in the footsteps of the neglected heroes: "Their example follow, follow their light / Sons of the patria, young Brazilians."[28] But rather than summoning his compatriots to free their country from foreign domination, Saldanha pleaded with them to assume their roles as "Pernambucanos" or "true Brazilians."[29] In what he would later call the "sacred cause of Independence,"[30] he argued that the blood that fell from their wounds had the power to produce future heroes, capable, like their ancestors, of liberating the region from domination.[31]

Through a careful reading of Saldanha's poetry and especially his Pindaric odes, it becomes clear that he appealed to and used history as an ideological tool for rescuing his contemporary Brazil. He believed in the possibility of an independent Brazilian nation, one where it was still possible to ameliorate the stark contrasts within Brazilian society—such as barbarism versus civility, the decadently rich and powerful versus the degradingly miserable and voiceless, and so forth—and usher in a more just "modern" epoch that was in line with the "lights of the century." In his search, Saldanha found inspiration in Pernambuco's ancestors, who served as a theoretical support to help his cause and open the doors of the present to the social and political truths propagated by the Enlightenment.

Saldanha addressed the population of Recife as autonomous political actors and not as malleable pieces in a hegemonic struggle for power. His poetical reading of the past was done with the hope of creating a tangible space of moral resistance through which liberty could flow. For that reason, the poet made no attempt to "amputate the past"; moreover, he exulted in a Brazilian race, including its Portuguese elements, and took pride in the virtuous characteristics of Brazil's mestizos and mulattos. His heroes have an aesthetic power that gave life to his very accurate portraits of the past. We see here an example of the political use of the past. His artistically sculpted impressions created a type of sublime beauty. His main heroes, Henrique Dias, a black man, and the Indian Felipe Camarão, did not fear death and were willing to sacrifice their very existence in order to defend the "patria."[32] In Saldanha's poetry, a transformed Recife assumed the center stage as the historic leader to defend the "patria" against any attempt to infringe upon the liberty of Brazilians. This transformation shattered the hierarchy of rhetorical mirrors that Pernambucanos used to judge themselves. Saldanha thus showed them a different image of the colonized self. Bravery, loyalty, and the stoic physical sacrifices of their ancestors dazzled his compatriots. For example, one reads that Felipe Camarão, the illustrious Brazilian, caused death to rain on the Dutch, thus forcing them to depart. In other words, Camarão, a Brazilian Indian, defeats the powerful white Dutch colonizers.

Saldanha, a man of African heritage who did not overtly address the question of race, had even more fabulous adventures to tell about Henrique Dias, the leader of the black militia. He wrote: "How unsuccessfully / You arrogant Belgian try to escape from the lightning! / The First Portuguese flag / Already trembles on the walls; / You Dutch, with rare luck, / Bring your pompous face down to the African arm." The poem ends reminding the reader that the whole world should know that the Brazilian people also created "more than human hearts, who [the Brazilians] do not envy either the Greeks or the Romans."[33]

This intervention of the nonwhite, colonized Brazilian-Pernambucano to save Recife for the Portuguese empire created fissures in the traditional history. The urban population of Recife read this "new history" with enthusiasm, an enthusiasm that created in them patriotic sensibilities—if one may judge from the popular nature of the revolt. It is important to note that even after the imperial government had sent troops to invade the city and hired a Scottish mercenary to bomb the port of Recife, enthusiasm for the revolt remained a tangible threat for many years to come.[34]

The Journalist and His Concern for the People

As mentioned earlier, there are numerous references to people memorizing and citing Saldanha's poems, yet due to the sophisticated construction of their verses, they were perhaps only read by a minority: Recife's lettered population. How, then, did Saldanha reach the barely literate masses? By turning from poetry to journalism! Saldanha, convinced of the acuity of his ideas, assumed the editorship of a periodical entitled *Argos Pernambucano*. Overcoming his initial reluctance to found a journal, he accepted the task because, as he wrote, "After having made the firm proposal to not write any periodical, we now see the necessity to change our minds and to write something."[35] Saldanha wrote a cogent analysis of the Brazilian constitution, hastily promulgated by Emperor Pedro I, and offered a compelling reason why it should be rejected: the constitution was not written by the people's representatives but, instead, hastily written by the king and a few of his advisers after the dissolution of the Brazilian Constituent Assembly in 1823. In *Argos*, he modeled his writing style after one of his most admired intellectuals: Thomas Paine.[36]

The similarity of styles found in the author of the *Common Sense* and the editor of *Argos* could surely not be a mere coincidence. Thomas Paine once wrote: "As it is my design to make those that can scarcely read understand, I shall therefore avoid every literary ornament and put it in a language as plain as the alphabet."[37] Compare this with Saldanha's opening number of *Argos*:

> We will write in a simple style because we write for the people, and for this rea-
> son, we will not frequently cite the different authors about which this material has
> been written. For as long as the people apprehend the truths, it is of little impor-
> tance to know which author first saw and patented them [the truths].[38]

Or, as expressed in the second number of *Argos*, "we developed and demonstrated our proposal with clarity and exactitude."[39]

Saldanha the journalist and astute observer of history adopted Paine's pedagogical style to further his goal: the creation of an enlightened and virtuous citizen. For example, the subject matter of *Argos* consisted almost entirely of a discussion and explanation of the project for the Brazilian constitution and the urgent necessity to reject it. Like Paine, Saldanha presented his ideas as "simple facts." He reminded his readers that there were numerous reasons to oppose the new constitution, but none so compelling as the idea that the king—and not the people—had promulgated the constitution: "if there were no more reasons to reject it, one would be enough: the fact that it was granted by the king." Furthermore, the journalist explained how, through the ages, it was the king who had perniciously promoted a type of forgetfulness that helped him to usurp the historical rights of the people.[40]

Saldanha's poetry employed the didactic power of example to provide his fellow citizens with a model of citizenship, thereby creating the idea of a Brazilian race, one that is respected and even envied all over the world. In *Argos* he applied the same concept, albeit in a simpler language, claiming that the true citizen was a soldier.[41] Moreover, he argued that citizenship in a free country was not granted; it had to be earned. Whosoever did not contribute— morally and physically—toward the prosperity of the nation was not worthy of being called a Brazilian.

Republicanism and the Americas

Saldanha gave material form to an ideal type of enlightened citizen. His political writings (during and after the Confederation of the Equator) also illustrate his (almost) obsessive attempt to create the necessary conditions for the emergence of people dignified enough to "inhabit the Brazilian climates." Saldanha was an avid reader of world history and philosophy. In his writings, the greatness of Hellenist culture collides with enlightened France, which, in turn, passes through Roman history and the recent North American Revolution, terminating with an encounter of local and national history. This capacity to trace a historic map, with the help of the ancient and modern writers, enabled him to provide his readers with republican models of virtue.[42]

The fear generated by the writings of this "mulatto"[43] (in Brazil, and, afterward, in France, Venezuela, and Colombia) was not due exclusively to his dark skin or his humble background. Saldanha threatened the forces in power with his attempt to inculcate the local population in Recife, which included a large number of slaves and free people of color, with republicanism, a noxious and dangerous concept in the political environment of post-independent Brazil and post-Napoleonic Europe. An anonymous proclamation issued to Brazilians during the revolt declared: "Here it is, then, Brazilians, attend to constituting ourselves in a manner analogous to the progress of the century in which we live: the American system should be identical; we repudiate oligarchic institutions, fitting only in aged Europe."[44] Even years after the defeat of the revolt, authorities feared that Saldanha, if successful, would eliminate the monarchical system in Brazil.[45]

According to Saldanha, Brazil had deviated from the American path. The march toward progress and enlightenment in Brazil was thwarted by the continued presence of the monarchy. Saldanha therefore concluded each edition of *Argos* with translated excerpts from *Des Droits e des Devoirs du Citoyen* (Rights and Duties of the Citizen), written by the French philosopher and republican Gabriel Bonnot de Mably.[46] The work can be read as an instruction book on how, resorting to a managed and nonfrenetic revolution, one could transform an absolute government into a constitutional monarchy, a lesson that, according to Saldanha, Brazil needed in 1824. Mably, a man who believed in the tangible possibilities of revolutions, opined that "a good citizen must remain hopeful, and is obligated, according to his position, his powers, and his talents, to work toward rending these revolutions useful to his country."[47] Saldanha followed this advice, and, as he would explain in the 1830s, he and his comrades all fought together in battle because they were believers in a "better destiny [for Brazil]."[48]

One of the first official acts of the new provincial government during the Confederation of the Equator was the immediate abolition of the slave trade. Providing the population with tangible proof that the new government would prioritize liberty and human rights, the act declared that slavery was in direct opposition to the principles of natural law and the "lights" of the century. Therefore the new leaders immediately suspended all trafficking of slaves in the port of Recife.[49] To better understand the radical nature of this move, it is important to note that, as Marcus Carvalho, a specialist in the history of Pernambuco, claims for the traditional elites, protecting the institution of slavery was more important than the maintenance of the monarchy or even their desire to keep the territory of Brazil intact.[50]

In a similar vein, the leaders of the revolt chose to temporarily adopt the constitution of Colombia, not only because of their admiration of Simón Bolívar but, more important, also because of a clause in the constitution that outlawed the use of all colonial racial categories. This declaration of a "constitutional racial equality"—at least on paper—must have been a motivating factor in the choice of a model for Pernambuco. As Saldanha would soon find out, though, despite the declaration of an end to legal racial discrimination, "Bolivar's views regarding people of African descent were rooted in the colonial past and the spectre of the Haitian revolution."[51]

Mably's intense interest in history and politics could also have influenced the Brazilian intellectual. We know that in addition to his poetry, journalistic pieces, and juridical works written in Venezuela, Saldanha also wrote a play about Atahualpa, the famous Inca emperor whom Pizarro captured and murdered, besides composing a history of the wars in his native state of Pernambuco. Joaquim de Mello also mentioned that Saldanha planned on writing a history of the Confederation of the Equator. Tragically, these are the works that were confiscated by the police during Saldanha's stay in France and never seen again.

Pindaric odes, a discourse written against the adoption of the constitution, articles in newspapers, an essay written in favor of the dissolution of marriage, historical narratives discussing the destruction of the great Incan civilization and the numerous and frequent revolts in his home state: Saldanha wrote all these for different publics and at different times. Yet when for just one moment we consider them as a whole, we see that located in the interstices of all these various writings is a new path that Saldanha so carefully carved out for his generation. In these interstitial spaces[52] we discover the glory of republicanism, which with Saldanha's flaming pen takes on a new connotation, an American one.

The tragic end of Atahualpa (1532), bloody battles against the Dutch invaders in Pernambuco (1634–1652), the independence war in North America (1770s–1780s), and, finally, an armed protest against the tyrannical powers of the new Brazilian monarch (1824)—looking on from a distance, the poet saw the common denominator that linked all these stories in America: the soul of its people. Saldanha accused the Brazilian monarch of adhering to a "vacillating and anti-American politics" and of subjecting America to the politics of the empire and of the Holy Alliance.[53] The revolutionary poet unveiled the duplicitous nature of the monarch and, with the help of history, offered a narrative of another possible political solution: an "American system." While the politics of Pedro I were viewed as being "anti-American,"[54] Brazil, so Saldanha reminded his readers, pertained to America.

Final Considerations

José da Natividade Saldanha was a Black Atlantic rebel who fought at home and abroad to usher in a period of political liberty, one in which all men were equal before the law.[55] His cause, he explained, was a holy one and was more important than that of the "immortal patriarch of American liberty, George Washington."[56] The omission of Saldanha's name from history books is indeed curious, for he clearly delineates, in his poetry and his political writings, an authentic revolutionary spirit in the tropical Atlantic. His experience of exile and, in particular, his travels in the United States and Europe reinforced his belief that the political future of Brazil was precarious if Brazil did not follow the example of its South American neighbors. Saldanha's vast erudition and travels influenced his writing style, a style that, at first, appears untranslatable due to his weaving together of localism and universalism. I hope, however, that I have illustrated that his entangled discourses were his unique contribution to the transatlantic Enlightenment.

Time was cruel to José da Natividade Saldanha. The generous friend of the dead who rescued the glorious deeds of Brazil's mestizo heroes from oblivion would, in turn, be forgotten. But it is still not too late to listen to the echoes of the revolutionary's melancholic voice. Or, as the exiled poet reminded his fellow citizens:

> And you who hear my sad song today,
> Share in the pain that afflicts me,
> And the echo that we hear shall cry out
> So that its memory will be made eternal.[57]

Notes

1. The separatist and republican revolt lasted from July to September 1824. To my knowledge, there are no English-language publications about this revolt.

2. Brazil declared its independence from Portugal in 1822. It was the only Latin American country that kept the monarchical system of government. Other new nation-states in the Americas (with the exception of Canada) declared themselves a republic.

3. Mendonça, "Pernambuco e sua Área de Influência," 406.

4. Bennett, "Writing in a Void," 82.

5. Gilroy, *Black Atlantic*, 6.

6. Suvin, "Displaced Persons," 121.

7. This section on Saldanha's life is based on the following sources: Costa, *Poesias*; Farias, *Mergulho no Letes*, chapter 4; Mello, *Biografia de José da Natividade Saldanha*; Mendonça, *Natividade Saldanha*; Muniz, "O Poeta da Confederação do Equador," 384–426.

8. The sonnet that Saldanha wrote in 1817 was dedicated to the youth in Pernambuco who volunteered to fight against the Portuguese rule in colonial Brazil. A copy of this sonnet can be found in Costa, *Poesias*, 10; and Mello, *Biografia de José da Nativadade Saldanha*, 11–12. In the sonnet, Saldanha calls for the "sons of the patria, young Brazilians" to follow in the footsteps of the great Henrique Dias, a black hero during the wars of the Dutch invasion in seventeenth-century Pernambuco.

9. Muniz, "O Poeta da Confederação do Equador," 392. According to Manoel Joaquim de Menezes, a doctor and lieutenant who participated in both the revolt of 1817 in Recife and the Confederation of the Equator in 1824 on the side of the imperial army, Saldanha was highly sought out for business problems ("*causas de commercio*"). See Moraes, *Biographia do Tenente Coronel e Cirugião*. I consulted both the original manuscript and the published edition of this work. Oddly enough, in the original, the part about Saldanha is missing. See Menezes, "Historia médica brasileira e revolução de Pernambuco."

10. Frei Caneca, who, along with Saldanha, was one of the intellectual leaders of the 1824 revolt, mentions that upon the poet's return to Pernambuco, Saldanha was also nominated as the auditor of war, proof that in Pernambuco there was no antagonism between the races, this idea being a "perverse intrigue" introduced by the "*mão fluminense*" (court and political elite in Rio de Janeiro). See Caneca, *Obras Políticas e Literárias*, 397–398. Saldanha's nomination was on October 25, 1823. See *Atas do Conselho do Governo Pernambucano*, 1:203.

11. This is the title of a book by Margaret C. Jacob, *Strangers Nowhere in the World: The Rise of Cosmopolitanism in Early Modern Europe.*

12. Nesbitt, *Universal Emancipations*, 2. Nesbitt succinctly argues that "one must understand the Enlightenment public sphere of intellectual debate not as a centralized European phenomenon, but instead as a widely dispersed and formally variegated component of the entire early-modern world-system" (66). See also chapter 1: "Saint Domingue and the Singularization of the Enlightenment." Laurent Dubois also argues that one must understand the Haitian Revolution as a "zone of engagement and debate with broader discourses," and that one must construct a "more integrated intellectual history of the Enlightenment." Dubois, "Enslaved Enlightenment," 12, 3. These same arguments, with respect to the Haitian Revolution, can, I argue, be applied to the Confederation of the Equator in Pernambuco.

13. When General Lima e Silva arrived in Recife on September 12, 1824, he immediately sought out Saldanha's house, which he then entered and searched. Upon leaving, he ordered all the furniture to be destroyed. See Freire, "Revolução de 1824," 285–287; and Muniz, "O Poeta da Confederaçao do Equador," 44. Muniz also alleges that a French man named Lieuthier hid Saldanha and managed to get him aboard a French ship, the *Edipo*. The plan, however, failed, but, with the help of Hamilton Bennett, the U.S. consul in Recife, the poet was able to escape to Philadelphia. See Muniz, "O Poeta da Confederaçao do Equador," 44; and Mello, *Biografia de José da Natividade Saldanha*, 67–69. This information is corroborated by a well-known local historian, F. A. Pereira da Costa, in *Anais Pernambucanos*, 439. Caitlin Fitz writes that merchant Joseph Ray, a U.S. citizen who lived in Recife at the time and is often cited as being active in the republican movement, helped seven to ten people of color to escape after the revolt, which would, according to the author, represent about 20 percent of the rebel leadership. See Fitz, "Stalwart Motor of Revolutions," 54.

14. See Mello, *Biografia de José da Natividade Saldanha*, 70–75.

15. The letter can be found in ibid., 76–79.

16. This information is from a French document dated March 25, 1825, written by the French ambassador in England to the minister of the interior in Paris. See a copy of this document in Rangel, *Textos e Pretextos*, 57–58.

17. While Saldanha was in Liverpool, he wrote a letter to the prefect of the police in Paris, complaining about the "spies" sent after him and about the confiscation of his mail and manuscripts. See ibid., 54–56.

18. I was able to verify that Saldanha did leave England on a ship destined to Colombia. A letter from Manuel de Carvalho Paes de Andrade, sent from Liverpool on June 4, 1825, contains the following observation: "Saldanha already left for Colômbia, but not without difficulties; the devil is still in his path; he left in one ship, and his clothes in another." Rio de Janeiro, Brazil, Instituto Histórico e Geográfico Brasiliero (IHGB), Documento 15, Lata 329.

19. The quote is from Ali, "Life and Times of Simón B," 150.

20. Chacon, *Da Confederação do Equador á Manifesto de Mundrucu*, 193. Chacon also includes a copy of the two writings referred to above.

21. For varied and confused accounts of his death, see Guimarães, *Vida e Morte de Natividade Saldanha*, 190–201; Chacon, *Da Confederação do Equador à Grã-Colômbia*, 11; Moraes, *Biographia do Tenente Coronel e Cirugião*, 30; and Freire, *Revista do Instituto Arqueológico*, 287.

22. See, for example, the juridical discourse he wrote while living in exile in Caracas, which starts out: "As men are naturally equal, and consequently free and independent . . ." Reproduced in Chacon, *Da Confederação do Equador à Grã*, 69–70. Note that these speeches he wrote in Caracas and Bogotá were written in Spanish and not Portuguese.

23. Many of the documents that I encountered had "missing pages" and ink poured over them in order to prevent future generations from discovering that there was a plan to erect a republic in Brazil. The plan is normally hidden in Brazilian historiography because it contradicts Brazil's myth of independence after a peaceful, nonconflictual process.

24. Martins, *História da Intelligência Brasileira*, 14, 36.

25. Alfredo Bosi includes Saldanha in the category of poets of little value (*"escasso valor"*). See Bosi, *História Concisa da Literatura Brasileira*, 89–92; Costa, *Dicionário Biográfico de Pernambucanos Célebres*, 591–598; and Nascimento, *O Recife pela Voz dos Poetas*. Luckily, the Foundation for the Historical and Artistic Patrimony of Pernambuco recently published an anthology of poets from Pernambuco that included Saldanha. The editor recommends Saldanhas's patriotic hymns to "all those Who Love Brazil." See Morais, *Dicionário bibliográfico de poetas pernambucanos*, 246–248.

26. For a recent example, see Bosi, *História Concisa da literature Brasiliera*, 89–92.

27. For example, Mello claims that his Elogy, dedicated to his friends who participated in the Revolution of 1824, "immediately spread and many people copied it." See Mello, *Biografia de José da Natividade Saldanha*, 63.

28. "Soneto à Mocidade Pernambucana," in ibid., 11–12; Costa, *Poesias*, 10.

29. See "Ode a Rabello," Epodo V, in Costa, *Poesias*, 74.

30. In a letter dated December 17, 1823, Saldanha refers to the independence movement as a "sacred cause" and argues that the Europeans who had not sworn allegiance to the cause should be deported. See the manuscript "Officios da Presidencia, 1800–1823," Recife, Pernambuco, Instituto Arqueológico, Histórico e Geográfico Pernambucano (IAHGP).

31. See "Soneto à sua Condemnação á Morte," in Mello, *Biografia de José da Natividade Saldanha*, 89; and Costa, *Poesias*, 44.

32. See, for example, his Pindaric ode dedicated to Felipe Camarão, in Costa, *Poesias*, 62–82.

33. See Saldanha's Pindaric ode dedicated to Henrique Dias, in Costa, *Poesias*, 61–66.

34. See, for example, the following documents: "Descrição de Fatos ocorridos na Revolução de 1824 em Pernambuco," Biblioteca Nacional (BN), Manuscripts, I-28, 32; "Cartas Anonimas," BN, Manuscripts, I-31, 33, 3; and a letter written in 1826 informing the government that many soldiers in the military still supported the defeated leaders of the revolt and its cause (Arquivo Nacional [AN], Caixa 74, 2, pacote 3).

35. I was unable to locate the first number of *Argos* in the State Archive. The above quote is therefore taken from Nascimento's study of periodicals in Pernambuco, *Periódicos do Recife—1821-1850*, vol. 4, *História de Pernambuco (1821-1954)*, 63–66.

36. Saldanha specifically cites Paine as one of the greatest intellectuals of the eighteenth century. He writes: "It is for certain that only after the Revolution in North America and after the writings of the famous Raynal, Condorcet, Mirabeau, Mably, Paine, and others that people know the true social principals [*sic*] and the rights of man." See *Argos Pernambucano*, June 7, 1824, 5.

37. See Keane, "Tom Paine and the People"; and Larkin, *Thomas Paine and the Literature of Revolution*, 75.

38. Nascimento, *História da imprensa de Pernambuco*, 63.

39. *Argos Pernambucano*, June 7, 1824, 5; Nascimento, *História da imprensa de Pernambuco*, 63. Paine's lucid and simple style contributed greatly to his popularity. Thomas Jefferson writes that "no writer has exceeded Paine in ease and familiarity of style, in perspicuity of expression, happiness of elucidation, and in simple and unassuming language." See Jefferson, *Writings*, 1451.

40. The quote is from a speech given by Saldanha to the Municipal Camara and reproduced in Mello's biography. I could not locate the original speech, but since Mello was a member of the city council at that time, and as he was concerned about recording history, the source seems reliable. See Mello, *Biografia de José da Natividade Saldanha*, 41. Saldanha repeats this same idea several times in the second number of *Argos Pernambucano*.

41. *Argos Pernambucano*, June 7, 1824, 6.

42. Margaret C. Jacob notes that "a preexisting set of assumptions, vocabularies, and experiences, identifiably cosmopolitan . . . made the international republican conversation happen more easily." See Jacob, *Strangers Nowhere in the World*, 11.

43. While in Colombia, Saldanha wrote an acrimonious letter to the lawyer Moraes Mayer. He objected to the repeated use of the term "mulatto" when referring to Saldanha during the hearings against the participants of the revolt. Costa, *Poesias*, XCI.

44. See *Publicações do Archivo National*, 124–125. The president of the revolt issued this proclamation, but, as noted above, Saldanha was credited with being the intellectual force behind the revolt, so I believe it is safe to assume that he wrote the official propaganda issued by the provisional government.

45. There is a transcription of a letter written in French that warns the authorities about the existence of a society formed to eliminate the monarchy in the New World. The so-called plot that the authorities uncovered originated in Colombia and was led by the agents of Carvalho, the president during the 1824 revolution. I consulted this letter in IHGB, Documento 15, Lata 329.

46. For more information on Mably and his republicanism, see Wright, *Classical Republican in Eighteenth-Century France*.

47. See ibid., 74.

48. The exact expression he uses in his Elogy dedicated to his friends who participated in the Revolution of 1824 was "all believers in a better destiny." This poem can be found in Costa, *Poesias*, 113–117; and Mello, *Biografia de José da Natividade Saldanha*, 63–66.

49. A complete copy of this document can be found in Costa, "Documentos Relativos a Prioridade de Pernambuco," 269–270. I do not doubt the veracity of this account, because I also encountered a reference to the end of the slave traffic in the book of minutes from the provincial government from July 3, 1824. See *Atas do Conselho do Governo de Pernambuco*, 289, 290–291. See also Costa, *Anais*, 387–388. General Cochrane, the Scottish mercenary hired to defeat the revolt, was very worried that the rebels would allow slaves in the republican armies. See "Officio do Brigadeiro F. de Lima e Silva ao Almirante Cochrane," 5 Set. 1824, in *Publicações do Archivo*, 317–318.

50. Carvalho, "Os Negros Armadas pelos Brancos," 881.

51. For information on the Colombian constitution and the race factor, see Helg, "Simon Bolivar," 471. There are several documents that mention the choice to adopt the Colombian constitution. See, for example, Costa, *Anais*, 72–73.

52. Homi K. Bhabha reminds us that "we should remember that it is the 'inter'—the cutting edge of translation and negotiation, the *in—between* space—that carries the burden of the meaning of culture. It makes it possible to begin envisaging national, antinationalist histories of the 'people.' And by exploring this Third Space, we may elude the politics of polarity and emerge as the others of our selves." See Bhabha, *Location of Culture*, 38–39.

53. This is part of a speech that Saldanha delivered in Pernambuco in 1823 when the question about the acceptance of the constitution was debated. For a transcription of this speech, see Mello, *Biografia de José da Natividade Saldanha*, 34–49.

54. See his speech in ibid., 41–46.

55. In his juridical piece written in favor of the dissolution of marriage, published in 1825 during his sojourn in Caracas, the force of his republican ideas remained unabated. He began by reminding his readers that "men are naturally equal and therefore free and independent," and then, in the same carefully constructed prose he used in Brazil, explained concepts such as natural rights, liberty, and independence. The speech ends by supporting a woman's right to divorce. See a copy of this speech in Chacon, *Da Confederação do Equador à Grã*, 69–70.

56. Mello, *Biografia de José da Natividade Saldanha*, 40–41.

57. This is the last stanza of the poem that he wrote in exile and dedicated to his "friends involved in the 1824 Revolution." It was first published in Recife in 1869. See also Mello, *Biografia de José da Natividade Saldanha*, 63–65; and Costa, *Poesias*, 113–117.

Bibliography

Archival Sources

Argos Pernambucano. Recife, Pernambuco. Arquivo Público do Estado.

Instituto Histórico e Geográfico Brasiliero (IHGB). Documento 15, Lata 329. Rio de Janeiro, Brazil.

Menezes, Manoel de Joaquim de. "Historia médica brasileira e revolução de Pernambuco em 1824 que foi causa da dissolução da Constituinte." Rio de Janeiro. Biblioteca Nacional (BN) Seção de Manuscritos, II-32, 1, 9.

Moraes, Mello. *Biographia do Tenente Coronel e Cirurgião-mor Reformado do Exercito Dr Manoel Joaquim de Menezes*. Rio de Janeiro, BrazilSeção de Obras Raras, 39, 10, 7.

"Officios da Presidencia, 1800–1823." Recife, Pernambuco. Instituto Arqueológico, Histórico e Geográfico Pernambucano (IAHGP).

Secondary Sources

Ali, Tariq. "The Life and Times of Simón B." *New Left Review* 40 (July/August 2006): 149–160.

Atas do Conselho do Governo de Pernambuco. Vol. 1, *1821–1824*. Recife: Assembléia Legislativa de Pernambuco; CEPE, 1997.

Bennett, Herman L. "Writing in a Void: Representing Slavery and Freedom in the Narrative of Colonial Spanish America." *Social Text* 93 (Winter 2007): 67–89.

Bhabha, Homi K. *The Location of Culture*. London: Routledge, 1994.

Bosi, Alfredo. *História Concisa da Literatura Brasileira*. 3rd ed. São Paulo: Editora Cultriz, 1994.

Caneca, Frei Joaquim do Amor Divino. *Obras políticas e literárias*. Vol. 2, *1875*. Collecionadas pelo Commendador Antonio Joaquim de Mello. Recife: Assembléia Legislativa, 1979, 2 vols. [1875].

Carvalho, Marcus J. M de. "Os Negros Armados Pelos Brancos e suas Independências no Nordeste, 1817–1848." In *Independência: História e Historiografia*, ed. István Jancsó, 881–914. São Paulo: Editora Hucitec, 2005.

———. "Rumores e Rebeliões: Estratégias de Resistência Escrava no Recife, 1817–1848." *Tempo* 3.6 (December 1998): 49–72.

Chacon, Vamireh. *Da Confederação do Equador à Grã-Colômbia (1796–1830): Escritos Políticos e Manifesto de Mundrucu*. Brasília: Senado Federal, 1983.

Costa, F. A. Pereira da. *Anais Pernambucanos*. Vol. 9, *1824–1833*. 2nd ed. Recife: Governo de Pernambuco, 1983.

———. "Documentos Relativos a Prioridade de Pernambuco na Questão da Emancipação dos Escravos (1817 e 1824)." *Revista do Instituto Arqueológico, Hisórico e Geográfico Pernambucano* 6.42 (1901): 260–282.

———. *Poesias de José da Natividade Saldanha*. Recife: J. W. de Medeiros, 1875.

De Farias, Amy Caldwell. *Mergulho no Lethes: Uma Reinterpretação Político-Histórica da Confederação do Equador*. Porto Alegre: EDIPUCRS, 2006.

Dubois, Laurent. "An Enslaved Enlightenment: Rethinking the Intellectual History of the French Atlantic." *Social History* 31.1 (February 2006): 1–14.

Fitz, Caitlin. "'A Stalwart Motor of Revolutions': An American Merchant in Pernambuco, 1817–1825." *Americas* 65.1 (2008): 35–62.

Freire, A Luna de. "Revolução de 1824." *Revista do Instituto Arqueológico, Histórico e Geográfico Pernambucano* 7.47 (1895): 209–300.

Gilroy, Paul. *The Black Atlantic: Modernity and Double Consciousness*. Cambridge, Mass.: Harvard University Press, 1993.

Guimarães, Argeu. *Vida e morte de Natividade Saldanha (1796–1832)*. Lisboa: Luz-Braz, 1932.

Helg, Aline. "Simón Bolívar and the Spectre of 'Pardocracia': José Padilla in Post-Independence Cartagena." *Journal of Latin American Studies* 35.3 (August 2003): 447–471.

Jacob, Margaret C. *Strangers Nowhere in the World: The Rise of Cosmopolitanism in Early Modern Europe.* Philadelphia: University of Pennsylvania Press, 2006.

Jefferson, Thomas. *Writings.* New York: Library of America, 1984.

Keane, John. "Tom Paine and the People." *Times Literary Supplement*, March 31, 1995.

Larkin, Edward. *Thomas Paine and the Literature of Revolution.* Cambridge: Cambridge University Press, 2005.

Martins, Wilson. *História da Intelligência Brasileira.* 3rd ed. Vol. 2. São Paulo: T. A. Queiroz, 1992.

Mello, Antonio Joaquim de. *Biografia de José da Natavadade Saldanha.* Recife: Manuel Figueiroa Faria & Filho, 1895.

Mendonça, Denis António de. "Pernambuco e sua Área de Influência: Um Território em Transformação." In *Independência: História e Historiografia*, ed. István Jancsó, 379–410. São Paulo: Editora Hucitec, 2005.

Mendonça, Kleber. *Natividade Saldanha: Traços de uma Época, de uma Poesia e de uma Vida.* Recife: Faculdade de Ciências Humanas, ESUDA, 1975.

Moraes, Mello. *Biographia do Tentente Coronel e Cirugião—mor Reformado do Exercito Dr Manoel de Joauim de Menezes.* Ed. J. J. do Patrocinio. Rio de Janeiro: Typographia Brasileira, 1861.

Morais, Lamartine. *Dicionário Bibliográficode Poetas Pernambucanos.* Recife: FUNDARPE, 1993.

Muniz, Arthur. "O Poeta da Confederaçao do Equador." *Revista do Instituto Arquelógico Histórico e Geográfico Pernambucano* 13.73 (1908): 384–426.

Nascimento, Luiz do. *História da imprensa de Pernambuco (1821–1954).* Vol. 4, *Periódicos do Recife, 1821–1854.* Recife: Universidade Federal de Pernambuco, 1969.

Nesbitt, Nick. *Universal Emancipation: The Haitian Revolution and the Radical Enlightenment.* Charlottesville: University of Virginia Press, 2008.

Publicações do Archivo Nacional. Rio de Janeiro: Arquivo Nacional, 1924.

Rangel, Alberto. *Textos e Pretextos: Incidentes da Chronica Brasileira a Luz de Documentos Conservados na Europa.* Tours: Arrault, 1926.

Suvin, Darko. "Displaced Persons." *New Left Review* 31 (January/February 2005): 107–123.

Wright, Johnson Kent. *A Classical Republican in Eighteenth-Century France: The Political Thought of Mably.* Stanford, Calif.: Stanford University Press, 1997.

Developmentalism, Tanzania, and the Arusha Declaration

Perspectives of an Observing Participant

Ikaweba Bunting

Throughout the African Diaspora, in the United States in particular, acknowledgment of a historical African identity among enslaved Africans and their descendants has been a contentious and dangerous proposition. Consequently, black folks shied away from doing so. That fearful and shameful avoidance of Africa and an African relationship has persisted through the transition from chattel to wage slavery, Jim Crow apartheid, and so-called second-class citizenship. Malcolm X, among others, confronted and challenged the psychological and political dimensions of this alienation. For example, in *Message to the Grass Roots*, he states:

> We are African, and we happen to be in America. We are not American. We
> are people who formerly were Africans who were kidnapped and brought to
> America. Our forefathers weren't the Pilgrims. We didn't land on Plymouth Rock.
> The rock was landed on us. We were brought here against our will; We were not
> brought here to be made citizens. We were not brought here to enjoy the constitu-
> tional gifts that they speak so beautifully about today.[1]

In his speech given at the founding rally of the Organization of Afro-American Unity, he articulates the identity-history-resistance nexus:

> This modern house Negro loves his master. He wants to live near him. He'll pay
> three times as much as the house is worth just to live near his master, and then
> brag about "I'm the only Negro out here." "I'm the only one on my job." "I'm the
> only one in this school." You're nothing but a house Negro. And if someone comes
> to you right now and says, "Let's separate," you say the same thing that the house

Negro said on the plantation. "What you mean, separate? From America? This
good white man? Where you going to get a better job than you get here?" I mean,
this is what you say, "I ain't left nothing in Africa," that's what you say. Why, you
left your mind in Africa![2]

Intellectual and ideological acceptance of these assertions of lost "mind,"
historical alienation, and the emancipatory imperative to separate from the
institutions that precipitated the damage were perhaps more easily verbalized
than lived for many. Returning from the Diaspora to Africa, immersing one-
self within an African social space, brings one face-to-face with the reality of
the damage and destruction engendered by the conquest and enslavement of
our ancestors. A person is confronted on the personal self-reflective level as a
descendent of the enslaved, suffering from "loss of mind," the internalization
of American chauvinism, and African denigration. The reality of the damage and destruction done to the land and communities from which we were
taken also poses challenges to the imaginations and preconceived notions
born of calculated misinformation and dreams of African renaissance.

Such sociocultural dynamics, coupled with an ever-evolving black consciousness, accompanied and facilitate me into the communities and lives of
the peoples of East Africa. That evolving consciousness determined that my
observations were generated from a premise and intent different from that of
classical missionary or European academics' participant observation. It was,
rather, from the premise of an observing participant.

The social research method born of European and American anthropological missionary-generated study of the "Other" was referred to as "participant observation." The phrase "observing participant" has been reversed
intentionally. Its purpose is to articulate social, cultural, and political consciousness of the participant. The idea of observant participation engages
objectivity and subjectivity by making a reflexive statement on positionality.
A long succession of missionaries, anthropologists, government administrators, and researchers from Europe and America came through Africa as well
as through the urban ghettoes and rural outback of Africa America to meth-
odologically examine the lives of the people whom they categorized as African subalterns and thus intrinsically a deviation from the "norm" of humanity
(meaning obviously a European or Western humanity). I observed in order to
participate, to join, to be emancipated, to be empowered, rather than participation to be able to observe, define, prescribe, and dominate. The difference is
significant. My experiences as an observing participant provided a practical
and organic method that facilitated cultural learning, emancipation, and the
recognition and understanding of the sociohistorical continuity of the shared

experiences among Africans globally. The army of empire builders trekked across the African world for various cultural, racial, religious, and economic motivations in order to participate in the sociocultural interactions of these African "Others." They observed, then interpreted, controlled, and prescribed to the subalterns. A power coefficient emerged in respect to the observers and the observed. That power relationship maintained the hierarchical structure of the imperial cultural, economic, and racial order. The observers claimed a superiority of perspective, intellectual capabilities, epistemology, world-view, and scientific method. As an African of the Diaspora, I had none of the superlative attributes of the dominant norm. I had no delusions of possessing the authority and normative power of a representative model of Occidental civilization. Upon entering continental African social space, in respect of the dominant norm I remained a subaltern "Other," the same as all Africans within the structure of the Occidental world order. Such a reality significantly contributed to determining perspective and positionality.

In the 1970s Tanzanians generally referred to Africans in the Diaspora as *Wanegro* (Wah-nay-grow). The common understanding was that *Wanegro* were Africans taken from Africa by *Wazungu* (Wah-zuun-gooh) (Europeans) and enslaved in the Americas. Use of the "*M/Wa*" prefixes in the Bantu lexicon of Kiswahili indicates singular and plural as well as an ontological category of being.[3] The plural "*Wa*" can also refer to historical and locative identity of peoplehood. Thus the Maasai people are *Wamassai*, or the Zulu people are *Wazulu*. In this instance, the plural form does not signify numerous individual Maasai or Zulu. Rather, it signifies a distinct peoplehood. Interaction between returnee Diaspora Africans and indigenous Africans in regards to identity evolved around such terms.

Wanegro in America are a distinct African people. This reality exists as a function of historical continuity, culture, and the racial designation attached to the land of their ancestral origins. By the 1970s Africans in America had rejected the moniker "Negro." They were defining themselves as Black Americans, Black people, and Afro-Americans. Their evolving search for a moniker expressing self-determined identity encountered the *Wanegro* identifier and generated many discussions and debates among political activists, intellectuals, journalists, members of the ruling party (Tanganyika African National Union [TANU]),[4] and even those in the President's Office. Eventually "*Warejiaji*," rather than "*Wanegro*," was the term mutually and officially agreed upon. "*Warejiaji*" translates as "returnees." There was even a committee established in the President's Office called the *Warejiaji* Committee. The *Warejiaji* Committee included officials from the Tanzanian Ministry of Foreign Affairs, the

President's Office, and individuals from the African American community living in Tanzania (exclusive of any U.S. government officials). The purpose of the committee was to assist Africans from the Diaspora wishing to settle in Tanzania and ease their social and cultural transition. Although a politically acceptable alternative to *"Wanegro,"* the word *"Warejiaji"* never gained popular traction. "Black American" became more common in the urban areas as more Africans from the Diaspora arrived. *"Wanegro"* persisted in the rural areas. Among Tanzanians who had considerable informal contact with Africans from the Diaspora, the term *"Wanigga"* (Wah-nee-gah) was also used, and African American–accented and culturally nuanced English (Ebonics) was referred to as speaking *kinigga*. What is of note in regards to these identifiers is that the people of the land recognized and acknowledged the historical identity and relationship they had with those Africans from the Diaspora who came to Tanzania.

The participation of an African from the Diaspora in the nation-building and African liberation project of Tanzania was a consolidation of Pan-African purpose for implementing a decolonizing methodology.[5] Enjoying the social and political space within which to work to bring to fruition such Pan-African purpose was a function of a proverbial perfect storm. This storm encompassed a confluence of social forces that influenced the philosophical, political, and artistic space of the African world, wherein I lived. Within this African world, the civil rights and Black Power movements in America; the defiance campaigns in South Africa; the armed, antiracist, and anticolonial struggles for national independence in Kenya, Algeria, and Ghana; and the crisis of the Congo engendered by U.S. Cold War policies that frustrated the emancipation of the Congolese people and subsequently resulted in the assassination of Prime Minister Patrice Lumumba were notable cross-fertilizing events that engendered ideas of resistance.[6]

Policies repressing black political movements and leadership in the United States were synchronically occurring during the period of my childhood and adolescence, the 1950s through the 1960s. Ideas and social movements that emerged from the generation of Africans in America who came of age during these years reflected the expression of these forces. Stimulated by the heightened consciousness and militancy of Black World War II veterans and the ideas of thinkers and activists such as W. E. B. DuBois, Kwame Nkrumah, Franz Fanon, Ella Baker, Fannie Lou Hamer, and Elijah Muhammed, among others, an active and militant impetus found expression in organizations such as the Nation of Islam, Mississippi Freedom Party, Congress of Racial Equality (CORE), Southern Christian Leadership Conference (SCLC), Student

Non-Violent Coordinating Committee (SNCC), Organization of Afro-American Unity, Black Panther Party for Self Defense, and the numerous Black Student Unions in colleges and universities across the United States. The social movements that germinated from these forces were nurtured in barbershops, hair salons, street-corner debates, and church sermons; by glimpses of militant and demanding black athletes, black artists, black writers, and social activists beginning to appear in the national media; together with the news reports of the brutal and violent repression of the growing black sociopolitical movement.

This conglomerate of endogenous African American expression of social and cultural self-determination emerged as Black Power. The transformation of the civil rights movement into the Black Power/Black Liberation Movement, together with the lethal and racist institutional repression, became the social and political landscape within which my departure from the United States took place. Central to being able to locate the Diaspora presence and activities within the continental African revolution and liberation movement is the indisputable reality of the historical and sociocultural continuity of the descendants of enslaved Africans in the Americas, Europe, and the Caribbean with the history and sociocultural evolution on the continent of Africa. The creation of a collective global African identity has roots in the plantation slave system of the Americas. The plantation system served as crucible for an amalgamation of the collective of political, spiritual, epistemological, linguistic, and cultural expressions of the different African peoples and societies represented within the masses of enslaved Africans into a Diaspora continuum of African historical and cultural reality.

The amalgamation of the sociocultural manifestation of the global African experience throughout the 600-year-old night (1400–2000) of the Occidental capitalist world dominion spawned the idea of a collective fate connecting the social and political welfare of Africans in the Diaspora to the newly independent nations of Africa. Influenced by the power and interconnectedness of these forces, students and political activists on both sides of the Atlantic began to identify the African anticolonial struggle and the antiracist black civil rights struggle as one within a global African peoples' liberation movement. For the African Diaspora, a new authenticity emerged as we began to embrace models of resistance from continental African liberation movements for challenging the paradigm of white supremacy and privilege. This new positional and conceptual dynamic was articulated as Black Power and revolutionary Pan-Africanism.

Positionality is a determinant of the social space occupied and the premises from which observations and analyses are made.[7] Whether the analysis, discourse, and output serve the purposes of a continuation of the dominant norm or that of resistance and emancipation on the part of the subaltern "Other" depends on the positionality of perspective and purpose. Sociocultural dynamics created by Africans during the civil rights African liberation epoch circa 1945 to 1975 brought about a renaissance of historical knowledge of self and kind such that my engagement with continental Africa could be none other than as an African from the Diaspora observing so as to learn how to act in a continental African social context simultaneously acknowledging our common condition and historically shared experience as Africans within the epoch of the Occidental modernist world order. Hence I was an observing participant in the nation-building and African liberation project of the people and government of Tanzania.

Tanzania and the African Diaspora

Tanzania, more than any other place at that historical juncture, constituted a welcoming space for Pan-African revolutionary aspirations. The ideological construct of its African-centered Arusha Declaration informed with ideas of *Ujamaa*, Pan-Africanism, and international anti-imperialist solidarity resonated with the heightened African consciousness and political militancy accompanying ideas of Black Power. Black Power articulated within a historical dialectical relationship with Africa and its Diaspora leads to Pan-Africanism.

The Arusha Declaration, as well as the constitution of TANU, incorporated values and objectives related to African philosophical ideas for social and economic organization, Pan-Africanism, and support for the African revolution, antiracism, and social justice worldwide. Subsequent to the pronouncement of the Arusha Declaration as the blueprint for national construction, the East African nation of Tanzania became a political and intellectual center for Pan African activists, progressive intellectuals, and social justice freedom fighters from Africa and the Diaspora. Tanzania positioned itself as a rear base of support and training for various national liberation movements of southern Africa and their armed militia. The Tanzanian national narrative was composed in this environment. A number of individuals and representatives of organizations from the African Diaspora, especially from the United States and the Caribbean, came to Tanzania to participate in this narrative of building a new African nation that had clearly declared its purpose of Pan-African unity, anti-imperialism, antiracism, and social revolution.[8]

My immigration to Tanzania was inspired by the declared Pan-African objectives and anti-imperialist revolutionary purpose of the government's policies. Among African nationalists, progressives, and political activists around the world, Tanzania gained considerable stature as an antiwhite supremacy Pan-African force. Perceiving Tanzania as such was, in part, a result of its Arusha Declaration, its internationalist positions taken in support of anti-imperialist and antiracist struggles around the world. The reception and support extended to Malcolm X by the Tanzanian minister of foreign affairs, Mohammed Babu, laid the foundation for the affinity toward Tanzania felt by African Americans. Adding to this was the convening of the Sixth Pan-African Congress in Tanzania and the call by President Julius Nyerere for a Pan-African Skills organization to facilitate Africans from the Diaspora to come to Tanzania and participate in nation building.[9] Tanzania's stature was also enhanced among anti-imperialist Pan-African forces in relation to the support it extended to the Congolese resistance to the U.S. and Belgian governments' efforts to undermine and defeat the Congolese people's anticolonial agenda, which included Pan-African unity and noncapitalist economic objectives. Tanzania extended material and logistical support in collaboration with Ernesto "Che" Guevara and the Cuban government and the Congolese anti-imperialist fighters.[10]

While living in Tanzania, the character of the discourse of nation building and anti-imperialism in a capitalist-, racialist-dominated world inculcated a critical perspective of the dominant narrative of history and global socio-economic relations as fabricated by Occidental cultural and political institutions. Antiracism and the extending of political and material support for African liberation and building of a socialist society informed the discourse of the national project and generated critical analysis and popular discussion regarding African issues that permeated social interactions. Being outside the direct influences and restrictions of Euro-American social discourse and cultural hegemony was and continues to be a liberating and empowering experience. Living in Tanzania under the rubric of *Ujamaa* and African liberation facilitated the purging of American chauvinism from the mental fiber of the descendents of enslaved Africans from the Americas. The liberating effects and cultural awareness engendered by the experiences inform my analysis of developmentalism and global relations. Knowledge and understanding regarding economic, social, and cultural power relationships between African peoples and the so-called International Community are essential for completing the emancipatory and unifying objectives of the global African revolution.

The Roots of Developmentalism

The expansion of capitalism from early mercantilism through colonial imperialism into twenty-first-century neoliberal globalization is a definitive illustration of the coexistent emergence of the culture and ethos of intervention,
empire, and white supremacy. This culture and ethos—expressed as "Manifest
Destiny," "The White Man's Burden," "Democracy Promotion," and, recently,
"Responsibility to Protect"—have been operationalized by way of the enterprise of the three C's of Civilization, Christianity, and Commerce.[11] The three
C's constitute the essential elements whereby European and Euro-American
adventurers, merchants, missionaries, and government agents motivated by
diverse interests determined to bring the backward, uncivilized, undemo-
cratic (*sic*) peoples and regions of the world into the light under the guid-
ance of Occidental civilization. They would do this by way of the gift of the
three C's encompassing the advantages of rational thought, enlightenment,
Western science, culture, episteme, technology, democracy, and the one true
God, a god whose image embodies European likeness. This is the Occidental
civilizing mission, Occidentalism. It is the core element of developmentalism.

Occidental social science discourse codified and promulgated the idea,
popularly and institutionally, of the superiority of European and American
culture and forms of social organization. Occidental social science also constructed a theorem to the effect that improvement in societal organization
and life chances for African peoples and societies is a function dependent on
the degree of assimilation of Americo-European culture and the replication
of the Americo-European socioeconomic paradigm of nation-state organization. It is also essential to acquiesce to the normalization of Occidental epistemological product.[12]

The dichotomous relationships generated by the nineteenth-century linear
sequential evolutionary model of society have been maintained throughout
the twentieth century and into the twenty-first century through terms like
"traditional" and "modern," "developed" and "underdeveloped," "least developed" and "highly developed," and, more recently, "emerging economies" versus "highly developed economies." Extending from this binary hierarchical
construct is an institutionalized axiom that emanates predominantly from
people and organizations of the Occidental world that assume the right and
responsibility to intervene in societies other than their own and alter the
"otherness" so as to normalize and reshape them into the image and desired
behavior of Occidental perfection.[13] This conviction and resultant practices
have emerged as a preeminent characteristic that defines relations among
the nations and peoples of the Occident (Europe, North America, Australia,

and New Zealand), on the one hand, and the peoples and nations of Africa, Asia, South America, and the islands of the seas, on the other.[14] The counterpart to this axiom that emerged within those nations and peoples objectified by Occidental institutional definition is the belief that the practice of programmed social intervention, coupled with the presence of Western institutions and European people, is necessary and essential for the reconstruction of postcolonial societies into viable nation-states. Paradoxically, it is asserted that this will facilitate independence.

An illustration of this mind-set and the symbolism attached to it is reflected in a case study of a so-called development worker from Denmark. Claus (a pseudonym) was recruited as a mason for a rural school construction project in Njombe, Tanzania. I accompanied Claus on his orientation field visit to the project. Escorted by the chairperson of the Njombe District Development Corporation to several construction sites, we began to wonder as we looked at the construction of school buildings in various stages of completion, "What is Claus really supposed to do?" Much of the construction was complete, and according to Claus, the work was of good quality and as professional as he had seen or done, for that matter. Later Claus mentioned his befuddlement, exclaiming to the chairperson that he saw no need for his skills and wondered what was the purpose of his post. The chairperson laughed heartily, replying, "Oh don't you worry, you just relax, find a nice woman and have a good time, when the people see we have our Mzungu (European) they will know that we are developing and that something is being done."[15]

This case study anecdote reveals several layers of the cultural, psychological, and economic manifestations of imperial developmentalism. It depicts an attitude and conceptualization on the part of the Tanzanian project director regarding the symbols of "development." His condescending and dismissive attitude toward the rural population and his understanding concerning European (white) people in relation to the idea and values of development—that is, modern civilization—are indicative of alienation, self-negation, and acquiescence to the ideology of the Occidental norm of white supremacy. The implication is that the physical structures of the school buildings were not enough evidence for the contributing villagers and that the project was incomplete symbolically until it established a connection with an international donor agency. The proof and confirmation of that connection was the physical presence of a white person.

The different attitudes and beliefs generated in the space of contact between the Occidental and African worlds are a central aspect in relation to control of power and knowledge, self-confidence, alienation, and the dependency syndrome. All are elements and phenomena related to the emancipatory project informing the reconstruction of African societies that the Arusha Declaration addressed. The case study referred to above reveals that it was not the technical skills and knowledge that were needed or lacking. Their existence was obviously evidenced by the existing construction.

The civilizing mission of the colonial project morphed into the development mission. The ideology of developmentalism emerged in tandem with the metamorphosis to accommodate the changes in the relationship of international capital and colonized territories after World War II. From July 11 through November 5, 1949, the first economic mission of its kind was organized by the International Bank for Reconstruction and Development (IBRD/World Bank). The mission visited Columbia. The terms of reference for their activities were to devise a comprehensive development strategy for an underdeveloped country.[16]

The ideology of developmentalism—its practices and programs of socioeconomic intervention for nation-state construction of former colonial territories—emerged from the historical context of imperialism and the civilizing mission. Neocolonialism defines the economic, social, and cultural relations between imperialist nation-states and postcolonial nation-states. The neocolonialist ideology is developmentalism.[17]

The Modernization Project—in particular, its cultural and epistemological components—are critically essential aspects of developmentalism.[18] The phenomenon has produced a distinct development discourse. Developmentalism is rooted in the matrix of empire, finance, trade, and missiology.[19] Social, cultural, and economic intervention or social engineering is a salient feature of that matrix in terms of custom and practice. Occidental development plans and projects utilize the social sciences to construct policies and institutions for the express purpose of controlled transformation or status quo maintenance. This is a model for social development that is predicated upon dissemination of sociological knowledge through education and training. This model disseminates its findings and conclusions in an academic social science sphere, but it does not respond to the need for operationalizing social knowledge for emancipatory action purposes.[20] The distance between the person or institution positioned as the user of such knowledge and the society producing it, of which the knowledge is about, is exemplified by the reified perspective regarding user, producer, and the need for operationalization for emancipatory purposes. A second model postulates the translation of social science knowledge into new know-how and change tools and the use of this knowledge to organize new social action relationships.

Developmentalism is informed by the belief that enlightened, rational, and planned socioeconomic and cultural interventions will rapidly result in the peoples and nations of Africa, Asia, and Latin America (all non-European peoples) confirming the supremacy, universality, and inevitable evolutionary progress of Occidental socioeconomic and cultural organization. Developmentalism is a progeny of imperialism in the same way as colonialism. A new colonialism emerges within the framework of neo-imperial globalization, which is a socially constructed manifestation of the idea of developmentalism into the twenty-first century.

The Age of Development

The age of development is this time period, when the ideology of developmentalism has grown to near universal acceptance. Development becomes institutionalized by way of the creation of a multiplicity of structures, doctrines, theories, and organizations for the explicit and inherent purpose of social and economic intervention. The benchmark announcing the birth of the age of development is considered to be the speech by American president Harry Truman delivered on January 20, 1949. Truman stated in his inaugural address that the "Southern Hemisphere is an underdeveloped area." Such determination by Truman provided the cognitive base for intervention from the North and subordination in the South.[21]

The gestation period of developmentalism and the cognitive base for the theory and practice of intervention have roots that precede President Truman's pronouncement, however. They are rooted in the expansion of capitalism, nineteenth-century imperialism, and the sixteenth-century idea of "mission." The idea of mission essentially is that it is the divine duty and responsibility of Europeans to save the pagan, savage "Other" from sin, damnation, and unenlightened darkness and bring him or her into the light of modernized, civilized, Christianized society.[22]

Industrialization, coupled with free-market economics leading to a high mass-consumption society model, is depicted as the pot of gold at the end of the development rainbow. It therefore follows logically that those states that are highly industrialized and technically mechanized with high rates of consumption must necessarily be the models of "being developed." Industrialization is an institutional axis of modernization, together with colonialism, developmentalism, and consumerism.[23] This link is epistemological, historical, and cultural in regards to the nations of the "subaltern peoples." Modernization implies the adoption of Occidental institutions and values. There is an explicit imperative that the "nonmodern" societies discard existing endogenous values and sociocultural institutions and replace them with modern

Occidental-style institutions.[24] An essential characteristic of this ideology is the conviction that through the application of social and economic engineering strategies based on theories of modernization, former colonial societies can be converted into modern replicas of Occidental societies at an accelerated rate.[25]

A belief in progress is a fundamental aspect of the modern worldview. The normalization of the concept of progress provides justification for the technical order of domination, control, and assembly line consumer culture. The cultural and ideological implications of the concept of progress and its influences have spread globally throughout all cultures and societies. Africa is linked to the concept of progress by way of the imperialist modernization project and the ideology of developmentalism.[26]

Development formulated as a universal human project was bequeathed to the newly independent governments of the former colonies by the international political economic apparatus constructed by the United States and its European allies in the wake of World War II.[27] The new governments were to derive legitimacy from being able to build a developing nation progressing toward becoming modern in the image and likeness of the colonial metropolitan capitals. The foundation of the model is simple. The peoples, cultures, and governments of Africa are economically, socially, and culturally backward and need to develop and develop fast. In this task of development, popular participation in national agenda setting is a burdensome luxury that must be relegated to political theater of periodic multiparty elections while economics occupies the central place on the ideological and pragmatic policy terrain that is not open to democratic participation or popular input. Developmentalism is the ideological guise under which the new postindependence ruling classes consolidate themselves and their alliance with transnational corporate capital.[28] In effect, therefore, development efforts of governments and agencies have basically tried to create a new modernized African state within the historical context of imperialist interventionist economics, bureaucratic structures, attitudes, and beliefs.

The discourse of development is infused with the culture and values of the Occidental worldview. For African societies' emancipatory self-determined social purpose, there is an inherent contradiction with the Occidental development model. The prosperity of the Occidental world is a function of the historical exploitation and impoverishment of the African world. How can that same system and its global structure in turn then be used for creating African prosperity? This paradox has continuously bedeviled African government leaders and politicians. Ignoring it perpetuates the impoverished status quo. Participating in it increases the suffering of the majority of the people and perpetuates the domination, rendering one a traitor to social justice. Resistance to it invites instability and undermining tactics deployed by convergent corporate and imperialist interests to maintain the present order. It is the imperialist contradiction within the neoliberal world order.

In Tanzania, the Kiswahili equivalent of development is *"Maendeleo."* Significantly, *"Maendeleo"* is a noun related to the verb form *"kuendelea,"* which means to continue an action, to carry through with what one is doing. It signifies forward progress and development in the political lexicon of Tanzania.[29] Local people use the word *"Wafadhili"* interchangeably as an inclusive term for foreign development assistance agencies, expatriate field staff, and their official government representatives. Literally the word means "benefactors." *"Wafadhili wanaleta maendeleo"* (foreign benefactors) bring development.[30] The two interesting factors to take note of are the conceptual conflation of philanthropy and development into a single idea, *"Maendeleo,"* and the externalization of the concept and project of development, *"wanaleta,"* meaning "they bring."[31] Indigenous perception reveals an obvious distance in the conceptual packaging whereby *Maendeleo* is the project that is conceived and resourced from outside of their day-to-day cognitive realms. Not only is it outside of their cognitive realms, but outside as well from livelihood activities—that is, those sets of activities, customs, and rituals that must be performed daily in order to produce and live. People thus experience a sense of alienation and ontological distance between themselves and the development project.

Several perspectives are attached to the word and concept of "development." One perspective conceives of development as a process whereby a development agency and its expert personnel come from various nations of the Occidental modern world of the disposable income countries and assume the role of superior knower in relation to the objects or target communities of people who are to be developed. The African community is a disadvantaged entity that must be reshaped with the new knowledge, technologies, and modern worldview that the development agency and its workers bring with them. Another view of development conceives of it as a welfare package to be delivered to a community. It is defined in terms of quantified growth in specified social indicators, such as increased income or consumption levels. Developmentalism, in this form, reduces the purpose of collective social interaction to that of merely the production of wealth through the application of science and technology. It is accompanied by the axiom that it is universally applicable and necessary for all societies. In this model, importance is placed on economic growth without concern for social welfare or how wealth is distributed. It necessarily engenders a closer relationship between the government and external organizations than between the local government and its own people. It spawns a view that the best ideas for social life are to be externally derived and that indigenous culture is an obstacle to economic growth. A custom is deliberately generated that ignores the use of local resources and the competence of the people. The people and local communities are reduced to being merely human capital, and a strict division is set up between "formal" and "informal" socioeconomic sectors informed with the idea that real knowledge production happens in the so-called formal sectors. Developmentalism in its neoliberal mode also embraces the tenet that economic growth cannot be achieved without a few people being rich and all others being poor.[32]

Developmentalism, as characterized above, is what Nkrumah defined as neocolonialism.[33] Nkrumah explained the nature of neocolonialism and enumerated various aspects of economic relations between former colonial territories and the former colonial powers. The essence of neocolonialism, according to Nkrumah, is that the state that is subject to a neocolonial relationship is theoretically independent, with all of the political trappings of sovereignty, but the economic reality is one of dependence and control by outside forces. Because of the dialectical relationship between economics and political policy, such a state's political policies and direction are also determined by external forces.[34]

For Nkrumah, this relationship was primarily one among states. He did not consider the possibility of control being exercised by a consortium of financial and political interests that are not specifically identifiable to any one particular state. When Nkrumah was writing, multilateral and bilateral donor and development agencies had not yet become the significant players in the political economy of twentieth-century African states and international relationships as they were by the later part of the twentieth century and the first decades of the twenty-first. Some characteristics of the neocolonial relationship Nkrumah described persist to this day. Nkrumah's analysis reveals that the rulers of neocolonial states derive their authority from the support they obtain from the external neocolonial powers—not from the will of the people.[35] This is no less accurate now than it was when Nkrumah first wrote about it. Within the development paradigm, the African state is stabilized by so-called development assistance in the social welfare sector (health, education, services) and the finance sector. In exchange, the state provides cheap compliant labor; access to minerals and natural resources, including land; markets; and political support in multilateral organizations to the governments and corporations of the Occidental world.

The relationship between the state and external organizations is closer than between the state and its citizens.[36] The African state is dependent on the external power entity for its very existence as a government of a "developing nation." This dependence ranges from managing and controlling the commanding heights of the economy to the provision of the simplest of social services. Multilateral organizations such as the World Bank and International Monetary Fund (IMF) and bilateral agencies like the United States Agency for Development (USAID), Canadian International Development Agency (CIDA), Danish International Development Agency (DANIDA), or Department for International Development (DIFID), and non-governmental organization (NGO) donors such as Save the Children, Oxfam, Action Aid, or CARE carry out these roles on behalf of the Occidental development apparatus or so-called International Community in cooperation with the neocolonial African government. Because the role of these organizations of the apparatus is so vital to the existence and stability of the governments, there must be a continual dialogue with, and deference to, the apparatus and its institutions. Their roles and identities sometimes overlap and fuse together.

The idea of a hierarchy from less developed to advanced, from primitive to modern, is essential to modernization and the idea of progress and thus intrinsic to the idea of development. Modernization theory assumes a unidirectional evolutionary account of social change governed by rational progress.[37] This assumption accompanies a hierarchical concept of order and progress. Inherently there is a top-down relationship in this evolutionary conceptualization. The ignoring of local human resources and competencies is as well a consequence of the underlying belief of developmental hierarchy.[38] It is part of the power and control equation linked to the production and distribution of knowledge.

The changes introduced by development finance and technical assistance projects (as opposed to private corporate finance) into the relationship between African states and the economies of the northern industrialized countries is the concrete dimension that characterizes, to some extent, the classical neocolonial relationship theoretically posited by Nkrumah.[39] The significant difference, however, is that rather than the transnational and multinational corporations that Nkrumah envisaged, the economies and governments of Africa have become most heavily dependent on the development apparatus. The development apparatus facilitates the transnational corporate agenda. This can be understood, then, as a stage in the evolution of imperialism or globalization.

It would contribute to a deeper understanding of the conditions of postcolonial Africa and realizing Pan-African unity for Africans of the Diaspora to understand developmentalism being a stage of imperialism following colonialism. Not only is developmentalism consequently an ideology, but it is also a condition, a set of relationships that transpired from the colonial condition—that is, that set of relationships between the societies that were conquered by Europe and the realm of Western economic, social, and cultural hegemony. The fact is that Nkrumah, like most of the independence anticolonial leaders of colonized territories, did not recognize developmentalism as an aspect of imperialism subsequent to colonialism being related to the ideas of progress. These leaders envisaged, believed, and planned for progress through social intervention and planning as something achievable and anti-imperialist.[40]

The Development Apparatus

The genesis of the development apparatus can be traced to the expansion of capitalism and the colonial/missionary adventures of Europe and the post–World War II institutionalization of the idea of accelerated social development utilizing programmed socioeconomic and cultural engineering. The development apparatus is a conglomerate of institutions, beliefs, and practices that have come into existence by way of the plans and experiments to promote accelerated economic growth, social change, and modernization in former colonial territories or communities of oppressed nationalities within Western capitalist societies. The development apparatus is established upon theoretical concepts of social science, specific cultural forms and interests, and international institutional structures. Within the development apparatus there is an interplay of socioeconomic forces expressed in class stratification, power contentions, ideological differences, disparate academic and intellectual interpretations, racial- and cultural-based divisions of labor and decision-making structures, as well as values and objective settings.[41]

The complex institutional structure and mechanism of the development apparatus consists of multilateral international organizations and financial agencies, bilateral and multilateral social intervention agencies, NGOs and charity organizations, government ministries, universities and training colleges, private capital, and private individuals. This array of interests and institutions all operate and function either exclusively or in part to institute, impart, bring about, plan for, participate in, or kick-start development.[42] These organizations and institutions are staffed by professionals covering areas in finance, economics, public health, anthropology, sociology, agricultural, and education. Reminiscent of the old colonial officers and bureaucrats, these development professionals have become experts in the social science of development intervention programming and practices. The professionalization and institutionalization of "development" as a social goal and a value have encouraged powerful interests for consolidating mechanisms that fortify the continuation of the set of relationships linked to the production and control of knowledge and discourse for the social construction of *truth* about the *Other*—in this case, Africa and the underdeveloped world.[43] The knowledge of development is produced, disseminated, and utilized by a global imperialist structure that I refer to as the development apparatus. This apparatus functions via a network of governments, organizations and institutions, applied programs, conferences, workshops, and consultancies.

Institutionally, at the top of our structure of the development apparatus is the Organization for Economic Cooperation and Development (OECD), an organization of twenty countries from Europe and North America. Its objective is to assist the economic growth of its member nations by cooperation and technical analysis of national and international economic trends and policies. Most of the finance invested in the development apparatus and to keep it functioning comes from the OECD. Within the OECD, there is the Development Assistance Committee (DAC). Members of the DAC coordinate the foreign aid policies of OECD countries. DAC members are Australia, Austria, Belgium, Canada, Denmark, Finland, France, Germany, Italy, Japan, the Netherlands, New Zealand, Norway, Sweden, Switzerland, the United Kingdom, and the United States.[44]

In just as significant a financial position of power and in a somewhat stronger political position of power are the Breton Woods institutions of the International Bank for Reconstruction and Development (IBRD), or World Bank as it is commonly known, together with the International Monetary Fund (IMF). The United Nations (UN) and its various departments such as the United Nations Development Program (UNDP), United Nations Education Science and Cultural Organization (UNESCO), United Nations International Strategy for Disaster Reduction (UNISDR), International Labor Organization (ILO), Food and Agricultural Organization (FAO), and Organization for Economic Cooperation and Development (OECD) are substantially dependent on funding from the OECD countries. The UN has both a symbolic and operational role that it plays in the development interface. It also provides a forum where the countries undergoing development intervention can dialogue and negotiate with the nations of the industrial North. However, the economic and military power differentials determine outcomes. Under the umbrella of the arrangements of the multilateral organizations of the development apparatus are the bilateral agencies of different Western industrial countries and the related NGOs. National governments of developing countries, local

NGOs, and local recipient communities or target groups complete the bottom tier of the structure.

This is the edifice that confronts Pan-African emancipatory self-determination and unity. Africans of the Diaspora are becoming increasingly more engaged in continental Africa as the African Union (AU) continues to implement the sixth region policy, which includes the Diaspora as an integral region of Africa. In light the inclusion of Diaspora and the realities and practices of institutions and agencies of the development apparatus for Africans in the Diaspora, it becomes even more vital to fully understand the culture of developmentalism and its power relations as well as the ethos informing it. What has development, as a phenomenon, created in Africa? How are challenges to its overwhelming power and breadth registered, co-opted, crushed, or successful? Intervention and development are linked to corporate purposes and the dialectics of late European imperialism and industrialization with accompanying epistemological and philosophical formulations.[45]

Developmentalism and its institutional manifestations are phenomenological consequences of historically determined relationships actualized during the period of mercantilist expansion and industrialization in Europe. Another manifestation of this phenomenon is the redefinition and rechronicling of the time-space continuum of the peoples of Africa as "precolonial," "colonial," and "postcolonial." These designations characterize the usurpation of endogenous historical experience and its relocation within the context of events and chronicles of Occidental socioeconomic and cultural experience. Similarly, the structures and functions of the nation-states of Africa have been fundamentally defined within the context of an Occidental social, political, and economic organization. They have been informed and underpinned with an ideology and ethos deriving primarily from the discourse of unilineal evolution and the dichotomy of developed–underdeveloped.[46] Interwoven with this is "paradox nationalism," by which I mean a nationalism that is simultaneously a creation and consequence of colonialism, and, at the same time, its emergence was a resistance to colonial domination. Nationalism in Africa generally did not occur as a collective expression of coinciding interests from the base of different polities. Rather, imperialism and colonization produced the territorial entities.[47] This laid the foundation for a psychocultural coherence based upon a common experience as victims of slavery, forced labor, colonial exploitation, racial discrimination, and cultural negation.[48] This reality made it just as easy and legitimate for Africans of the Diaspora—as for any person from any of the many ethnopolitical groups within the borders of Tanzania—to have a nationalist sentiment toward Tanzania.

As people's resistance to colonialism and imperialism consolidated and made substantial advances, it acquired nationalist characteristics. Freedom fighters and activists, ironically, found themselves struggling to take over a state whose very essence was predicated upon the subjugation and exploitation of the indigenous population within its territorial boundaries.[49] The inheritance of the colonial state, as it were, put constraints upon the revolutionary nationalism of the oppressed. Independence absorbed the revolutionary upsurge. Resistance to colonial exploitation, rather than becoming a social revolution, was rechanneled via the emerging petty bourgeoisie into an exercise of consolidation of the new nation-state. This process was defined as development. The shift from revolutionary nationalism to developmentalism for the most part put the new leadership in a position diametrically opposed to the aspirations of the African people's revolutionary upsurge.[50] Development supplanted revolution.

The institutions of the World Bank, IMF, General Agreement on Trade and Tariffs, and the UN, all elements of the development apparatus, formed the institutions of new transnational imperialism.[51] World War II was a catalyst that brought about the disintegration of the old colonial world of Europe from which the United States benefited considerably. The new international political economy resulting from the war enabled the United States to impose its own division of the world based on the accessibility of open door neocolonialism to the hegemony of finance capital and production.[52] According to Nabudere, "A system of multilateral institutions was worked out to guarantee this new division of the world and just as with the old style imperialism, military arrangements were made to back it up."[53]

These inherent contradictions within the states of Africa converge in the political, economic, and social crises that currently manifest in the African world. The relationship between Africa and the Occidental empire has gone through a series of changes. The struggles and subsequent nationalism that brought about the political independence of African societies altered the structure of governmental control and the relationship of governed and the government. However, despite these political changes, and much to the frustration of the workers and peasants of Africa, political independence in Africa did not bring about the social, cultural, and economic changes that were envisaged by the former colonial subjects (or objects). The persistence of economic and cultural domination has been described as neocolonialism.[54] What has emerged from neocolonialism claiming universal appeal is developmentalism. Everybody wants development and progress, and the development apparatus is the global structure that has been erected to engineer and manage development.

The Arusha Declaration, *Ubuntu*, *Ujamaa*, and *Undugu*

The Arusha Declaration was intended to counter the imperialist structure and ideological purpose of developmentalism, de-linking Tanzania from the imperialist world order and creating a new African model of a society emerging from colonialism. It was diametrically opposed to the capitalist mode of production and social organization, instead placing people and social welfare as the paramount purpose of all economic and social activity as opposed to profit and wealth accumulation by capitalist interests. The Arusha Declaration was TANU's declared policy for establishing an African-centered socialist and self-reliant nation. At the time of its implementation in February 1967, the Arusha Declaration was heralded by many as the blueprint for "African Socialism"—*Ujamaa*. The Arusha Declaration included the TANU creed, the policy of *Ujamaa na Kujitegemea* (Socialism and Self-reliance) and *Mwongozo* (Leadership Code), party membership, and the Arusha Declaration. The government structure and the policy of *Ujamaa* were replaced by a neoliberal free market democracy structure as African economies and governments came under increasing pressure from Western financial institutions through structural adjustment programs and conditionality reflective of the shift in U.S. and British political and economic policies to the right.[55]

However, central to the Declaration is *Ubuntu*. The word "*Ubuntu*" originates in the Bantu lexicon. It is an African philosophical construct that provides location for us in relation with the world. According to *Ubuntu*, there exists a common bond between humans in a society, and it is through this bond, through our interaction with our fellow human beings, that we acquire identity and human qualities. Within this cultural world of *Ubuntu* we affirm our humanity when we acknowledge the humanity of others. This dependent humanity defines what it means to be truly human in the African worldview. The acknowledgment of the humanity of others is expressed and realized through social interaction characterized as respect, listening, decency, tolerance, and consensus, as well as equity.[56]

Ubuntu is described as the essence of being human. *Ubuntu* speaks of the fact that one's humanity is inextricably bound up in that of others. I am human because I belong. *Ubuntu* values wholeness and compassion. A person with *Ubuntu* is welcoming, hospitable, warm and generous, willing to share, available to others, willing to be vulnerable, and affirming of others, and does not feel threatened that others are able and good, for they have a self-assurance from knowing that they are an integral part of a greater whole. The quality of *Ubuntu* gives people resilience, enabling them to survive and emerge still human despite all efforts to dehumanize them. *Ubuntu* has its roots in humanist African philosophy, where the idea of community is one of the building blocks of society. J. S. Mbiti, in his seminal work *African Religions and Philosophies* (1969), describes the African ontological perspective as "I am because we are and since we are I am." This is in essence the idea of *Ubuntu/ Ujamaa/Undugu*. It predicates the person's existence upon the collective life of all and upon the community. It depicts a cause-effect relationship between the collective and the person. This collectivity is the extended family, including those who occupy this world, the living dead, and the ancestors. The idea of the interconnectedness of life and family has strong cultural and spiritual significance. In general, African belief systems conceive of ancestors in a continuous relationship among those living on this plane of existence. Their living memory is the spiritual manifestation of the collective living history and thus the link to the "Divine Entirety."[57]

It is important to venerate one's ancestors and eventually to become an ancestor worthy of veneration. To ascend to ancestorhood, the community must flourish. If it does not, no one will be there to remember and venerate you. Therefore to ensure one's life and immortality, one must adhere to community values and respect one's community's rules. One goes through a ceremonial rite of passage that symbolizes the formal ties with the current community members and those who have passed on. Harmony of the communal social self is ensured by *Ubuntu* principles being articulated in the social discourse.[58] These principles are incorporated in the Arusha Declaration and infused into the national ethos of Tanzania.

The principle of caring for each other's well-being was promoted and a spirit of mutual support fostered. Each individual's humanity is ideally expressed through his or her relationship with others and theirs in turn through recognition of the individual's humanity. The Arusha Declaration acknowledges both the rights and the responsibilities of every citizen in promoting individual and societal well-being. Kindred to the idea of *Ubuntu* is *Undugu*. *Undugu* translated into English means fellow siblings, relatives, shared ancestry, shared histories, shared earth, and shared community of experience. In Tanzania, this concept of *Undugu*, common blood, ancestry, history, values, and locale is an articulation of *Ubuntu*. It constituted part of what informed the philosophical idea of *Ujamaa* (familyhood or community). It was based on the concept of equality, joint action, and unified responses. *Ubuntu* as *Ujamaa* posits the belief that there can be no freedom, social justice, or realization of full human potential without equality of personal worth and access. It was equality that colonialism had fundamentally distorted and destroyed. The Tanzania political lexicon subsequent to the Arusha Declaration mandated that all citizens, including politicians, refer to each other as *Ndugu*. Often *Ndugu* would be translated into English as comrade. Comrade, however, as a word indicating fellow socialist or Communist, did not carry with it the full essence of the word "*Ndugu*" and what it symbolizes in the Bantu lexicon. "*Undugu*" carries a meaning much more than comrade. It carries with it the idea of shared life, mutual responsibility for well-being, and collective identity.

The concept of self-reliance as a pillar of *Ujamaa* was aimed at transforming Tanzania from a colonial society into a society based on the interests of all on equality and justice. It also meant transforming the people of Tanzania from colonial objects into mentally liberated subjects able to determine their own destiny within the overall framework of *Ujamaa*. This idea of transformation, equity inclusion, and people-centeredness informed the organization and the operating principles of the new state. Self-reliance and *Ujamaa* are a state of mind, and in its formulation it not only means an economistic self-reliance in the material sense but also independent and endogenously informed thought free of the hegemonic and Afri-pessimistic Occidental epistemological and cultural determinations and policies.[59]

Nyerere imbued his role of African head of state with the philosophical and cultural values of *Ubuntu/Ujamaa/Undugu*. A subtext of his work and methods was to establish and valorize endogenous African creative and intellectual endeavors. Thus the approach to the process of national construction and social cultural reconstruction of the different societies in Tanganyika to forge a national African society was one of education, institution building, and cultural reaffirmation. The method of facilitating the social campaigns for mobilizing grassroots support through participation debates, consultations, workshops, and seminars was underpinned by Nyerere's pedagogical appreciation that education and learning are necessary components for creating a just social environment and that all situations for social interaction should provide an opportunity for praxis of what has been learned.

The principles for governance within the philosophical framework of *Ubuntu/Ujamaa/Undugu* were set out in the Arusha Declaration. The declaration stated: "The objective of *Ujamaa* is to build a society in which all members have equal rights and equal opportunities; in which all can live in peace with their neighbors without suffering or imposing injustice, being exploited, or exploiting; and in which all have a gradually increasing basic level of material welfare before any individual lives in luxury."[60]

The Arusha Declaration is a synthesis of *Ubuntu/Ujamaa/Undugu*. It enumerated a set of principles asserting that all human beings are equal; every individual has a right to dignity and respect; every citizen is an integral part of the nation and has the right to take an equal part in government at local, regional, and national levels; every citizen has the right to freedom of expression, movement, religious belief, and association within the context of the law:

> Every individual has the right to receive from society protection of life and of property held according to law; every individual has the right to receive a just return for his or her labor; all citizens collectively possess all the natural resources of the country in trust for their descendants. In order to ensure economic justice the state must have effective control over the principal means of production; and it is the responsibility of the state to intervene actively in the economic life of the nation to ensure the well-being of all citizens, and to prevent the exploitation of one person by another or one group by another, and to prevent the accumulation of wealth to an extent which is inconsistent with the existence of a classless society.[61]

This passage captures what in essence is the contradiction between the African peoples' aspirations and national ethos and that of the modernist development model constructed by imperialist powers.

The Arusha Declaration and Leadership Code outlined a set of values and protocols of leadership informed by the ideas of *Ubuntu/Ujamaa/Undugu*. Popular participation was mobilized as a social movement that engaged in a massive grassroots program of building structures, a program directed at ensuring that national policy formulation would be substantiated by a bottom-up process. The conception of self-reliance and community and individual liberation being contingent upon collective liberation and participation is an important principle of unity that informed *Ujamaa* and was to be engendered by it.

As an intellectually articulated and culturally informed philosophy and a practically implemented policy, the Arusha Declaration, infused with African philosophical concepts of *Ubuntu/Undugu/Ujamaa*, is a real-life expression of the historically felt need for Africans to become masters of determining their own destiny. The concept, the policies, the strategies, and the campaigns for realizing a national society with an ideology of *Ujamaa* as articulated in the Arusha Declaration promoted the mental and intellectual freedom of Africans in an effort to formulate national responses that would support such a paradigm. The ideas of the Arusha Declaration resonated with the ideas and programs that had been articulated by the Universal Negro Improvement Association (UNIA), Booker T. Washington, and the Nation of Islam, as well as the civil rights and Black Power movements as expressed in public statements and speeches by Martin Luther King Jr. and the Student Nonviolent Coordinating Committee (SNCC). These same ideas articulated and implemented in Africa were resonating with those African voices in the Diaspora expressing and calling for similar purposes of self-determination, emancipation, and African unity.

In reference to *Ujamaa*, Nyerere explained that it was not an accident or coincidence in the choice of the word "*Ujamaa*" to define socialist policies, nor was it a result of trying to find a Kiswahili equivalent for the English word "socialism." Rather, it is an indigenous concept, an African word emphasizing the African cultural-centeredness of the policies Tanzania intended to follow.[62] Understood as cultural and cognitive self-determination, *Ujamaa*, the philosophy and the policies informed by it, is an effort of Africans to control the discourse of the creation of a unified national society from disparate enthnopolitical protonations historically disenfranchised by the colonial experience. The effort was based upon an African-centered perspective, assessment, and philosophical apprehension of what is needed and how it should be achieved. The use of the word "*Ujamaa*" was to make it cognitively and culturally accessible to the majority of the people in the context of their cultural organization.

The Pan-African values of the Arusha Declaration set up a purpose for continental unity and peace. Continental integration is essential to reviving Africa. The idea of African integration had to be articulated as a broad, sweeping vision of a renascent Africa. A philosophical basis is important for African unity to be realized. A Pan-African philosophy conceptualizes continental integration as a necessary aspect of fulfilling Africa's destiny. Linked to this destiny is the destiny of its Diaspora. Nyerere's call to Africans from the Diaspora to come and participate was a confirmation in real time of the historical continuity and inclusion reuniting Africans and relocating the aspirations and identity of the lost/found children of those who were taken away.

Ubuntu as a community dynamic is at the core of Pan-African ideology asserting the common destiny of African humanity. The most important socioeconomic transaction is the social contract between the state and the society. This was at the core of the Arusha Declaration. *Ubuntu/Ujamaa/Undugu* is a sociospiritual philosophical construct located in the African communal cultural idea of unity between the social, spiritual, material, and metaphysical. A tragedy of Africa's shared sociocultural experience has been the imposition and internalization of exogenous values under the rubric of a Eurocentric Christianity and an Arabized Islam that negate the cultural and historical African sociocultural text. To a significant degree, conflicts on the continent are actually violent phases of a conflict between Eastern, Western, and indigenous African worldviews that only superficially coincide with religious beliefs or political ideologies. They are in essence struggles for the control of economic resources and political power within the badly structured nation-states created by the colonialists.[63]

Conclusion

Significantly, until its post–Arusha Declaration period, throughout its history, Tanzania was one of the most stable nations in Africa and did not suffer social distortions and violent conflicts. During the Arusha Declaration era, Tanzania provided material and political support as well as the physical space for the liberation movements from Zimbabwe, Namibia, Mozambique, Angola, and South Africa to organize, train, and pursue national liberation. Tanzania became home to millions of refugees from Zaire, Uganda, South Africa, Mozambique, Kenya, Ethiopia, Somalia, Malawi, Namibia, Zimbabwe, Rwanda, and Burundi. It also hosted the largest group of Diaspora Africans to return to live and work in Africa between the years 1964 and 1980. Thus it is imperative for Africana scholars, Pan-Africanists, and social justice activists to examine the Arusha Declaration as an indigenous template that institutionalized African philosophy and values, thereby empowering the capacity for Tanzania and its people to play that historical role in the emancipation and liberation of African peoples. The ideology of *Ujamaa na Kujitegmea* was used to transform a conquered, enslaved, and colonized people and territory that had been part of a European empire into a Pan-African, anti-imperialist, antiracist social movement that emerged as an independent nation based upon African cultural, social, and spiritual worldviews.

The essential precept of this social philosophy is that the singular purpose of social organization is the well-being of humanity and to provide the wherewithal for all to realize their human potential free from injustice and lack of access to basic needs. For its alleged failure, *Ujamaa* still elicits controversy and liturgical-like denouncements. The reason is rooted in the relationship of Eurocentric hegemony, neocolonial power relationships, a lack of holistic phenomenological understanding, and the study of state formation of formerly colonized peoples. The Arusha Declaration was an indigenous blueprint societal construction. Today the people of Tanzania—especially the educated and entrepreneurial elite—have rejected the ideas of the Arusha Declaration as well as *Ubuntu* and have instead opted to embrace the neoliberal free market paradigm based on competition (with its inherent winners and losers) along with capital accumulation within the global order.

It is important for our/the Pan-African purpose of unity and prosperity for African peoples to acquire knowledge and understanding about the struggles of the nationalist and Pan-African revolution on the continent and its com-plicated dimensions of class, ethnicity, and cultural alienation. Africans in the Diaspora are for the most part unfamiliar with the actual institutions and mechanisms that perpetuate the continued oppression and exploitation of African peoples on the global scale. The reasons are historical as much as they are rooted in ignorance among Africans of the Diaspora, and the con-tinent has been propagated and promoted continuously for centuries. Afri-cans of the Diaspora, especially those in the United States, have been kept ignorant of the shared sentiments and struggles of Africans since the Haitian Revolution. Part of the reason that these strategies are successful is related to the degree to which the denigrating stereotypes about Africa have been internalized and how this impacts personal human development as well as perspectives of African social realities, particularly in the areas of econom-ics, political power, and identity. There is an unresolved affliction blocking conscious awareness and actions that could address the reality of our his-torical oppression, exclusion, and powerlessness that causes psychological dependence such that Africans in America, both in the historical Diaspora and the more recent Diaspora, assimilate the chauvinistic hubris of American jingoistic supremacy-patriotism. This chauvinism can be purged. Those from the Diaspora who came to Tanzania and East Africa in the 1970s were chal-lenged by the African and global reality. We were allowed space to purge our-selves of the American cowboy cultural chauvinism and to relocate into the world community of peoples. I imagine similar choices were presented to our ancestors, as Malcolm X noted. When presented with the chance to separate to leave, physically or socioculturally or both, many of us balk and ask, Where shall we go? Where can we find a better place than this? America? This good white man?[64] With our humanity confirmed as we have reconnected to the source and flow of the African historical continuum, we know now there is a place to go, and although we must continue our struggle we can reconstruct our own world that is better than here and now!

Notes

1. Breitman, *Malcolm X Speaks*.

2. Ibid.

3. Jahn, *Muntu*.

4. TANU was the nationalist party established in 1954 by Tanzanian nationalists led by Mwalimu Julius Kambarage Nyerere. TANU successfully organized the people of the former British colony to expel British colonialism from Tanganyika and formed the first indepen-dent African government.

5. Mwakikagile, *Nyerere and Africa*; Smith, *Beyond the African Tragedy*.

6. DeWitt, *Assassination of Patrice Lumumba*.

7. Milner, "Race, Culture and Researcher Positionality," 388–400.

8. Mwakikagile, *Nyerere and Africa*.

9. Ikaweba Bunting, interview, in "Heart of Africa," 309.

10. Guevara and Camiller, *African Dream*.

11. Bannon, "Responsibility to Protect," 1157–1164.

12. Depelchin, *Silences in African History*; Said, *Culture and Imperialism*; Fanon, *Wretched of the Earth*; Fanon, *Studies in a Dying Colonialism*.

13. Ani, *Yurugu*.

14. Smith, *Beyond the African Tragedy*; Sachs, *Development Dictionary*; Cernea, *Putting People First*.

15. Bunting, "Ethnographic Study of the Development Interface."

16. Escobar, "Power and Visibility," 428–443.

17. Shivji, "Democracy Debate in Africa," 79–91; Shivji, *Where Is Uhuru?*; Shivji, "Pan Africanism," 208–220.

18. Harvey, *Condition of Post Modernity*.

19. Missiology, or mission science, is the area of practical theology that studies the mandate, message, and work of the Christian missionary. Missiology is a multidisciplinary and cross-cultural reflection on all aspects of the propagation of the Christian faith, embracing theology, anthropology, history, geography, theories and methods of communication, comparative religion, Christian apologetics, methodology, and interdenominational relations. Because mission science considers both the positive and the negative consequences, as well as the strategies, of the spread of Christianity, missiology also touches on the environmental impact of evangelization and charitable work, including practical facets of international politics and economic development. One of its most difficult challenges is to distinguish between Christian practices that are essential to Christianity and therefore must be practiced by Christians in all cultures and other strictly cultural expressions of Christianity that can be changed and adapted to a different culture. http://www.knowledgerush.com/kr/encyclopedia/Missiology/.

20. Cernea, *Putting People First*.

21. Sachs, *Development Dictionary*.

22. See Rogate Mshana's compelling work, *Insisting Upon People's Knowledge to Resist Developmentalism: Peasant Communities as Producers of Knowledge for Social Transformation in Tanzania*.

23. Ibid.; Giddens, *Consequences of Modernity*.

24. Hadjor, *Dictionary of Third World Terms*.

25. Booth, *Rethinking Social Development*; Booth, "Marxism and Development Sociology"; Hobart, *Anthropological Critic of Development*; Mazrui, *Cultural Forces in World Politics*; Long, *Battlefields of Knowledge*; Brokensha, *Indigenous Knowledge Systems*.

26. Ani, *Yurugu*.

27. Coulson, *African Socialism in Practice*.

28. See also Shivji, "Democracy Debate in Africa," 79-91; Shivji, *Where Is Uhuru?*; and Shivji, "Pan Africanism or Imperialism?," 208-220.

29. Kiswahili, *Kamusi ya Kiswahili Sanifu.*

30. Bunting, *Ethnographic Study of the Development Interface.*

31. Kiswahili, *Kamusi ya Kiswahili Sanifu.*

32. Mshana, *Insisting Upon People's Knowledge.*

33. Nkrumah, *Neocolonialism.*

34. Calinicos, *Marxism and the New Imperialism*; Babu, *African Socialism*; Nkrumah, *Neocolonialism.*

35. Nkrumah, *Neocolonialism.*

36. Mshana, *Insisting Upon People's Knowledge.*

37. Hobart, *Anthropological Critic of Development.*

38. Mshana, *Insisting Upon People's Knowledge.*

39. Nkrumah, *Neocolonialism.*

40. Musseveni, *Sowing the Mustard Seed*; Ani, *Yurugu*; Cabral, *Unity & Struggle*; Nyerere, *Azimio la Arusha*; Nyerere, *Uhuru na Ujamaa.*

41. Bunting, *Ethnographic Study of the Development Interface.*

42. Ferguson, *Anti-politics Machine.*

43. Escobar, *Encountering Development*; Escobar, *Power and Visibility*; Mudimbe, *Invention of Africa.*

44. Todaro, *Economic Development.*

45. Sachs, *Development Dictionary*; Mazrui, *Cultural Forces in World Politics*; Mudimbe, *Invention of Africa*; Said, *Culture and Imperialism*; Rahnema, "Under the Banner of Development," 37–46.

46. Davidson, *Black Man's Burden*; Wallerstein, "Culture as the Ideological Background," 31–55; Mudimbe, *Invention of Africa*; Chinweizu, *West and the Rest of Us*; Williams, *Destruction of Black Civilization.*

47. Davidson, *Black Man's Burden.*

48. Mondlane, *Struggle for Mozambique*; Nyerere, *Uhuru na Ujamaa*; Nabudere, *Imperialism in East Africa.*

49. Babu, *African Socialism.*

50. Bunting, "In Search of a New Africa"; Bunting, interview, in "Heart of Africa."

51. Calinicos, *Marxism*; Hoogvelt, *Sociology of Developing Societies.*

52. Calinicos, *Marxism*; Hoogvelt, *Sociology of Developing Societies.*

53. Nabudere, *Imperialism in East Africa*, 81.

54. Turok, *Africa What Can Be Done?*; Rodney, *How Europe Underdeveloped Africa.*

55. Nyerere, *Azimio la Arusha.*

56. Murithi, *African Union*; Louw, "Ubuntu and the Challenges of Multiculturalism," 15–36.

57. Mbiti, *African Religions and Philosophies.*

58. Eze, "What Is African Communitarianism?," 386–399; Dirk, "African Concept of Ubuntu."

59. Nyerere, *Uhuru na Ujamaa.*

60. Ibid.

61. Nyerere, *Azimio la Arusha*; Ngowi, "Economic Development and Change," 259–267.

62. Hodd, *Tanzania after Nyerere*; Coulson, *African Socialism*;Nyerere, *Uhuru na Ujamaa.*
63. Ngwodo, "Debt, Despots and Domination."
64. Breitman, *Malcolm X Speaks.*

Bibliography

Ani, Marimba. *Yurugu: An African Centered Critique of European Cultural Thought and Behavior.* Trenton, N.J.: African World Press, 1994.

Asante, Molefi. *Kemet, Afrocentricity and Knowledge.* Trenton, N.J.: African World Press, 1990.

Babu, Abdulrahman Mohamed. *African Socialism or Socialist Africa.* London: ZED Press, 1981.

Bannon, Alicia. "The Responsibility to Protect: The U.N. Summit and the Question of Unilateralism." *Yale Law Journal* 115 (2006): 1157–1164.

Booth, David. "Marxism and Development Sociology." *World Development* 13 (1985): 761–787.

———. *Rethinking Social Development: Theory, Research and Practice.* London: Longman, 1994.

Breitman, George. *Malcolm X Speaks.* New York: Grove Press, 1965.

Brokensha, David. *Indigenous Knowledge Systems and Development.* Latham, Md.: University Press of America, 1980.

Bunting, Ikaweba. "An Ethnographic Study of the Development Interface; Power Knowledge, Culture and the Phenomenon of the Development Community." Ph.D. diss., University of Wales, 1997.

———. "The Heart of Africa: Interview Julius Nyerere on Anti-Colonialism." *New Internationalist* (February 1999): 309.

———. "In Search of a New Africa." *New Internationalist* 277 (1996): 12.

Cabral, Amilcar. *Unity & Struggle.* London: Heinemann-African Writers Series, 1967.

Calinicos, Alex. *Marxism and the New Imperialism.* London: Bookmark, 1994.

Cernea, Michael. *Putting People First: Sociological Variables in Rural Development.* Oxford: World Bank, Oxford University Press, 1991.

Chinweizu. *The West and the Rest of Us.* London: Sundor, 1975.

Coulson, Andrew. *African Socialism in Practice.* Nottingham: Spokesman, 1979.

Davidson, Basil. *The Black Man's Burden: Africa and the Curse of the Nation State.* London: Universal Library, 1992.

Depelchin, Jacques. *Silences in African History.* Dar Es Salaam: Mkuki na Nyota, 2004.

DeWitt, Ludo. *The Assassination of Patrice Lumumba.* London: Verso, 2000.

Escobar, Arturo. *Encountering Development: The Making and Unmaking of the Third World.* Princeton, N.J.: Princeton University Press, 1995.

———. "Power and Visibility: Development and the Invention and Management of the Third World." *Journal of Cultural Anthropology* (1988): 428–443.

Eze, Michael. "What Is African Communitarianism? Against Consensus as a Regulative Ideal." *South African Journal of Philosophy* (2008): 386–399.

Fanon, Frantz. *Black Skins White Masks.* New York: Grove Press, 1967.

————. *Studies in a Dying Colonialism*. London: Earth Scan Publication, 1989.

————. *Wretched of the Earth*. New York: Grove Press, 1963.

Ferguson, James. *The Anti-politics Machine*. Minneapolis: University of Minnesota Press, 1994.

Giddens, Anthony. *The Consequences of Modernity*. Cambridge: Polity Press, 1991.

Guevara, Che E., and Patrick Camiller. *The African Dream: The Diaries of the Revolutionary War in the Congo*. New York: Grove Press, 2000.

Hadjor, Kofi B. *Dictionary of Third World Terms*. London: I. B. Tauris, 1992.

Harvey, David. *The Condition of Post Modernity*. Oxford: Blackwell, 1989.

Hobart, Mark. *An Anthropological Critic of Development: The Growth of Ignorance*. London: Routledge, 1993.

Hodd, Michael. *Tanzania after Nyerere*. London: Pinter Publishers, 1988.

Hoogvelt, Ankie. *The Sociology of Developing Societies*. Hampshire, England: Palgrave McMillan, 1976.

Jahn, Janheinz. *Muntu: African Culture and the Western World*. New York: Grove Press, 1989.

Long, Norman. *Battlefields of Knowledge: Interlocking of Theory and Practice in Social Research and Development*. London: Routledge, 1990.

Louw, Dirk. "The African Concept of Ubuntu and Restorative Justice." In *Handbook of Restorative Justice: A Global Perspective*. New York: Routledge, 2006.

————. "Ubuntu and the Challenges of Multiculturalism in Post Apartheid South Africa." *Quest; An African Journal of Philosophy* (2001): 15–36.

Mazrui, Ali. *Cultural Forces in World Politics*. London: James Curry, 1990.

Mbiti, John. *African Religions and Philosophies*. New York: Anchor Press, 1969.

Milner, H. R. "Race, Culture and Researcher Positionality: Working Through Dangers Seen, Unseen and Unforeseen." *Educational Researcher* (2007): 388–400.

Mondlane, Eduardo. *The Struggle for Mozambique*. London: Zed Press, 1969.

Mshana, Rogate R. *Insisting Upon People's Knowledge to Resist Developmentalism: Peasant Communities as Producers of Knowledge for Social Transformation in Tanzania*. Frankfurt: Verlag für Interkulturelle Kommunikation, 1992.

Mudimbe, V. Y. *The Invention of Africa: Gnosis, Philosophy and the Order of Knowledge*. London: James Curry, 1988.

Murithi, Timothy. *The African Union: Pan Africanism, Peace Building and Development*. Burlington, Vt.: Ashgate, 2005.

Musseveni, Yoweri. *Sowing the Mustard Seed*. London: Macmillan, 1997.

Mwakikagile, Godfrey. *Nyerere and Africa: The End of an Era; Relations Between Africans and African Americans: Misconceptions, Myths and Realities*. Atlanta: Protea Publishing; New Africa Press, 2002.

Nabudere, D. *Imperialism in East Africa*. London: Zed Press, 1981.

Ngowi, Honest. "Economic Development and Change in Tanzania since Independence: The Political Leadership Factor." *African Journal of Political Science and International Relations* (2009): 259–267.

Ngwodo, Chris. "Debt, Despots and Domination." http://www.odiousdebts.org.

Nkrumah, Kwame. *Neocolonialism: The Last Stage of Imperialism*. London: Panaf Books, 1965.

Nyerere, Julius. *Azimio la Arusha*. Dar Es Salaam: Tanganyika African National Union (TANU), 1967.

———. *Uhuru na Ujamaa*. Dar Es Salaam: Oxford University Press, 1968.

Othman, Haroub. *Reflections on Leadership in Africa, Forty Years after Independence*. Brussels and Dar Es Salaam: Institute of Development Studies and VUB University Press, 2000.

Rahnema, Majid. "Under the Banner of Development." *Development: Seeds of Change* (1986): 37–46.

Rodney, Walter. *How Europe Underdeveloped Africa*. Dar Es Salaam: Tanzania Publishing House, 1971.

Sachs, Wolfgang. *The Development Dictionary: A Guide to Knowledge as Power*. London: Zed Books, 1992.

Said, Edward. *Culture and Imperialism*. New York: Vintage Books, 1993.

Shivji, Issa. "The Democracy Debate in Africa: Tanzania: Taylor & Francis Ltd, Review of African Political Economy." *Africa in a New World Order* 50 (1991): 79–91.

———. "Pan Africanism or Imperialism? Unity and Struggle towards a New Democratic Africa." *African Sociological Review* (2006): 208–220.

———. *Where Is Uhuru? Reflections on the Struggle for Democracy in Africa*. Cape Town: Fahamu Books, 2009.

Smith, Malinda. *Beyond the African Tragedy*. Hampshire: Ashgate, 2006.

Taasisi ya Uchunguzi wa Kiswahili. *Kamusi ya Kiswahili Sanifu*. Dar Es Salaam: Oxford University Press, 2005.

Todaro, Michael. *Economic Development*. London: Longman, 1997.

Turok, Ben. *Africa What Can Be Done?* London: Zed Books, 1987.

Tutu, Desmond. *No Future without Forgiveness*. New York: Doubleday, 1999.

van Dijk, Teun, A. *Elite Discourse and Racism*. Newbury Park, Calif.: Sage, 1993.

van Hensbroek, Boel P. *Political Discourses in African Thought*. Westport, Conn.: Praeger, 1999.

Wallerstein, Immanuel. "Culture as the Ideological Background of the Modern World-System." *Theory, Culture and Society* (1990): 31–55.

Williams, Chancellor. *The Destruction of Black Civilization*. Dubuque, Iowa: Kendall/Hunt, 1971.

II. CRAFTING CONNECTIONS

Strategic and Ideological Alliances

Garvey in Oz

The International Black Influence on
Australian Aboriginal Political Activism

John Maynard

The influence of Marcus Garvey's black nationalist movement on the mobilization for Australian Aboriginal self-determination in the 1920s remains little known in the dominant Australian or international historical scholarship. Historians and political scientists have given scant regard to the interconnections between oppressed Aboriginal people and racialized struggles of people in other parts of the world. Instead, their focus has tended to emphasize a binary examination of race relations between blacks and whites. In particular, their studies of external influences on Aboriginal political activism have focused on white Christian and humanitarian influences in Australia. Furthermore, most studies of an organized Aboriginal political agenda are locked into the ingrained misconception that Aboriginal political activism had its beginnings during the vibrant 1960s.

Given the reality of globalization and tense international relations, it is timely to explore the historical, political, cultural, and economic relationships between Aboriginal people and other oppressed groups across the twentieth century. Garvey himself historically remains a man clouded in misinformed derision, yet he was an inspiring and charismatic figure whose influence crossed the oceans in all—and sometimes in unrecognized—directions.

Garvey's international influence both at the time and into the future would be substantial. When Ghana achieved its independence in 1957, the first president of the new nation, Kwame Nkrumah, confessed that he attended Universal Negro Improvement Association (UNIA) meetings in Harlem, New York, when he was a student in the United States. Similarly, when Nigeria won its independence in 1960, the first governor general, Nnamdi Azikiwe, also respectfully acknowledged the influence of Garvey. Many later notables, including Malcolm X, Martin Luther King Jr., Elijah Muhammad, and Nelson Mandela, afforded Garvey due recognition in the struggle.[1] Malcolm X was forthright in his estimation on the impact of Garvey: "All the freedom movements that are taking place right here in America today were initiated by the work and teachings of Marcus Garvey."[2]

Recognition of early international black connections in Australia has been documented in the past, including reference to Australian connections to Marcus Garvey.[3] Indeed, Tony Martin writes, "The Sydney, Australia UNIA branch was undoubtedly the furthest from Harlem. It illustrated how, in those days before commercial air travel and television, and before even the widespread use of radio, Garvey and the UNIA were nevertheless able to draw communities from practically all over the world together into a single organization with a single aim."[4] Evidence also suggests that there were Australian delegates at the 1920 UNIA convention in New York.[5] Who these delegates were remains a mystery.

How did the message of Garveyism spread all the way to Sydney, and who were the members of the Sydney branch? Clearly, Garvey and his message struck a grassroots response "in the hearts and minds of black people from an astonishing variety of social and cultural backgrounds"[6] that reverberated around the globe. Even Ho Chi Minh, the legendary Vietnamese freedom fighter, was another twentieth-century leader who attended UNIA meetings in New York in the early 1920s while a merchant seaman.[7] The role of merchant seamen in the spreading of Garvey's ideas cannot be underestimated. The capacity to spread this message globally was achieved through Garvey establishing a worldwide network of information. Moreover, he had the ready agents to do his bidding, and many "of those who did this work for him were seamen."[8] This network across the sea-lanes of the world was the crucial ingredient that played its part in establishing links to Australia. Paul Gilroy's work has established transatlantic black movements and global connections, and his concept of the "Black Atlantic" forced us to "think outside the fixed and misleading boundary lines of nation states."[9] This maritime migration of people and ideas was instrumental not only in the passing of goods but also, in Elizabeth Baldwin's words, in "the political struggles that flowed back and forth across the ocean."[10]

The Aboriginal Waterfront Connection

During the early decades of the twentieth century, a number of Aboriginal men worked on the Sydney waterfront, and through their intercultural exchanges with international black seamen on the docks of Sydney, the future Aboriginal leaders of the 1920s—including one, Fred Maynard—acquired knowledge of the works of Frederick Douglass, Booker T. Washington, W. E. B. DuBois, and Marcus Garvey. Through discussion, the Aboriginal dockworkers learned of a mind-set and ideology that was already being actively pursued overseas. They thus realized that they were not alone. Aborigines drew inspiration from the African American experience. The racism, prejudice, and oppression to which they were subjected in Australia were being battled elsewhere around the globe; they consequently needed to take part in a global strategy to tackle them for themselves. It is therefore understandable that international black movements and ideologies would form the core of the political directives and rhetoric of the future Aboriginal leaders.

Sources illustrate that international black literature was available and sought in Australia, as were black writers. Correspondence sent to Carter G. Woodson, editor of the *Journal of Negro History* (and regarded by many as the "Father of Negro History"[11]) gives evidence of that. It once more highlights the maritime connections for a writer. A. Goldsmith, who described himself as a "Negro Exile," sent his correspondence to Woodson from Port Melbourne in 1920. Goldsmith informed Woodson that the "Negro papers I read out here [are] *The Crisis*, the *Brownies Book*, '*Crusader*,' '*Journal of Negro History*,' '*The Negro World*,' the '*Emancipator*.'"[12] Goldsmith inquired of Woodson's intellectual appraisal: "what do you think of them?"[13] He enclosed nine shillings and sixpence to Woodson for his subscription for the *Negro History* journal.[14] In 1924 an Aboriginal man named Tom Lacey sent a letter to Amy Jaques Garvey. The letter substantiates the Australian interest in international black literature and newspapers. Lacey hinted at their potential for propaganda: "I would be very grateful to you if you could advise me how to get some of your American papers, *The Negro World* and other papers, so that I could distribute them among our people as it might help to enlighten them a bit."[15]

It is important to consider not just the impact of a newspaper like the *Negro World* but also the attempts of white authorities to stamp out its circulation. Indeed, "the *Negro World* penetrated every area where black folk lived and had regular readers as far away as Australia," says historian Tony Martin:

It was cited by colonial powers as a factor in uprisings and unrest in such diverse places as Dahomey, British Honduras, Kenya, Trinidad and Cuba. These powers therefore had no illusions concerning the appeal of its message of racial self-reliance and its anticolonialist tone to oppressed black people. During its entire existence, therefore, the paper was engaged in a running battle with the British,

French, United States and other governments, all of which assiduously sought to engineer its demise, or, failing that, to restrict or prevent its circulation.[16]

The sheer size and speed of the UNIA's rise unquestionably unsettled the authorities in several countries, not least the United States. The Bureau of Investigation and its later director, J. Edgar Hoover, became increasingly ambivalent toward this upsurge of black agitation, and the bureau's agents were compiling dossiers of evidence and activities:

> It has been ascertained that there has been considerable correspondence between the officers of the Universal Negro Improvement Association in New York and prominent coloured men in foreign countries, and that such correspondence or exchange of views American Negroes and prominent coloured men in other countries . . . cannot fail to have its effect in due time in the establishment of a closer relationship between the coloured races of the world. . . . It is the intention of the association to raise funds and send agents . . . to spread the propaganda. This is to be accomplished not by public lectures, but by establishing personal relations of friendship with the more radical natives of each country and leaving them the work of getting the message to the masses.[17]

Clearly an international network to oppose inequality was under way, and people were attracted to Garvey's message of self-determination and justice. It was just such interaction that unquestionably attracted Australian Aboriginal interest.

Black Seamen and the Coloured Progressive Association

The first indication of serious international black influence upon later Aboriginal political mobilization is the formation in Sydney in 1903 of the Coloured Progressive Association (CPA). This organization and its links to Aboriginal people were undoubtedly a result of working connections on the Sydney waterfront, at that time a major and busy international port. The CPA's membership largely comprised African Americans, West Indians, Africans, Indians, and Islanders, and there is evidence that Aboriginal people were also involved.[18] The great majority of the international black men could not have been nationals but would have been foreign transitional seamen.

This particular period in Australia was one that witnessed high levels of overt racism. The implementation of the "White Australia" policy, with its significant long-term ramifications, was a famous product of the era.[19] This clearly racist act aimed to exclude colored immigrants from Australia, particularly Asians. This enforced "White Australia" mentality had its origins in the anti-Chinese riots that erupted during the gold rush period. Deep racist and prejudicial attitudes resurfaced when South Sea Islanders were kidnapped into the Queensland sugar industry as laborers. In 1920 Australian prime minister Billy Hughes proudly declared that the "White Australia" policy was the country's greatest achievement since federation in 1901.[20] As one contemporary critic put it, "Australia first put a tax on coloured people, increased the tax, afterwards limited the number, and finally prohibited their entry."[21] These international black seamen would have had a foreboding experience in Australian ports at the time. One Jamaican seaman displayed his disgust by refusing to turn out for the customs inspection. He was forced to appear in court and replied to the magistrate:

> "We went to Newcastle, had to pass customs; went to Wallaroo, had to pass customs; came to Port Adelaide had to pass customs. Once I was undressed, and they made me come up. There are 12 of us coloured men on the ship, and we want to know why we should be singled out. The ship is chartered, and we came to work the ship, not to live here. We do not see why we should have to pass the customs every time we come into port." Defendant was ordered to forfeit two days' pay, and to pay £2 1/- costs. As he left the court he bowed to the magistrate and said, "Good Morning Sir."[22]

In 1904 a deck crew of twenty lascars had left a ship docked in Melbourne and camped on shore, refusing point blank to return to the vessel. They complained to authorities of ill-treatment working on an Australian-owned vessel, *Argus*, and that they had been assaulted by the captain. "Eight of the men complained that they had been struck by the captain. They all declined to go on board unless there was a fresh captain. They would sooner go to gaol."[23] The following day the men appeared before the city court and received no support for their pleas of abuse. The captain appeared exonerated, but the crewmen were brave enough to stand up in the face of penalized abuse:

> The 21 Lascar seamen who went on strike from the steamer Argus on Sunday, owing as they alleged to ill-treatment by the captain were before the city court today. Captain Sutherland said he had not touched any of the men, and he had heard no complaints.
>   The Bench, after hearing further evidence ordered 18 of the men back to the steamer, whilst the others, who were said to have caused the trouble were remanded for a week.[24]

Twenty years later conditions for international black seamen remained harsh in Australian ports. A crew of West African seamen went on strike while their ship was in dock at Newcastle. It was noted in the press that the captain of the vessel would "have to support them on board or pay a penalty of £100 a man if they remain off the ship more than 24 hours."[25] Although some white groups opposed the restrictive policies that targeted black visitors,[26] similar severe experiences for black seamen were the norm in other ports around the globe during the early decades of the twentieth century. Many black seamen were forced to live in poverty in English ports like London, Liverpool, Cardiff, and Hull:

> Dumped from tramp steamers or attracted by the prospect of casual work ... black seamen found it hard to get another ship, harder still to find work ashore. Most white seamen rejected them as shipmates; white dockers, too, refused to work alongside them. Having spent the small sums they had been paid off with, having pawned any spare clothes and other belongings, destitute seamen tramped from port to port, desperate for work. Their quest was endless and almost hopeless. Help from compatriots and parish hand-outs kept them from starving.[27]

The formation of the CPA in Sydney was undoubtedly a result of similar experiences. Black people congregated for comfort and support in the face of mutual hardship, isolation, and, at times, hostile racism. International black commentators were scathing of the "White Australia" policy: "There is Australia, a great empty continent containing five million people where it could easily support one hundred million. It is being held for white settlers who do not come, while coloured people are being kept out. Let Australia open its doors to its natural coloured settlers."[28]

Knowledge of the CPA would have undoubtedly faded from memory and history had it not been for the visit to Australia of one highly identifiable black icon. Heavyweight boxing sensation Jack Johnson, a black American, visited Australia in 1907 contesting and decisively winning three fights. An advertisement in the *Referee* on Wednesday, March 13, 1907, drew attention to Johnson's imminent return to the United States and that an organizing body called the CPA of New South Wales was holding a farewell function in his honor. The organization was described as a "solid influential Sydney body."[29] Some of the organization's officeholders were named: "Mr. W. Grant is grand president, Mr. H. Gilbert treasurer, and Mr. G. Phillips secretary."[30]

The farewell to Johnson, at Leigh House in Sydney, evidently well attended and an undoubted success, was given sarcastic racist coverage in the *Truth*:

Fig. 5.1. The Coloured Progressive Association farewell for Jack Johnson; Sydney, 1907. Johnson is in the back center of photo in the light tweed suit. Fred Maynard is seated to Johnson's left, center of the three men seated. Courtesy of John Maynard.

the gorgeous mirrors of the dance-room reflected the gyrations of the coloured cult of the city. . . . White men (a very few) ambled around with full black, half and quarter caste beauties. . . . Three white ladies toed the "shazzy" in amazing shoulder cut evening dresses. One of these charmers had on a blazing red costume, and she made a paralysing start in a waltz.[31]

Jack Johnson was described as looking magnificent when he arrived in a light square-cut tweed suit. He moved at ease among the crowd throughout the evening but did not take to the dance floor himself. Highlights of the dancing during the night presents further evidence of the maritime background of those present: "a quadrille was in progress shortly after 11 o'clock, and some sable dancers were displaying bell bottomed trousers with great effect."[32] Despite its glaringly offensive tone, the article presented historical evidence of the CPA at the time. The president, an elderly "coloured" gentleman and a former steamtug captain, W. Grant, indicated to the reporter that the organization had established a membership of "40 or 50 and had been in existence about four years." Moreover, "he also let it be distinctly understood that the

Black Progressives didn't like the Commonwealth restrictive legislation. They want an open black door, which coons can enter at their own sweet will."[33] It evidently never occurred to the journalist that Aboriginal people could have been a part of the evening. Obviously educated and elegantly attired, Aboriginal men and women were out of the realm of his imagination: "The coloured gentlemen and ladies were almost entirely of the American type. The Coloured Progress [*sic*] Association does not evidently include the La Perouse [an Aboriginal community in Sydney] shade."[34] But a photograph of the event (which clearly identifies Jack Johnson and the West Indian boxer Peter Felix) shows that future Aboriginal activist Fred Maynard was present at Johnson's farewell in Sydney.[35]

No further mention or account of the CPA has to date been found. Johnson, for his part, was an inspiring highly politicized and outspoken individual. He returned to Australia in 1908 and won the heavyweight championship of the world by stopping Tommy Burns. The news of Johnson's victory spread rapidly through Aboriginal communities in Australia and reverberated around the globe.

The Sydney Australian Branch of the UNIA

At the height of its power in the early 1920s, the UNIA had successfully established chapters in forty-one countries—including Australia. The *Negro World* provides information on the background and activities of the Sydney UNIA branch. Moreover, a letter sent by the Australian UNIA's secretary, Robert Usher, and published in 1923 indicates the excitement and enthusiasm of the Sydney group; Usher marveled that the impact of Garvey and his organization was "resounding throughout the length and breadth of this small continent."[36] Despite a few difficulties, the branch was now up and running, and money was being spent to ensure its growth. Usher pointed out that many black people in Australia were suffering from low self-esteem and confidence, "but there are some of us who are doing our best to not only keep ourselves out of the mire, but to pull our brothers out as well."[37]

The Sydney branch intended to adamantly spread information about Garveyism in order to break ignorance within Aboriginal communities and provide inspiration: "we are doing our best to bring them in line."[38] Usher was aware of Garvey's proposed world tour and expressed the hope that he might include an Australian visit because "we would like him to visit the Sydney Division."[39] A U.S. federal surveillance report states that in 1923, Garvey had taken steps to undertake a world tour, including a month in Australia. It was noted that the "various branches of the UNIA are being requested to immediately arrange for Garvey's appearance before the branches."[40] Garvey himself took notice of the Sydney branch and its support, thus acknowledging the Australian members: "I have discovered that the same kind of loyalty is manifested by the foreign divisions of the organisation. The moment I landed in New York I received a cable from Sydney, Australia, where we have a division, who manifested their loyalty 100 percent, after hearing and reading in the Sydney papers of my arrest here a few weeks ago."[41]

A 1924 letter written by Tom Lacey to Amy Jaques Garvey helps clarify the makeup and operation of the Sydney branch. "Dear Madam;" the letter reads, "I do hope you will excuse me for taking the liberty of writing to you, but I am doing so in the interests of our people."[42] Lacey's letter moved on to pledge to Garvey and his movement the support of 10,000 Aboriginal people in New South Wales as well as 60,000 Aboriginal people nationally. He stressed, "we have a great deal of work in front of us to do. What I mean by that is the native [A]boriginals of this state, New South Wales."[43] Lacey confided that they were planning to expand the organization and that they had a national focus at the forefront of their agenda. "We have not had the time to organize the other four states yet," he explained, "but I think there are about fifty or sixty thousand; that is as far as we can reach at the present time."[44]

Lacey had been a member of the Sydney UNIA branch since 1920 and had recently been elected the organizer of the Sydney chapter:

> I myself take a great interest in the work. Nearly all my time is taken up with it. I started in 1920, that is four years ago, and they made me organizer this year, 1924. I hope before long you will be able to send us a delegate down here to Australia, as it would mean a great help to us.[45]

His letter reveals that the Aboriginal political fight was hampered by the tight control exerted over many Aboriginal people confined on reserves by both missionaries and government Protection Boards: "We have a bit of trouble to see some of our people, as the missionaries have got the most of them, and we have great difficulty in reaching them. The authorities won't allow us to see them unless we can give them (the Aboriginal Board) a clear explanation of what we want them for."[46] Lacey recognized the negative long-term effects of confinement to missions and reserves for the Aboriginal population. The authorities "have got their minds so much doped that they think they can never become a people,"[47] he grumbled. But Aboriginal people recognized Garvey as a great leader and a source of hope: "[Garvey] has done wonderful work since he started, and we will still continue to pray for him, that he may have great success in his great work."[48] Lacey furthermore mentioned that his sister was also involved in the Sydney UNIA branch and that she was about to offer some evidence that Aboriginal people in Australia had taken up the initiative to inform the international black community of their plight in Australia: "My sister Mrs Hassen, is treasurer of this branch. She is also going to write to you, and send some Australian papers."[49]

Despite such an optimistic tone and outlook, only a few months after this correspondence news of the establishment of the Australian Aboriginal Progressive Association (AAPA) was announced in Sydney, and, significantly, there was no further recognition of a Sydney UNIA branch after that. The Aboriginal leaders had obviously realized that an organization of their own would be of much greater advantage. They nevertheless continued to draw on the influence and ideology of Garvey's movement for their own fight, such as by cleverly unpacking Garvey's ideals and remodeling them to represent their own experience in Australia. They built their platform around Garvey's call for pride in culture, a solid economic base, and strong association to one's land of birth.

The AAPA's president, Fred Maynard, and Treasurer Tom Lacey would attract widespread media attention in the years to come. In the *Voice of the North* from January 11, 1926, Maynard was already described as an "orator of outstanding ability and in the not far distant future will loom large in the politics of this country." Lacey asserted that given the opportunity, Aboriginal people were capable of gaining the same position "as the coloured people of the United States of America, who have their colleges and universities."[50] A newspaper account of Lacey likens him to Moses and thus places him on the same echelon as Garvey, the "black Moses":[51]

> From end to end of N.S.W. [New South Wales] the name of Lacey is known and admired. He is a keen debater and will be hailed as a modern Moses. The slogan "No more slavery in N.S.W" will reverberate throughout the length and breadth of the continent, and will not only have the effect of breaking the chains off the aboriginals in prison gangs of Western Australia, but will straighten out every grievance which the native people are enduring under the respective Australian governments.[52]

The AAPA

In Sydney, the newly formed AAPA tapped into the growing Aboriginal grassroots discontentment. A combination of increased harsh government actions, including the revocation of tens of thousands of acres of Aboriginal farming lands, the separation of Aboriginal children from their families, and returning Aboriginal World War I veterans, served as the catalyst for an eruption of Aboriginal political protest. The AAPA held its first conference at St. Davids Church and Hall in Surrey Hills in Sydney in April 1925. The new organization was instantly front-page news in the Sydney press, and over 200 Aboriginal people attended this inspiring first Aboriginal civil rights convention, many having traveled a great distance from across the state. The imprint of Garveyism was deeply embedded in the platform of the new movement. The logo, motto, and much of the political rhetoric of the AAPA were adopted from the doctrine of Garveyism. The clarion call of Garvey's UNIA was "One God! One Aim! One Destiny!"[53]—the same motto appeared on the AAPA's letterhead. In his poem "Africa for the Africans," Garvey cried:

> Europe Cries to Europeans. Ho!
> Asiatics claim Asia, so
> Australia for Australians
> And Africa for Africans

"Australia for Australians" was the same battle cry as the one featured on the AAPA logo. It was no coincidence. Marcus Garvey had written in his manifesto, "We are organized for the absolute purpose of bettering our condition, industrially, commercially, socially, religiously and politically."[54] In its four years in the public spotlight, the AAPA continued to publish demands in the media that resonated with Garvey's influence. For example, President Fred Maynard stated that the AAPA encouraged Aboriginal self-respect through spiritual, political, industrial, and social ideals. The Aboriginal political movement was thus enthusiastically charged with enforcing government change with regards to Aboriginal affairs.

The AAPA opened its own offices on Crown Street in Sydney in 1925, assisted in establishing a home for Aboriginal girls who had run away from white employers, and, despite severe opposition from the Protection Board, became an officially registered company with the Register General. It would establish thirteen branches across the state with an active membership of over 600 Aboriginal members and went on to hold four annual conferences in Sydney, Kempsey, Grafton, and Lismore, at which papers were delivered by Aboriginal people on issues including housing, education, health, employment, land, and children—issues that remain on the agenda even today, some ninety years later.

The AAPA had a ready base of followers eager to align themselves with this new movement. One man wrote from a far-back settlement, stating that

someone should come and tell them about the "Freedom Club."[55] Sydney
became a crucible of Aboriginal radicalism, as many of the people who came
there were refugees hunted and hounded from their homes across the state
but were prepared to flee in an attempt to protect their children. AAPA leaders were readily given the opportunity to speak politics in places like Salt
Pan Creek and La Perouse, where they had large audiences of supportive and
encouraging Aboriginal people who were sick and tired of the government's
negligence and inability to listen to any Aboriginal grievances.

In late 1925, at the AAPA's second convention held in the coastal town of
Kempsey, over 700 hundred Aboriginal people were in attendance for three days.
The title of President Maynard's paper and address presented on the occasion
deserves greater scrutiny. Although the original paper on which the address was
based does not survive, the title mentioned in the press report, "The Other Fellow," certainly has a strong postcolonialist ring to it. It takes little imagination to
realize to whom, in fact, Maynard was referring. Aboriginal people during this
period were strategically categorized as the maligned and marginalized "Other."
Maynard closed the Kempsey conference with a powerful resolution that was
forwarded to the press and all levels of Australian government:

> As it is the proud boast of Australia that every person born beneath the South-
> ern Cross is born free, irrespective of origin, race, colour, creed, religion or any
> other impediment. We the representatives of the original people, in conference
> assembled, demand that we shall be accorded the same full right and privileges
> of citizenship as are enjoyed by all other sections of the community.[56]

This kind of a reflection of the articulate and well-read Maynard again
bespeaks uncanny comparisons with Marcus Garvey. Both men were powerful and inspiring speakers. As young men they had carried and studied a
dictionary to improve their vocabulary, and both had a great appreciation of
the North American thinker Ralph Waldo Emerson. Speaking at Kempsey,
Maynard quoted Emerson by saying, "If a man built a better house or even a
better mouse trap than the other man, though he be in the dense woods the
world would make a beaten track to his door."[57] Garvey, for his part,

> "preached with telling force and earnestness Emerson's gospel of self-reliance."
> Furthermore, Ferris (William H. Ferris, editor of the *Negro World*) averred that
> "there is something in Emerson's advice to 'Hitch your wagon to a star,' which was
> undoubtedly the same inspiration as the advice that Garvey used in his exhorta-
> tion to 'lift up yourselves men, take yourselves out of the mire and hitch your
> hopes to the stars; yes, rise as high as the very stars themselves.'"[58]

Fig. 5.2. Fred Maynard and his sister Emma; Sydney, 1927.
Courtesy of John Maynard.

Up until this time, the enforced policy of isolation on tight restrictive reserves had prevented Aboriginal groups from mobilizing a united front of opposition. Marginalization thus not only meant being denied access to the urban space but also being precluded from mounting effective campaigns to confront the issues of disadvantage. In the face of such restrictions, Fred Maynard proved an inspiring leader. In 1927 he penned a three-page letter of protest to the New South Wales premier, which remains one of the most powerful statements ever written by an Aboriginal activist:

> I wish to make it perfectly clear, on behalf of our people, that we accept no condition of inferiority as compared with the European people. Two distinct civilisations are represented by the respective races. On one hand we have the civilization of necessity and on the other the civilization co-incident with a bounteous supply of all the requirements of the human race. That the European people

by the arts of war destroyed our more ancient civilization is freely admitted, and
that by their vices and diseases our people have been decimated is also patent, but
neither of these facts are evidence of superiority. Quite contrary is the case....
The members of [the AAPA] have also noted the strenuous efforts of the Trade
Union leaders to attain the conditions which existed in our country at the time
of invasion by Europeans—the men only worked when necessary—we called no
man "Master" and we had no King.[59]

Hard as it is to believe, by the mid-1930s both leaders—Garvey in the United
States and Maynard in Australia—were but fading memories. Garvey was
a target for the Bureau of Investigation, which had him convicted and jailed
on trumped-up mail fraud charges. Being a West Indian, he was eventually
deported in 1927 and never again allowed to return to the United States. Maynard and the AAPA in Australia were hounded out of existence by the police
acting on orders of the New South Wales Aborigines Protection Board. The
forced demise of the AAPA in the public political arena in Australia also meant
the onset of the organization's erasure from Australian history and memory.

In conclusion, it may be said that some historians continue to minimize the
impact of early urban black leaders like Fred Maynard and Marcus Garvey in
the sphere of black political protest, rather than recognize that the movements for which they stood were the forerunner of all the activism that followed them in Australia and the United States, respectively. If we understand
that the AAPA had a strong influence on Aboriginal activists for decades to
come, we will recognize that the AAPA was not just an aberration or short
blip on the radar but an enduring movement that left a lasting legacy.

One important realization is that Maynard and the AAPA largely existed
outside the view, recognition, and influence of the wider white populace. The
former's momentum was and is closely connected to the grassroots Aboriginal community activism, which was pivotal for the AAPA's success but also
accounted for its eventual historical oblivion. Finally, the interaction between
Aboriginal activists and Garveyites was the foundation stone of the Aborigines' political platform. As high profile 1970s Aboriginal activist Gary Foley
recently reflected, "the early Aboriginal activists were in fact much more
politically sophisticated than had been previously thought. . . . The strong
influence of Marcus Garvey, the 'father of Black Nationalism,' on certain
Indigenous Australian political activists . . . highlights the way in which Garvey's ideas were adopted and adapted to Australian conditions by Fred Maynard and others."[60] The legacy of these revelations are that young indigenous
people can take great pride in their people's long fight for equality and justice
in their own country.

Notes

In memory of Tony Martin, a good friend and the ultimate Garvey scholar. Tony Martin died unexpectedly on January 17, 2013, aged seventy, at Westshore Medical Hospital, Cocorite, Trinidad. R.I.P.

1. Martin, *Race First*, 360; Stein, *World of Marcus Garvey*, 1; Hahn, *Political Worlds of Slavery and Freedom*, 155–156.

2. Hahn, *Political Worlds of Slavery and Freedom*, 157.

3. Higman, "Jamaicans in the Australian Goldrush," 38–43; Martin, *Marcus Garvey*, 99.

4. Martin, *Marcus Garvey*, 99.

5. Martin, *Race First*, 42.

6. Fredrickson, *Black Liberation*, 152.

7. Martin, *Marcus Garvey*, 64–65.

8. Ibid., 48.

9. Baldwin et al., *Introducing Cultural Studies*, 161.

10. Ibid., 176.

11. Low, *Encyclopedia of Black America*, 868

12. Carter G. Woodson Files, Library of Congress, Washington, D.C., Reel 1, Series 2, Correspondence 1912–1950.

13. Ibid.

14. Ibid.

15. *Negro World*, August 2, 1924.

16. Martin, *Race First*, 93.

17. Federal Surveillance of Afro Americans (1917–1925): the First World War, the Red Scare, and the Garvey movement, -25 reels: Index film A563, Harvard—Widener Library, "British Secret Report on Unrest Among the Negroes," October 7, 1919.

18. Maynard, *Fight for Liberty and Freedom*, 19.

19. All government parties campaigned in favor of a "White Australia" policy during the first general election in 1901, and the restrictive legislation was among the first laws enacted by the national parliament. It was not until 1967 that a more positive practice was adopted, one that allowed for a flow of colored immigrants into Australia. Murphy, *Dictionary of Australian History*.

20. Larkins, *Dictionary of Australian History*, 223.

21. *Daylight*, November 29, 1924, 809.

22. *Daylight*, August 31 1925, 920.

23. *Sydney Morning Herald*, February 23, 1904, 5.

24. *Sydney Morning Herald*, February 24, 1904, 10.

25. *Northern Daily Leader*, September 5, 1925.

26. *Daylight*, July 31, 1923, 618 (for instance, the Seamen's Union had passed a "resolution in favour of black labour on ships" in Australian waters).

27. Fryer, *Staying Power*, 294–295.

28. *Crisis* 23.3 (January 1922), Schomberg Center for Research in Black Culture, New York Public Library, Harlem, N.Y.

29. *Referee*, March 13, 1907.

30. Ibid.

31. Ibid.

32. Ibid.

33. *Truth*, March 17, 1907.

34. Ibid.

35. Maynard family photograph.

36. *Negro World*, May 5, 1923.

37. Ibid.

38. Ibid.

39. Ibid.

40. Federal Surveillance of Afro Americans (1917–1925): The First World War, the Red Scare and the Garvey Movement, Lamont Library, Harvard University, Index film A563.

41. Hill, *Marcus Garvey*, 4:570.

42. *Negro World*, August 2, 1924.

43. Ibid.

44. Ibid.

45. Ibid.

46. Ibid.

47. Ibid.

48. Ibid.

49. Ibid.

50. *Voice of the North*, January 11, 1926.

51. Cronon, *Black Moses*.

52. *Voice of the North*, October 10, 1927.

53. Levine, *Unpredictable Past—Explorations*, 112.

54. Garvey, "Philosophy and Opinions," 55.

55. *Macleay Chronicle*, August 19, 1925.

56. *Macleay Chronicle*, October 7, 1925.

57. "A.N.A.," February 7, 1926, 57, National Library of Australia.

58. Hill, *Marcus Garvey*, 1:lxvi.

59. Maynard, F 1927 correspondence.

60. Maynard, *Fight for Liberty and Freedom*, v.

Bibliography

Archival Sources

Australian Natives Association (ANA). February, 7, 1926, 57. National Library of Australia.

Carter G. Woodson Files, Library of Congress, Washington, D.C., Reel 1, Series 2, Correspondence 1912–1950.

Crisis 23.3 (January 1922). Schomberg Center for Research in Black Culture, New York Public Library, Harlem, N.Y.

Daylight, July 31, 1923, November 29, 1924, and August 31, 1925. Mortlock Library, South Australia.

Federal Surveillance of Afro Americans (1917–1925): The First World War, the Red Scare, and the Garvey movement, -25 reels: Index film A563, Harvard—Widener Library, "British Secret Report on Unrest Among the Negroes," October 7, 1919.

Macleay Chronicle, August 19 and October 7, 1925. New South Wales State Library, Sydney.

Fred Maynard Correspondence, "Letter to the Premier." New South Wales State Archives, Sydney, New South Wales Premiers Department Correspondence Files, A27/915.

Negro World, May 5, 1923, August 2 and September 20, 1924. Schomberg Center for Research in Black Culture, New York Public Library, Harlem, N.Y.

Northern Daily Leader, September 5, 1925. New South Wales State Library, Sydney.

Referee, March 13, 1907. New South Wales State Library, Sydney.

Sydney Morning Herald, February 23 and 24, 1904. New South Wales State Library, Sydney.

Truth, March 17, 1907. New South Wales State Library, Sydney.

Voice of the North, January 11, 1926, and October 10, 1927. New South Wales State Library, Sydney.

Secondary Sources

Baldwin, Elaine, Brian Longhurst, Scott McCracken, Miles Ogborn, and Greg Smith. *Introducing Cultural Studies*. London: Pearson, 2004.

Cronon, Edmund David. *Black Moses: The Story of Marcus Garvey and the Universal Negro Improvement Association*. Madison: University of Wisconsin Press, 1987.

Fredrickson, George M. *Black Liberation: A Comparative History of Black Ideologies in the United States and South Africa*. New York: Oxford University Press, 1985.

Fryer, Peter. *Staying Power: The History of Black People in Britain*. London: Pluto Press, 1984.

Garvey, Marcus. "Philosophy and Opinions." In *Great Documents in Black American History*, ed. George Ducas and Charles Van Doren. New York: Praeger, 1970.

Hahn, Steven. *The Political Worlds of Slavery and Freedom*. Cambridge, Mass.: Harvard University Press, 2009.

Higman, Barry. "Jamaicans in the Australian Goldrush." *Jamaica Journal* 10 (1976): 38–45.

Hill, Robert, ed. *The Marcus Garvey and Universal Negro Improvement Association Papers*. Vol. 1. Berkeley: University of California Press, 1983.

———. *The Marcus Garvey and Universal Negro Improvement Association Papers.* Vol. 4. Berkeley: University of California Press, 1985.

Larkins, John. *Dictionary of Australian History.* Adelaide: Rigby, 1980.

Levine, Lawrence L. *The Unpredictable Past: Explorations in American Cultural History.* New York: Oxford University Press, 1993.

Low, W. Augustus, and Virgil A. Cliff, eds. *Encyclopedia of Black America.* New York: De Capo Press, 1988.

Martin, Tony. *Marcus Garvey, Hero.* Dover, Mass.: Majority Press, 1983.

———. *Race First.* Dover, Mass.: Majority Press, 1976.

Maynard, John. *Fight for Liberty and Freedom.* Canberra: Aboriginal Studies Press, 2007.

Murphy, Brian. *Dictionary of Australian History.* Melbourne: Fontana/Collins, 1982.

Rolinson, Mary G. *Grassroots Garveyism.* Chapel Hill: University of North Carolina Press, 2007.

Stein, Judith. *The World of Marcus Garvey.* Baton Rouge: Louisiana State University Press, 1986.

Africa for Africans and Asia for Asians

Japanese Pan-Asianism and Its Impact in the Post–World War I Era

Keiko Araki

> [The average Westerner] was wont to regard Japan as barbarous while she
> indulged in the gentle arts of peace: he calls her civilized since she began to
> commit wholesale slaughter on Manchurian battlefields.
> –Kakuzō (aka Tenshin) Okakura, *The Book of Tea* (1906)

Frustrated with Japan's low status in world politics, a number of Japanese intellectuals and political leaders supported Pan-Asianism from the latter half of the nineteenth century through the end of World War II. Intellectually, Pan-Asianism began "as a reaction to Western colonialism and over time developed into national independence movements" in countries such as China, India, and the Philippines.[1] Asian revolutionaries, and in particular those exiled to Japan, shared the idea of Asian solidarity against Western colonialism. Early Pan-Asianists in Japan, therefore, strongly opposed the Meiji government's course of Westernization and romantically embraced a distinctly Asian path.

Japan had been incorporated into the modern world against its will. In 1854 the country had opened up in response to the "request" of Commodore Matthew Perry, whose steamships symbolized the superior technology of the West. This incident was followed by a chain of unequal treaties into which Japan entered with Western states, typically leaning heavily in the latter's favor. Under the Meiji Restoration, after the overthrow of the Tokugawa feudal government, Japanese political leaders promoted industrialization and militarization.[2] They abolished the old Japanese system by modernizing their political, economic, and social spheres. Fully cognizant of the fact that any country without a strong government had little say in world affairs, they were determined to build a new nation-state with a rich economy and a strong army. From the late nineteenth century through the early twentieth century, Japan nearly achieved this goal. Nonetheless, Europe and the United States continued to assert their agenda in world politics.

However, as a consequence of the Russo-Japanese War (1904–1905) and Japan's rise in status in the international sphere, the Japanese government and the larger Japanese populace began to embrace Pan-Asianism. Pan-Asian philosophy developed out of "a vague feeling of Asianness into a clear concept of regional integration, for which regional solidarity and identity, however defined, were deemed necessary bases."[3] After World War I, many Japanese Pan-Asianists began to take the more hegemonic position that Japan was suited to save (and lead) the whole of Asia. They adopted the slogan of "*hakkō ichiu*," or "the eight corners of the world under the one heaven of benevolent imperial rule,"[4] from *Nihon Shoki*, Japan's oldest official history book completed in A.D. 720, to idealize an empire in which Japan was supreme. While Pan-Asianists in other Asian countries cautiously observed Japan's activities, in Japan, Pan-Asianism came to be used to justify Japan's colonialism in Asia until the end of World War II.[5]

"Asia for Asians" and "Africa for Africans"

Japanese Pan-Asianists argued that the unity of Asian people was needed to prevent Western encroachment. Fully aware of the racialized aspects of Western imperialism and international politics, some Pan-Asianists, such as Ryōhei Uchida and Kametarō Mitsukawa, likened the international standing of Asians with the status of black people. Recognizing that Japan would have to have a more advanced position in world politics, these Pan-Asianists furthermore claimed to be representing all people of color who were subjected to European oppression. They paid special attention to the rhetoric of Marcus Garvey and his black nationalist movement because of his charges of imperialism and racism as decisive defects of Western democracy.

Kokuryū-kai (Black Dragon Society), a Pan-Asianist political group led by Ryōhei Uchida, published the English-language magazine the *Asian Review* to dispel misconceptions made by Europeans and Americans of Asian peoples via a "mutual exchange of ideas and opinions,"[6] and "to honestly express the Japanese point of view before the world's eyes."[7] Many articles addressed racial violence around the world, including the lynching of black Americans in the United States as well as discussions of white domination in world politics.

Kokuryū-kai, in its determination to become the voice of the voiceless, stated that the *Review*'s "intention is not only to champion the cause of Japan but [that] of all Asian and African countries."[8] An article entitled "Coloured and Whites" was a response to a white American reader who, claiming "to love Japan and to admire the Japanese people," felt uncomfortable when she found that the magazine referred to the Japanese as "coloured," a term usually applied to black Americans. The *Asian Review* explained that when "we employ the word 'coloured,' we refer to the Asian and African peoples including the Negroes also." The article then proceeded to protest against the American reader's description of black Americans as "a bestial and low people" and pointed out that "there may be undesirable elements among the Negroes, just as there are wicked persons among the Americans and Europeans. For the fault of a few to accuse the whole race, however, cannot be justified by any logic."

In fact, Japan played a unique and vital role in Garvey's conception of a future black nation. He followed the Russo-Japanese War and argued that people of African descent, along with a victorious Japan, could overthrow the existing racial order: "what the yellow race did the black race could also do."[9] Japan's mere existence provided him with a strong case in point to challenge the idea of an absolute, fixed racial order. Garvey, a Jamaican Pan-Africanist, was then building up his movement in the United States. In 1914 he organized the Universal Negro Improvement Association (UNIA) and proposed an "imagined community"[10] of Africans at home and abroad that would transform the European racial hierarchies, which "degraded" the "black race" into a nation on its own. According to Garvey, a fully developed black nation-state should assert the rights of Africans and people of African descent across the globe. His "Back-to-Africa" movement saw Liberia as a place where Africans from abroad could help build a strong nation-state.[11] Ironically, Garvey viewed his black nation-state as a form of empire and in his speeches often used the terms "nation" and "empire" interchangeably.

Interested in its own parallels with the Garvey movement, the *Asian Review* made reference to a November 1920 interview of Garvey in the *Tokyo Asahi Shimbun* by Masuichi Midoro, a New York correspondent for the paper. After the UNIA convention in 1920, Midoro interviewed Garvey at his Harlem office and wrote a series of three long articles entitled "Yellow Peril or Black Peril: Newly Recurring Fear for White People." In the series, he discussed the Garvey movement and its divided reception in the United States. In making the connection of the oppression of blacks with anti-Japanese sentiments among the American people, however, Midoro observed that white Americans feared, above all, an alliance between Japan and China.[12] The *Asian Review* completely downplayed the possibility of such an alliance. Instead, it stressed cooperation between blacks and Asians. The *Asian Review* attributed anti-Japanese sentiment in China and Korea to European and American propagandists, a view shared by Garvey and other black leaders. "It is clear even to [the] dullest intellect that the union of all the colored peoples including the yellow and the Negro races will create a serious menace to the white people."[13]

The Japanese intellectual who introduced the Garvey movement most systematically to Japanese readers is Kametarō Mitsukawa. While joining several political associations, he established two study groups: Roso-kai (The Society of Mature Men) in 1918 and Yuson-sha (The Continued Existence Society) in 1919, both of which claimed to welcome members of all generations, ideologies, and genders, though the latter organization was comprised more so of intellectuals associated with right-wingers such as Shūmei Ōkawa and Ikki Kita, as well as other ideologues.[14] Mitsukawa advocated Pan-Asianist redemption and the reconstruction of Asia. Viewing world history as a racial conflict between the East and the West, he asserted that Asia should be united against European imperialism. While his "Asian Monroe Doctrine" remained an unclear concept at that time, according to Yuichi Hasegawa, it did not necessarily mean intervention in China but sought protection of Asia from Western encroachment. Mitsukawa also made note of the growing tide of socialism, but paid closer attention to nationalist movements.[15]

Reflecting upon the UNIA's first international convention in 1920, Mitsukawa wrote an article on Garvey and the UNIA, "Kokujin Afurika-shugi no Houga" (Signs of Black Africanism), for *Ajia Jiron* (Asia Commentaries), another Kokuryū-kai publication.[16] In the article, he revealed some doubt about the idea of "Africa for the Africans," since Africa had been a real "dark continent," its residents "totally ignorant and in the dark, only constituting a primitive nation." While he did not dismiss Garvey's ideas as empty theory, he thought that they could become a reality if three conditions were met: first, the development of inland areas via a strong railroad infrastructure; second, the placement of Egyptians and South Africans in positions of leadership; and third, via ethnic mixing with other "superior" nations as much as possible. At that time, Mitsukawa took a particular interest in other nationalist movements in Ireland, Egypt, India, and South Africa. He concluded that the overall unity of "Africans" regardless of race was the key to success of the resistance to European domination in Africa.

In 1925 Mitsukawa published *Kokujin Mondai* (The Negro Problem) (fig. 6.1), which focused on the Garvey movement, highlighting the UNIA tricolor red, black, and green Pan-African flag on the title page. The book was actually completed in 1922 but had been lost during the Kanto earthquake of 1923.[17] In the spring of 1925 the manuscript was rediscovered. In his book, Mitsukawa begins with a discussion of the "science" of races and varieties of "black" populations

Fig. 6.1. The title page from Kametarō Mitsukawa, *Kokujin Mondai* (The Negro Problem), published in 1925, incorporates Garvey's UNIA/Pan-African Flag. Courtesy of Waseda University Library.

in the world before tracing the preconditions of the Garvey movement in African American history, the Atlantic slave trade, and the European colonization of Africa. He argued that World War I could be considered a watershed creating this new movement, after which "the black problem is no longer just about slavery in the United States," but about "the agonies of rebirth of the 150,000,000 people, as a nation, who have suffered for thousands of years."[18] Despite acknowledging the fact that blacks did not comprise a "nation," Mitsukawa thus regarded the Garvey movement as nationalist based on the fact that Garvey's aim was the complete withdrawal of Europeans from Africa and the establishment of a black nation-state in the motherland.[19]

Mitsukawa did not hesitate to express his passionate empathy with black people: "The author has devoted his mind and body to the struggle to recapture Asia from deprivation, while looking for comrades for a decade. Africa, which is exploited like Asia; Negro people, who are oppressed like yellow people—these things inevitably hurt my spirit."[20] Describing the Japanese proposal of racial equality at the Paris Peace Conference of 1919 as a bombshell for "white autocracy," he questioned whether world peace could be possible when excluding "colored" nations.[21]

Mitsukawa refrained from estimating how soon the ideals of "Negro Africa" would be realized, but he believed that the return of ten million black people would not be difficult.[22] Obviously, he had a more positive view of the possibility of black redemption in this book than in his 1920 article in *Ajia Jiron*, in which he continued to regard Africans as "savage" and suggested that they should intermarry with other races and follow other "superior" religions.[23] In Mitsukawa's view, his point was proved by the very existence of African Americans, whom he considered as developed and civilized, and thus to be distinguished from "savage" Africans.[24] The book consequently reveals Mitsukawa's own thinking in problematic racial hierarchies, yet received positive reviews. As one journalist wrote in *Hōchi Shimbun*:

> We have known too much about Europe and Europeans. We know other people's kitchen, while not knowing about our own kitchen. How stupid it is to be ignorant of the fact that everything in the European kitchen was taken away from our own kitchen? *Kokujin Mondai* provokes us to get out of this stupidity. We must know Asia. We must know colored peoples. We must deal with our own kitchen. . . . *Kokujin Mondai* raises such a big question.[25]

Mitsukawa advocated that Japan unite with other Asian countries in the fight, and as "the oldest brother" it should take the lead.[26] In his opinion, the Japanese did not properly handle their responsibility of protecting China from European forces.[27] At the same time, he realized that Japan had its own problematic legacy in this regard. Dismissing Japanese brutality during the colonization of Korea in 1910, he argued, "I believe such brutal acts are not seen now."[28] What the Japanese needed, according to Mitsukawa, in order to "win Korean people's minds" was quite simply "love toward Koreans."[29]

Mitsukawa and Garvey both understood that racial unity against European imperialism was most important; however, they both oversimplify differences of culture. The author Hiroko Sato indicates that the premier fault of Mitsukawa's *Kokujin Mondai* was its ambiguous definition of "blacks" as including African blacks, American blacks, and Pacific "natives." According to Sato, Mitsukawa found hope in Garvey's movement despite being unaware of African and African American realities.[30] Accepting this element of the hierarchical European concept of world order, Mitsukawa and Garvey pursued the uplift of "blacks" and/or "Asians" as groups within the assigned (white) order. Garvey thought that what unified "blacks" was their shared predicament stemming from the history of slavery, colonization, and racial discrimination. This echoes the outcry of Tenshin Okakura, another prominent Pan-Asianist, that "Asia is one." As Kenichi Matsumoto rightly suggests, this idea of unity is based on the understanding that "to the down-trodden Oriental the glory of Europe is but the humiliation of Asia."[31] Mitsukawa equated Garvey's black Africanism with his own Asianism "to prove that the world was not created just simply for white people."[32]

Guardian of "Darker" Peoples Before the League of Nations

The Japanese government came to speak for other nations and peoples of color when it presented a proposal for racial equality at the Paris Peace Conference of 1919. The proposal was initially submitted as an amendment to the covenant:

> The equality of nations being a basic principle of the League of Nations, the High Contracting Parties agree to accord as soon as possible to all alien nationals of states, members of the league, equal and just treatment in every respect making no distinction, either in law or in fact, on account of their race or nationality.[33]

The incident gave many blacks in the United States the impression that Japan sought to be the ally and/or guardian of all "darker peoples," and that the proposal was an objection on the part of a leading nation of color to a world system dominated by whites. James Weldon Johnson saw "Japan, so far . . . [as] perhaps the greatest hope for the colored races of the world," stressing the point that "nothing appeals to modern white civilization except power."[34]

Among black leaders, expectations of Japan were embodied in the International League of Darker Peoples (ILDP), an organization that had originally been established to collect information on black radicals (unbeknownst to them) in Harlem in the middle of 1918. Rev. R. D. Jonas, a white preacher and a founding member, was an agent for the British and the U.S. Bureau of Investigation.[35] The ILDP was a front for Jonas, who was actually working for British and U.S. intelligence, to learn about the activities of "radical" black organizations and individuals in the United States. Despite Jonas's true intentions, unknowingly, notable black leaders, including Madam C. J. Walker, Chandler Owen, Adam Clayton Powell Sr., A. Philip Randolph, and Garvey, attended a meeting at Walker's magnificent home to launch the ILDP. Walker was so enthusiastic about the goals of the organization—to send a delegation to the Paris Peace Conference to present a proposal on racial harmony—that she considered leaving portions of her estate to the organization.[36] F. B. Ransom, her attorney and general manager, repeatedly warned her against identifying "with too many people . . . of fanatic ideas." Walker nonetheless defended the aims and activities of the organization and its members.[37]

On January 7, 1919, members of the ILDP went to the Waldorf Astoria to meet with Ruiko Kuroiwa, the editor of the *Yorozu Choho*, a daily newspaper published in Tokyo, and a member of the Japanese delegation to Paris. Randolph presented the ILDP's proposal, asking Kuroiwa for cooperation.[38] Kuroiwa reportedly replied in a fairly noncommittal way, "Japan has always had at heart these things you propose. . . . The people of my country have accepted the invitation in the broadest sense."[39] However, the same report informs us that, in private, Kuroiwa went much further, endorsing "cooperation between the Japanese and the dark people of Asia and Africa." The ILDP organ, the *World Forum*, in turn, was optimistic and reported from the meeting that "with the characteristic calmness and imperturbable solidness of the Japanese, the aforementioned representative assured the delegation of his unqualified and genuine approval of the darker peoples making common cause against the common enemy—race prejudice based upon color."[40]

The ILDP then organized a mass meeting with the Japanese envoy en route to the Paris Peace Conference on January 16, 1919. During that meeting, Jonas was supposed to speak on "Building a New World" and A. Philip Randolph on "Terms of Peace and the Darker Peoples."[41] Kuroiwa apparently was not too impressed with the event, however, only scratching a few lines in his notebook: "Negro Madame Walker and a few other interested visited and posed together for a photograph."[42] The ILDP faded away after the withdrawal of Madam C. J. Walker and Adam Clayton Powell Sr. in February 1919.[43]

While Garvey was one of the launching members of the ILDP, he seemed to maintain a certain distance from the organization. On January 16, 1919, the UNIA held a meeting in Harlem at the same time as the ILDP's abovementioned meeting.[44] The UNIA had already selected a delegation led by the Haitian national Eliézer Cadet, traveling under a French passport to Paris to submit to the conference the UNIA's peace proposal, adopted at the UNIA mass meeting in the previous year.[45] On March 7 Cadet met

Baron Nobuaki Makino, the Japanese deputy ambassador plenipotentiary and former foreign minister, to request that he submit the UNIA's peace proposal on behalf of the UNIA. After listening to Cadet, Makino stated that the UNIA "movement was to be taken seriously and that it was important" for blacks to be united. However, he declined to submit the UNIA's proposal since it was inappropriate for him to do so as a representative of Japan.[46] After this attempt to submit the UNIA's proposals ended in vain, Cadet concluded that the participation of any nation-state other than "the four great allied powers" at the conference was "pure camouflage" and that the League of Nations was "a sham."[47]

The Japanese proposal of racial equality, amended by the Japanese delegation to be less offensive by avoiding the word "race," gained a majority vote, eleven out of seventeen.[48] But President Woodrow Wilson, a native of the American South and a segregationist who, along with the British delegates, had strongly opposed the proposal, ruled that it needed unanimous approval, and it was therefore rejected. Randolph's *Messenger* observed that "Japan raised the race issue and threw a monkey wrench into the league of white nations which well nigh knocked the peace conference into pieces. It was successfully side-tracked however."[49]

After the session, C. D. B. King, one of the Liberian delegates, who later became the president of Liberia, asked French president Georges Clemenceau to insert the following remarks into the official record of the plenary session of the Paris Peace Conference, during which Makino had given a speech:[50] "As an African, and the only member of the Negro race present, I beg your kind permission to express my sincerest thanks and heartfelt gratitude to my most distinguished and honorable colleague, Baron Makino, for his great and admirable speech just delivered, on the question of the equality of races."[51]

Underneath this sympathy lurked the frustration and sense of hypocrisy that the Liberian felt in the midst of a conference where the principles of democracy and self-determination were highly advocated. H. F. Worley, the American financial adviser to the Republic of Liberia who had joined the conference as one of the Liberian delegates, reported King's dissatisfaction with "his isolation from the conference."[52] He remarked that

Liberia is an Ally and not an enemy and we object to being treated as enemies. We object to this discussion going on at which Liberia is not represented. Liberia's fate is being determined and she has no voice in the matter. Liberia wants a voice in discussing the responsibilities. . . . Even if a Mandatory is given regarding Liberia, she at least has the right advanced by President Wilson of self-determination as to what Government shall have the Mandatory over her.[53]

Rhetoric of "Race War": Japan as an Ally

Even after the failure of the racial equality proposal, black leaders expected Japan to play a leading role among "the darker peoples." Garvey occasionally mentioned the coming "race war," particularly in the South. A "race war" between blacks and whites would then be unavoidable, and black people would have to stop supporting their old masters.[54] "The next war will be between the Negroes and the whites," Garvey remarked, according to a report of the Bureau of Investigation, which had him under surveillance—after all, "with Japan to fight with us, we can win such a war."[55] When Masuichi Midoro, a correspondent for the *Tokyo Asahi Shimbun*, visited Garvey at his office in Harlem after the 1920 UNIA convention, he asked how and when the movement would realize its goals. Garvey reportedly answered, "in roaring spirits," adding that "if necessary, there will be a war. In the next 20 or 50 years, our ideals will be realized."[56]

Other influential African American publications considered it the duty of black people to side with the Japanese and to form alliances with Asian peoples to fight against racism and imperialism. For instance, the *Crusader*, a Harlem newspaper launched in 1918 by the Afro-Caribbean writer and founder of the African Blood Brotherhood Cyril Briggs,[57] articulately described that duty as "NOT TO FIGHT AGAINST JAPAN OR MEXICO, BUT RATHER TO FILL THE PRISONS AND DUNGEONS OF THE WHITE MAN ... THAN TO SHOULDER ARMS AGAINST OTHER MEMBERS OF THE DARKER RACES."[58] A Chinese student in Milwaukee responded in the next issue, "expressing ... deepest appreciation and admiration." The student explained that "one of the most treacherous methods of the white people to dominate the darker races is to intrigue and plot among the dark peoples themselves.... That the revolt of the Koreans and the boycott of the Chinese against the Japanese are partly due to the pernicious influence of the Occidental peoples is apparent."[59] Likewise, Garvey claimed that Europeans had incited anti-Japanese agitations in China and Korea: "White capitalists have gone into China and have poisoned the minds of the Chinese against themselves and against the Japanese. They have been subsidizing certain Chinese to fight among themselves, to divide up their soil into two republics. They have subsidized the Chinese to reject every proposal of Japan."[60]

Albeit critical of Garvey's movement, W. E. B. DuBois shared the former's views on Japan, as is evidenced by his belief that British propaganda had made "the white world think the only enemy of China is Japan."[61] In the *Crisis*, DuBois compared the size of Japanese holdings in China to those of European nations and addressed the contradictions of European concerns with regard to Japan: "why is it seemingly the custom to continually speak of 'Japanese aggression' and not one word about the huge holdings of these other nations?" He concluded that "the world certainly seems to have a double standard of international justice and it seems quite time that the real aggressors ceased using Japan as a smoke screen."[62]

When Kokuryū-kai published an article on "Lynching in America" in the *Asian Review*, several black newspapers—including the *Chicago Defender*, the *California Eagle*, and others—either reprinted or referenced the article.[63] However, the tone of the *Messenger* was quite different from that of other black papers. It bluntly noted the "hypocrisy of the Japanese which brutalizes the Chinese, oppresses most shamefully the Koreans, crushes and abuses the Japanese working classes, and disenfranchises more Japanese . . . than the United States disfranchises Negroes in the South." According to the editors of the *Messenger*, the Japanese article was to "serve the Japanese ruling class in a two-fold manner. It will inspire the Japanese masses with the fatalistic determination never to come under the yoke of American imperialism. Next, it will create discontent with America on the part of that portion of the population—Negroes."[64]

When the *New York Times* reported that the Japanese government was working in Beijing to exercise its influence on the selection of the Chinese delegation to the Paris Peace Conference, the UNIA's organ, the *Negro World*, republished the article under the provocative title "JAPAN MOBILIZING THE SENTIMENTS OF YELLOW RACES; Can You Understand This, Mr. Negro?"[65] In June 1919 the *Negro World* published an article entitled "CHINESE KNOW HOW TO FIGHT INJUSTICE,"[66] which briefly dealt with the May Fourth Movement and its spread. The May Fourth Movement was a student-led anti-imperialist demonstration in Beijing against the Treaty of Versailles, which mandated the transfer of the German concessions in Shandong to Japan and not to China. The article regarded the Chinese boycott of Japanese products as "a weapon negroes can use" but did not analyze the movement's causes and background. Garvey was steadfast in his belief that "in another twenty years Japan and China are going to get together" despite the intention of "white capitalists" to divide them.[67] When the Chinese delegation demanded China's right for self-determination as an independent nation at the Washington Naval Conference in 1921, Garvey overlooked the fact that the demand was also addressed to the Japanese. He argued "Asia for the Asians" and asked for it to be admitted as a principle comparable to the principle of "Africa for the Africans."[68]

Garvey's approval of Japan was strategic, and its underlying intention was to give black people an independent voice in world politics. In his view,

blacks "would be able to hold the balance of power in the world" if they supported Japan.[69] Garvey actually understood the Japanese imperialistic attitude toward Asia, even if he did not seriously consider the fundamental
problems of Japan's relations with other Asian nations. He accepted Japan's
leading position but refrained from making the public point of it being an
"imperialist" agenda. His goal was not to address the nuances of the constel-
lations of power between Asian nations, but to find allies and means for the
black freedom fight and structure a coordinated and strategic attack against
European hegemony. Although Garvey welcomed cooperation between black
people and the Japanese, his ultimate goal was for black people to stand on
their own feet and to be aware of possible threats from any direction, as is
evident in the following statement:

> Three babies are born; one yellow; one white; and one black. Soon the yellow
> baby gets guns and ammunition and puts on a uniform. The white baby does the
> same thing; grows up to manhood. All that time what do you think the negro
> baby is doing? Why standing looking on. Bye and bye [*sic*] a time comes for
> action. What occurs? They shoot that negro, and . . . that has been going on ever
> since America has been discovered.[70]

Garvey, like the *Messenger*, did make a critical assessment of the Japanese,
"for when we look to the Anglo-Saxon we see him full of greed, full of avarice,
with no mercy, no love, no charity. We go from the white man to the yellow man, and we see the same unenviable characteristics in the Japanese."[71]
Although he acknowledges this as problematic, his overall goal was to ally
with any nonwhite nation that was powerful enough to stand up to Europe.
Japan, as far as Garvey was concerned, was therefore more advanced than
China. He believed that the advances within one racial group should lead
the less advanced in lifting up the entire race. Hence conscious black people, such as UNIA members and "New Negroes," could awaken and lead the
unconscious black masses. This came from a perceived awareness that African Americans and blacks in the Caribbean held a unique position, which
rendered them an intimate understanding of whites. It was knowledge they
could, conceivably, share with their counterparts in Africa as a way to undermine white supremacy.

Garvey related to Asians' awareness about European colonialism: "The
Japanese has [*sic*] discovered it, the Sleeping Chinaman, at last, has awakened
from his slumber and discovered it and the sleeping, superstit[i]ous Indian
and Hindu Moslem has discovered it, through Mahatma Gandhi." He continued identifying the UNIA with Japan and the black masses with China:

"thank God, the Universal Negro Improvement Association has discovered it, through the new Negro."[72] William Pickens, a National Association for the Advancement of Colored People (NAACP) field secretary, made the point clearer by likening the Chinese to the black masses as well:

> Consider that Limitation of Arms Conference and be wise: Four hundred million Negroes are not represented, 65,000,000 Japanese are represented. Why? Because the Japanese, the fewer in number, are organized. The Chinese are more nearly like the Negroes; they are numerous, but loosely organized. . . . If China were as well organized as is Japan, China would be the greatest power represented in Washington today. For an individual Chinese is worth as much as an individual Japanese, or more.[73]

According to Garvey, nations and/or groups of people were classified not by color but by what they achieved, or, more precisely, by what they contributed to human civilization: "The prejudice of the world is not so much against skin—It is not so much against color—It is against what you have not done."[74] To avoid future discrimination, black people consequently would once again have to build up a civilization. After all, according to Garvey, black people had been leading in that regard in ancient Egypt. Their condition was therefore temporary and could be improved by their own doing. "They [Europeans] were prejudiced against the Japanese 70 years ago. . . . Since the Japanese have achieved[,] what has happened? Our proud and haughty President has issued an invitation from the White House to nations of equal standing to come and meet in Washington to discuss the question of disarmament."[75] However, he doubted the European initiative to proceed with disarmament. "Japan knows well that it is a scheme to rehabilitate Europe at the expense of Asia. But Asia is not going to disarm, not until all the others have completely disarmed."[76] This statement was in reference to the Washington Naval Conference planned for November 1921 to discuss disarmament. Garvey sent a telegram to the secretary of the conference. In it he warned the organizers not to repeat the mistake of the Paris Peace Conference, which had failed to establish true world peace, as that conference had not ended the colonization and subjugation of people of color.[77] Garvey left for D.C. to make his own case for disarmament.

After World War I, U.S. military intelligence compiled many reports on the possibility of a race war between the United States and Japan and feelings of empathy between African Americans and the Japanese nationals. Japanese nationals were reported to have attended UNIA meetings and even to have given speeches. The U.S. government cautiously watched their activities in any case. A few had personal contacts with Garvey, as well as with other

UNIA leaders. In October 1919 one Japanese contemporary "was reported to have said that Garvey's statement about the 'day of the war of races' was good agitation for Japan."[78]

The First International Convention of the UNIA, held in August 1920 in New York, was of particular interest to the Japanese. Several reports from special agents in the Bureau of Investigation mentioned that two Japanese visited Garvey in order to establish business contacts with the UNIA.[79] One agent collected information about a Japanese person who was seen around a cricket club formed mostly by West Indians in New York who were connected to the Garvey movement.[80] It was also reported that in San Francisco, Los Angeles, and Seattle, several Japanese attempted to establish branches of the Colored People's Union, an organization that was intended to include all colored races of the world, in cooperation with UNIA members with (East) Indians.[81]

The San Francisco Board of Education ordered Japanese and Korean pupils to attend Oriental schools with the Chinese. In 1913 California passed the Alien Land Law, targeting the Japanese, and prohibited persons ineligible for citizenship from owning land or property. The Immigration Act of 1924 finally banned persons ineligible for citizenship from immigration to the United States, which was seen as an effective way to restrict immigrants regarded as undesirable, such as the Japanese.[82] Faced with exclusion, a few Japanese American residents turned to the Garvey movement. In January 1921 *Shinsekai* (New World), a San Francisco–based Japanese American newspaper, published a series of eleven columns on the Garvey movement entitled "Awakening Movement of Darker Peoples, 400,000,000 Blacks Starting Nation-Building, Should Rise up in Accordance with Yellow People."[83] Focusing on the UNIA's First International Convention, the series praised Garvey's scheme to build an independent nation-state in Africa and to have an independent economy among blacks. *Shin-sekai* inserted a quote (evidence seems to indicate that the speech was never made) allegedly from one of Garvey's speeches in which he asserted that "the United States is white man's country,"[84] and then moved on to claim that Asia was "yellow man's" country. Lamenting their lack of a leader like Garvey, the paper encouraged the Japanese in the United States to follow the Garvey movement in order to develop a community and a responsibility for their homeland. "If such an honest person did such a thing, how would our community be flourishing? We should blame ourselves, but we do not have a person like Garvey."[85] *Shin-sekai* apparently found it useful to "embellish" Garvey's rhetoric to mobilize Japanese Americans in an atmosphere of increasingly anti-Japanese sentiment in the United States.

Garvey, however, recognized the difference in treatment of Japanese/Japanese Americans and blacks in the United States and attributed it to the existence of Japan as a protector. He argued that "the Japanese and Chinese are not lynched in this country because of the fear of retaliation. Behind these men are standing armies and navies to protect them . . . but Negroes, representing an undignified and unorganized nation, are lynched."[86] Indeed, the *Chicago Defender* provided a case in point when it published an editorial titled "Texas and the Yellow Peril,"[87] which introduced the story of two Japanese families that faced white opposition when they attempted to move to Texas. On their arrival at the station, they were "told [by members of the American Legion and prominent citizens] that it would be dangerous for them to attempt to settle on the property purchased." The editorial showed sympathy with the fact that the Japanese encountered "color prejudice" but pointed out that the Japanese were different from blacks. The Japanese person "has behind him an army and a navy." The same incident was reported in a Japanese American newspaper, *Nichi-bei Shu-ho* (Japanese-America Commercial Weekly), published in New York. According to that account, the families agreed to go back to California reportedly after a settlement of $10,000, including compensation and the actual price that they had already paid for the land.[88] Since no such offer was ever extended to African Americans, the Texas settlement consequently must have been perceived by them as emblematic of the diplomatic arm of the mighty Japanese nation that protected, to a degree, the rights of Japanese Americans.

Conclusion

At the turn of the twentieth century, Japanese Pan-Asianists were desperate to transform the racial texture of international politics. Black leaders such as Garvey also recognized the necessity of breaking down the racial world order that connected the destinies of African Americans with that of colonized peoples in Africa. To obtain respectable treatment, both Japanese Pan-Asianists, such as Uchida and Mitsukawa, and leaders like Garvey thought it useful to regard all "Asians" and all "blacks" as two collective actors that together could overturn the old racial world order. Black people in the United States made the astute observation that Japan was a nonwhite nation that had successfully defeated a white imperial power (that is, the Russo-Japanese War of 1904–1905). Japan became the third largest naval power in the world after World War I and had become a member of the "Big Five," which included the United States, Great Britain, France, and Italy, all of whom made up the Supreme Council at the Paris Peace Conference in 1919. Japanese victory over white Russia contradicted the primacy of social Darwinism and the inferiority of nonwhite peoples. Garvey and others took note of this evidence and claimed that "what the yellow race did the black race could also do."[89] While Japanese Pan-Asianists saw themselves as the vanguard and the voice of a unified Asia under Japan against European and American imperialism, for black people the existence of the Japanese state provided a strong case in point to overcoming the view of an absolute and fixed racial order and the ability of a nonwhite nation to stand up against the hegemony of whiteness on a variety of fronts.

Notes

This chapter emerges out of a working paper produced in 2007 entitled "Building a New Racial World Order: Intersecting Pan-Asianism and Pan-Africanism In a Post-WWI World." All translations are solely the responsibility of the author.

1. Saaler and Szpilman, "Introduction," 6.

2. For Japanese modern history, see, for example, Wakabayashi, *Modern Japanese Thought*.

3. Saaler, "Pan-Asianism in Modern Japanese History," 9.

4. For "*hakkō ichiu*," see Miwa, "Pan-Asianism in Modern Japan," 22–33. The English translation of "*hakkō ichiu*" is from Miwa's work.

5. For example, Sun Yat-sen in China questioned if Japan would choose to be "the hawk of the Western civilization of the rue of Might, or the tower of strength of the Orient." Brown, "Sun Yat-sen," 85.

6. *Asian Review* 1.1 (February 1920): 27.

7. *Ajia Jiron* 4.4 (April 1920): 78.

8. *Asian Review* 1.5 (July 1920): 459. Following quotes in ibid.

9. Quoted in "Report by Bureau Agent Harold Nathan," February 8, 1922, in Hill, *Marcus Garvey*, 4:492.

10. Anderson, *Imagined Communities*.

11. Garvey intended to send scientists, mechanics, and artisans to Liberia to build infrastructure, including educational institutions. Reports of the Convention, August 8, 1920, in Hill, *Papers*, 2:559.

12. *Tokyo Asahi Shimbun*, November 24, 25, 26, 1920.

13. *Asian Review* 2.1 (January 1921): 50–52.

14. Szpilman, "Between Pan-Asianism and Nationalism," 85–100; Szpilman, "Kaidai," 1:445–447.

15. Hasegawa, "Mitsukawa Kametarō no Taibei Ninshiki," 266–267, 298.

16. *Ajia Jiron* 4.10 (October 1920): 30–32. Following quotes in ibid.

17. The English title, "The Negro Problem," is based on the letter of thanks from Amy Jacques Garvey, Garvey's wife, to Kametarō Mitsukawa, who apparently sent an autographed copy of the book to the UNIA. Amy Jacques Garvey to Kametarō Mitsukawa, February 11, 1926, in Hill, *Papers*, 6:340.

18. Mitsukawa, *Kokujin Mondai*, 1–2.

19. Ibid., 3–4.

20. Ibid., Dai-gen (an epigraph), 3.

21. Ibid., 1.

22. Ibid., 288.

23. Ibid., 306.

24. Mitsukawa, *Sekai Gensei to Dai-Nippon*, 87–88.

25. Ikeda, "Kokujin Mondai no Kosatsu: Mitsukawa-shi no Chojutu wo Yomu" (A Study of Negro Problem: Reading Mr. Mitsukawa's Work), *Hōchi Shimbun*, January 25, 1926, in Mitsukawa Kametarō Papers, in Modern Japanese Political History Materials Room, National Diet Library.

26. Mitsukawa, *Sekai Gensei*, 95–101, 112.

27. *Ajia Jiron* 3.10 (October 1919).

28. Mitsukawa, *Sekai Gensei*, 156–157.

29. Ibid., 159.

30. Sato, "Japanese Views," 34–35.

31. Okakura, *Awakening of Japan*, 101; Okakura, *Ideals of the East*, 1; Matsumoto, *Takeuchi Yoshimi*, 93–94.

32. Mitsukawa, *Kokujin Mondai*, 4.

33. On the process of the Japanese delegation's racial equality proposal, see Shimazu, *Japan, Race and Equality*.

34. *New York Age*, May 24, 1919, 4.

35. Jonas was born in Wales around 1868 and came to the United States with his father when he was six years old. In 1917, after being arrested on suspicion of working for pro-German propagandists, he was employed by U.S. military intelligence in Chicago to inform against "black subversion" and pro-German agitation. In late 1918 he moved to New York and organized the ILDP, mainly among preachers. For details on Jonas, see Hill, *Papers*, 1:531–532.

36. Mme. C. J. Walker to F. B. Ransom, January 10, 1919, Madam C. J. Walker Collection, Indiana Historical Society (hereafter cited as Walker Collection).

37. F. B. Ransom to Mme. C. J. Walker, January 11 and 25, 1919; Mme. C. J. Walker to F. B. Ransom, January 27, 1919, all in Walker Collection.

38. The ILDP prepared and probably handed Kuroiwa a petition, which has not been found. However, the copy of the covering letter is stored in the Walker Collection. It is dated December 30, 1918, written in Japanese under the name of Jonas, with English sentences of almost the same contents attached above the leaders' names on the margin of the letter. A picture of the meeting was published alongside a Japanese article, "Koku-jin Hakugai Monogatari" (Black Persecution Story) (*Kaizo* 12.11 [November 1930]), written by Hiroichiro Maedako, who was a writer for *Nichi-bei Shu-ho* (Japanese-America Commercial Weekly). He is mentioned as a radical Japanese in the above report.

39. Report of Capt. Dalrymple, Military Intelligence, April 5, 1919, 10218–324/1/273X(50), RG165, U.S. National Archives and Record Administration (NARA).

40. *World Forum* 1.1 (January 1919), in 10218–296(3) 273X(50), RG165, NARA.

41. Another speaker mistakenly noted on the handbill is "Prof. R. R. Wright, Jr., on 'For Those who Stay at Home.'" Richard R. Wright Sr. (1855–1947) was then the president of the Georgia State Industrial College for Colored Youth and also the father of Richard R. Wright Jr. (1878–1967), the author of *87 Years Behind the Black Curtain*, who should not be confused with Richard Wright (1908–1960), the author of *Native Son*. See also Werner, p. 155n25.

42. Diaries of Ruiko Kuroiwa, January 7, 1919, in the Newspaper Library at the Japan Newspaper Museum, Kanagawa.

43. Bundles, *On Her Own Ground*, 263.

44. 10218–296 (2) 2-1 273X (50), RG165, NARA.

45. The UNIA peace proposals included: "(1) That the principle of self-determination be applied to Africa and all European controlled colonies in which people of African descent predominate; (2) That all economic barriers that hamper the industrial development of Africa be removed; (3) That Negroes enjoy the right to travel and reside in any part of the world even as European[s] now enjoy these rights; (4) That Negroes be permitted the same educational facilities now given to Europeans; (5) That Europeans who interfere with, or violate African tribal customs be deported and denied reentry to the continent; (6) That the segregatory and proscriptive ordinances against Negroes in any part of the world be reported and that they (Negroes) be given complete political, industrial and social equality in countries where Negroes and people of any race live side by side; (7) That the reservation land acts aimed against the natives of South Africa be revoked and the land restored to its prescriptive owners; (8) That Negroes be given proportional representation in any scheme of world government; (9) That the captured German colonies in Africa be turned over to the natives with educated Western and Eastern Negroes as their leaders." Bureau of Investigation Reports, November 12, 1918, Hill, *Papers*, 1:288.

46. Eliézer Cadet to the UNIA, April 19, 1919, Hill, *Papers*, 1:409.

47. Eliézer Cadet to *L'essor*, June 10, 1919, Hill, *Papers*, 1:416–417. Japan was one of the Big Five powers; however, Japanese delegates did not participate in the Big Five's top-level meetings since Japan did not send top leaders to the conference.

48. The Japanese delegation attempted to insert in the preamble of the covenant the following sentence: "by the endorsement of the principle of equality of nations and just treatment of their nationals." For more details on the process, see Shimazu, *Japan, Race and Equality*, 13–37.

49. *Messenger*, March 1919, 5.

50. President King later rejected Garvey's "Back-to-Africa" movement, which targeted Liberia as a pioneering black nation-state to achieve full development with the help of Africans abroad. He decided instead to lease a part of the Liberian land to Firestone Tire and Rubber Company.

51. C. D. B. King to M. Clemenceau, April 30, 1919, RG59, 763.72119/5119, NARA.

52. H. F. Worley to William A. Phillips, April 23, 1919, RG59, 763.72119/5122, NARA; Contee, "Document," 140.

53. Memorandum by H. F. Worley, April 22, 1919, RG59, 763.72119/5122, NARA.

54. *Negro World*, December 3, 1921, in Hill, *Papers*, 4:204–206.

55. Bureau of Investigation Reports, December 5, 1918, in Hill, Papers, 1:305–306; also in RG165, OG10218–261/14, NRA.

56. *Tokyo Asahi Shimbun*, November 24, 1920.

57. See, for instance, Gottesman, "Cyril V. Briggs and the American Left."

58. *Crusader* 3.4 (December 1920): 12.

59. *Crusader* 3.5 (January 1921): 29.

60. Speech by Marcus Garvey, *Negro World*, November 19, 1921, in Hill, *Papers*, 4:187.

61. *Crisis* 23.3 (January 1922): 103. DuBois's novel, *Dark Princess*, published in 1928, shows that he also shared a view of the possible unity of darker races fighting against white supremacy. His visit to Manchuria and Japan in 1936, as a guest of the Japanese government, confirmed his affirmative views of Japan and its colonialism. DuBois, *Dark Princess*; W. E. B. DuBois, "Japanese Colonialism," *Pittsburgh Courier*, February 13, 1937, in Lewis, *W. E. B. DuBois*, 83–84.

62. According to data originally published in the *Boston Post*, England owned 27.8 percent of the total land of China; Russia 42.3 percent; France 3.4 percent; and Japan 5.6 percent. *Crisis* 21.4 (February 1921): 168.

63. *Asian Review* 2.4 (May–June 1921): 321; *Chicago Defender*, July 16, 1921; *California Eagle*, July 16, 1921; *Messenger* 3.3 (August 1921): 225.

64. *Messenger* 3.3 (August 1921): 225.

65. *Negro World*, November 30, 1918, in Hill, *Papers*, 1:299; *New York Times*, November 22, 1918.

66. *Negro World*, June 14, 1919, 2.

67. Speeches by Marcus Garvey, November 13, 1921, in Hill, *Papers*, 4:186.

68. Ibid., 4:187.

69. Bureau of Investigation Report, December 3, 1918, in Hill, *Papers*, 1:309.

70. Report by Special Agent J. T. Flournoy, November 12, 1921, in Hill, *Papers*, 4:215–216; also in RG165, 10218–261/33, NARA.

71. Speech by Marcus Garvey, January 1, 1922, in Hill, *Papers*, 4:326.

72. Speech by Marcus Garvey, February 5, 1922, in Hill, *Papers*, 4:486. Yuichiro Onishi describes Japan as the "New Negro of the Pacific" in "New Negro of the Pacific."

73. William Pickens to the *Negro World*, December 17, 1921, in Hill, *Papers*, 4:284.

74. *Negro World*, September 17, 1921, in Hill, *Papers*, 4:39.

75. Ibid.

76. Speeches by Marcus Garvey, November 13, 1921, in Hill, *Papers*, 4:189.

77. Marcus Garvey to the Secretary, International Conference on Disarmament, November 12, 1921, in Hill, *Papers*, 4:167–169.

78. Report by the War Department, October 20, 1919, RG165, 10218–364/12, NARA.

79. Report by Special Agent P-138, October 21, 1920, OG258421, RG65, NARA; Report by Special Agent P-138, October 22, 1920, in Hill, *Papers*, 3:62; Report by Special Agent P-138, November 5, 1920, in Hill, *Papers*, 3:71.

80. Reports by Special Agent P-138 in October and November 1920, OG258421, RG65, NARA; Reports by P-138, BS202600-667, RG65, NARA.

81. J. J. Hannigan, Commandant, Twelfth Naval District, to the Director, Office of Naval Intelligence, December 3, 1921, in Hill, *Papers*, 4:236–237; Office of Naval Intelligence, Report of the week ending March 18, 1922, in Kornweibel, *Federal Surveillance of Afro-Americans*, Reel No. 23, Frame Nos. 686–689.

82. For early Japanese immigration, see Ichioka, *Issei*.

83. *Shin-sekai*, January 4–15, 1921.

84. *Shin-sekai*, January 13, 1921.

85. *Shin-sekai*, January 15, 1921.

86. *Negro World*, March 29, 1919, in Hill, *Papers*, 1:397.

87. *Chicago Defender*, January 15, 1921. Following quotes in ibid.

88. *Nichi-bei Shu-ho* 1018 (January 15, 1921).

89. Quoted in "Report by Bureau Agent Harold Nathan," February 8, 1922, in Hill, *Papers*, 4:492.

Bibliography

Allen, Ernest, Jr. "Waiting for Tojo: The Pro-Japan Vigil of Black Missourians, 1932–1943." *Gateway Heritage* (Fall 1995): 38–55.

Anderson, Benedict. *Imagined Communities: Reflections on the Origin and Spread of Nationalism.* Rev. ed. London: Verso, 2006.

Brown, Roger H. "Sun Yat-sen: 'Pan-Asianism,' 1924." In *Pan-Asianism: A Documentary History.* Vol. 2, *1920-Present*, ed. Sven Saaler and Christopher W. A. Szpilman, 75–85. Lanham, Md.: Rowman & Littlefield, 2011.

Bundles, A'Lelia. *On Her Own Ground: The Life and Times of Madam C. J. Walker.* New York: A Lisa Drew Book, 2001.

Contee, C. G. "Document: The Worley Report on the Pan-African Congress of 1919." *Journal of Negro History* 55 (1970): 140–143.

DuBois, W. E. B. *Dark Princess.* 1928. Reprint, Jackson: University Press of Mississippi, 1995.

Gallicchio, Marc. *The African American Encounter with Japan and China: Black Internationalism in Asia, 1895–1945.* Chapel Hill: University of North Carolina Press, 2000.

Gordon, Andrew. *A Modern History of Japan: From Tokugawa Times to the Present.* Oxford: Oxford University Press, 2008.

Gottesman, Isaac Herschel. "Cyril V. Briggs and the American Left: 1917–1925." M.A. thesis, University of Wisconsin–Madison, 2000.

Hasegawa, Yūichi. "Mitsukawa Kametaro no Taibei Ninshiki" (Kametaro Mitsuoka's View of the United States). In *Taisho-ki Nihon no Amerika Ninshiki* (Japanese Views of the United States during the Taisho Era), ed. Yuichi Hasegawa. 259–304. Tokyo: Keio University Press, 2001.

Hill, Robert A., ed., *The Marcus Garvey and Universal Negro Improvement Association Papers.* Vols. 1–7. Berkeley: University of California Press, 1983–1990.

Horne, Gerald. *Race War: White Supremacy and the Japanese Attack on the British Empire.* New York: New York University Press, 2004.

Ichioka, Yuji. *The Issei: The World of the First Generation Japanese Immigrants, 1885–1924*. New York: Free Press, 1988.

Kearney, Reginald. *African American Views of the Japanese: Solidarity or Sedition?* New York: State University of New York Press, 1998.

Koshiro, Yukiko. "Beyond an Alliance of Color: The Africa American Impact on Modern Japan." *positions: east asia culture critique* 11.1 (2003): 183–215.

Lauren, Paul Gordon. *Power and Prejudice: The Politics and Diplomacy of Racial Discrimination*. 2nd ed. Boulder, Colo.: Westview Press, 1996.

Lewis, David Levering, ed. *W. E. B. DuBois: A Reader*. New York: Henry Holt, 1995.

Lipsitz, George. "'Frantic to Join . . . the Japanese Army': The Asia Pacific War in the Lives of African American Soldiers and Civilians." In *The Politics of Culture in the Shadow of Capital*, ed. Lisa Lowe and David Lloyd, 324–353. Durham, N.C.: Duke University Press, 1997.

Matsumoto, Kenichi. *Takeuchi Yoshimi "Nihon-no Asia-shugi," Seidoku* (Intensive Reading of Yoshimi Takeuchi's "Japanese Asianism"). Tokyo: Iwanami Shoten, 2000.

Mitsukawa, Kametarō. *Kokujin Mondai* (The Negro Problem). Tokyo: Nitori Meicho Kanko Kyokai, 1925.

———. *Sekai Gensei to Dai-Nippon* (Current Situation of the World and Great Japan). Tokyo: Kouchi-sha, 1926.

Miwa, Kimitada. "Pan-Asianism in Modern Japan: Nationalism, Regionalism and Universalism." In *Pan-Asianism in Modern Japanese History: Colonization, Regionalism and Borders*, ed. Sven Saaler and J. Victor Koschmann, 21–33. New York: Routledge, 2007.

Okakura, Kakuzo. *The Awakening of Japan*. New York: Century, 1904.

———. *The Book of Tea*. New York: Duffield, 1906.

———. *The Ideals of the East with Special Reference to the Art of Japan*. London: John Murray, 1903.

Onishi, Yuichiro. "The New Negro of the Pacific: How African Americans Forged Cross-Racial Solidarity with Japan, 1917–1922." *Journal of African American History* 92.2 (2007): 191–213.

Pitkin, Walter B. *Must We Fight Japan?* New York: Century, 1921.

Prashad, Vijay. *Everybody Was Kung Fu Fighting: Afro-Asian Connections and the Myth of Cultural Purity*. Boston: Beacon Press, 2001.

Saaler, Sven. "Pan-Asianism in Modern Japanese History: Overcoming the Nation, Creating Region, Forging an Empire." In *Pan-Asianism in Modern Japanese History: Colonization, Regionalism and Borders*, ed. Sven Saaler and J. Victor Koschmann, 1–18. New York: Routledge, 2007.

Saaler, Sven, and Christopher W. A. Szpilman. "Introduction: The Emergence of Pan-Asianism as an Ideal of Asian Identity and Solidarity, 1850–2008." In *Pan-Asianism: A Documentary History*. Vol. 1, *1850–1920*, ed. Sven Saaler and Christopher W. A. Szpilman, 1–41. Lanham, Md.: Rowman & Littlefield, 2011.

Sato, Hiroko. "Japanese Views on the Racial Problems in the United States." *Kiyo (Annals)* 34 (1973): 23–36. Institute for Comparative Studies of Culture, Tokyo Woman's Christian University.

Sawada, Jiro. *Kindai Nihon-jin no Amerika-kan—Nichi-ro Sensou igo wo Chu-shin ni* (Modern Japanese Views of America—Mainly after the Russo-Japanese War). Tokyo: Keio University Press, 1999.

Shimazu, Naoko. *Japan, Race and Equality: The Racial Equality Proposal of 1919*. London: Routledge, 1998.

Stein, Judith. *The World of Marcus Garvey: Race and Class in Modern Society*. Baton Rouge: Louisiana State University Press, 1986.

Stoddard, Theodore Lothrop. *Rising Tide of Color against White World-Supremacy*. New York: Scribner, 1920.

Szpilman, Christopher W. A. "Between Pan-Asianism and Nationalism: Kametarō Mitsukawa and His Campaign to Reform Japan and Liberate Asia." In *Pan-Asianism in Modern Japanese History: Colonization, Regionalism and Borders*, ed. Sven Saaler and J. Victor Koschmann, 85–100. New York: Routledge, 2007.

———. "Kaidai" (Bibliographical Notes). In *Mitsukawa Kametarō: Chiiki, Chikyu jijo no Keimou-sha* (Kametarō Mitsukawa: An Educator of Regional and Global Affairs), 1:441–475. Tokyo: Takushoku Daigaku, 2001.

Taylor, Quintard. "Blacks and Asians in a White City: Japanese Americans and African Americans in Seattle, 1890–1940." *Western Historical Quarterly* 22.4 (1991): 401–429.

Tinker, Hugh. *Race, Conflict and the International Order: From Empire to United Nations*. London: Macmillan Press, 1977.

Wakabayashi, Bob Tadashi, ed. *Modern Japanese Thought*. Cambridge: Cambridge University Press, 1998.

Convenient Partnerships?

African American Civil Rights Leaders
and the East German Dictatorship

Anja Werner

In 2006 a multiauthored volume was published tracing the relationship between the United States and the Communist East German (GDR, or German Democratic Republic, 1949–1989) dictatorship. From its cover smiled Angela Davis dressed in a blouse of the East German Communist youth organization (FDJ, or Free German Youth) standing next to the equally smiling dictator Erich Honecker, the general secretary of the Socialist Unity Party's (SED) Central Committee and, after 1976, also the East German head of state.[1] While covering a broad range of subjects, however, none of the articles actually focused on the connection between African American civil rights activists and the East German dictatorship depicted on the cover. The volume thus reflects a dilemma: even though African American civil rights leaders actually represent a crucial link between both countries during the Cold War, this relationship has not yet been explored in a more thorough analysis.[2]

In the following, I focus on connections between African Americans' fight for freedom and the East German establishment, taking four particularly well known civil rights activists as examples: W. E. B. DuBois, Paul Robeson, Angela Davis, and Martin Luther King Jr., whereby especially King, above all, allows me to include the perspective of the East German opposition. As the space of this article is limited, I cannot thoroughly discuss this last point, but its inclusion appears to be vital in order to highlight the complexity of interaction between African American activists and both the leadership and representatives of the opposition in East Bloc countries. It also needs to be taken into account that during the comparatively short time period of roughly forty years, the East German dictatorship changed, especially when

Honecker replaced Walter Ulbricht in 1971 at a time of East-West détente and the Communists set out to strive for recognition and prestige in the Western world. Moreover, other prominent African Americans also visited the GDR: Communist leader Henry Winston came to see Robeson in an East Berlin hospital in 1963[3] and returned as a guest of the GDR committee on human rights in May 1972, on which occasion he spoke up in support of Davis.[4] During a November 1971 visit to the GDR on the occasion of the opening of an Angela Davis exhibit, Claude Lightfoot, a leading member of the Communist Party USA (CPUSA), thanked the GDR for its tight solidarity during Davis's trial.[5] Musicians and artists such as Harry Belafonte and Louis Armstrong visited the GDR, while the cartoonist Ollie Harrington actually moved there.[6]

The relationship between black Americans and the GDR is multifaceted. East German propaganda—in line with Marxist theories that require force to overthrow the existing capitalist order[7]—preferred more radical African American civil rights leaders who embraced Communism. This suggests that the GDR's major goal was to agitate against the United States rather than to support wholeheartedly the black freedom fight. The East German Communist propaganda machine therefore had difficulty in depicting King, the best-known proponent of nonviolent resistance in the African American context, who did not even flirt with Communism. The East German opposition, in turn, which grew under the protection of East German churches, unsurprisingly, was inspired by King. After all, the events of 1989 are also referred to as the "Peaceful Revolution" that brought down the East German dictatorship in an explicitly nonviolent fashion. "No violence" was the message chanted during demonstrations, and it was also a guiding spirit emanating from the peace prayers in Leipzig since 1981. But while activists in Leipzig's St. Nikolai Church sang "We Shall Overcome" in the fall of 1989, not all of them were necessarily aware of the fact that they were borrowing symbols from the earlier African American fight for civil rights.[8]

I structured my article into four parts. First, I provide an overview of the history of black intellectuals and German thought, also including Afro-German contexts, which serves as a framework. The second part examines the attitudes of African American leaders toward the GDR. The third section subsequently discusses how they interacted with members of the SED dictatorship as viewed from the perspective of Communist propaganda and censorship. The fourth part focuses on the dilemma that King presented for the East German dictatorship with his potentially explosive nonviolent activism that actually strengthened the East German opposition.

Larger Contexts: Black Germany

African Americans and Germans have interacted on various levels since at least the American Revolution.[9] African Americans came to Germany for many different reasons. In the twentieth century, for the most part they were either students or members of the military, besides tourists and celebrities. African Americans also studied in German universities since the late nineteenth century, as did DuBois and Davis.[10] Earlier examples of black intellectuals in Germany may also be traced, above all Anton Wilhelm Amo, the eighteenth-century African philosopher,[11] and James W. C. Pennington, who was awarded an honorary Ph.D. degree from the University of Heidelberg in 1849.[12] They all contributed to vibrant intellectual and cultural exchanges between black and German cultures. Another facet should be added: during the Third Reich, refugee scholars from Nazi Germany contributed to educating a future African American elite at historically black colleges and universities in the South.[13]

African American history is intertwined with Afro-German history. Germans of African descent combine a rather heterogeneous mix of heritages, including both African and African American roots;[14] however, their percentage in the population is very low in comparison with that of African Americans.[15] An older generation of Afro-Germans today—such as Hans-Jürgen Massaquoi and Marie Nejar—was born between the two world wars to German women and African diplomats or sailors.[16] Then, of course, there were the German children of black Belgian and French occupation troops after World War I. All of them lived through the Third Reich, whereby the Nazis forced especially the latter, the so-called *Rheinlandbastarde*, to undergo sterilizations.[17]

The Afro-German heritage of the post–World War II period is as divided as the country was then. Those in the West were often the children of African American GIs.[18] Afro-Germans in the East, in turn, were typically the sons and daughters of African students.[19] Moreover, at times of civil war, Namibian children were brought to the GDR since the late 1970s. While they were housed and schooled in institutions separate from the rest of society, they nonetheless became Germanized during several years of schooling in the GDR. In exceptional cases, an African child came to grow up in an East German foster family.[20] At the same time, the East German dictatorship made sure that Namibian refugee children—just like visiting African adults—would not become overly involved with the population. If an African man had children while in the GDR, they would ultimately be separated once the African's visa expired and he was forced to return home. The German mother was left behind with her "brown" child. Today, Afro-Germans are also the children of immigrants and refugees.

Since the 1980s Afro-German culture has become more vocal and thus visible. Personal accounts alongside solid research have been published since then. The subject of black GIs in West Germany during the 1960s civil rights movement is the topic of ongoing research.[21] Moreover, African American cultural influences may be traced in Germany. For instance, whether Germans knew it or not, they were influenced by techniques of nonviolent resistance such as sit-ins, which provided inspiration for protest movements in West Germany as well as for the opposition in East Germany. In reunified Germany today, activists continue to stage regular sit-ins against nuclear power.[22] Finally, enthusiasm for music derived from black culture such as hip-hop, which has become commercially successful around the globe, is now the subject of doctoral dissertations as to its reception specifically in the GDR.[23]

Contacts between people of African descent and white mainstream Germans left an imprint on the civil rights movement and eventually reflected back on German culture. African Americans who had traveled to Germany as students prior to the 1960s attest to the fact that German philosophers shaped African American thought.[24] Leroy Hopkins traced such a black intellectual history between the United States and Germany in his "Black Prussians."[25] Ingeborg Solbrig discussed African American intellectuals visiting Germany for educational purposes before the world wars, most notably DuBois and Alain Leroy Locke, who took an interest in Johann Gottfried Herder's *Negro Idyllen*.[26] DuBois, of course, had studied in Berlin from 1892 to 1894 and returned to what was then East Germany in 1958 for an honorary Ph.D. degree.[27] Ironically, DuBois is celebrated today as the first black recipient of a Ph.D. degree from Harvard University, when, in fact, a white establishment had prevented him from obtaining the—in the 1890s—more prestigious German degree.[28] Moreover, the political and social activism of the Frankfurt School inspired Angela Davis during her West German student days in the mid-1960s.[29]

Hopkins concluded that in the three generations from James W. C. Pennington via DuBois to Davis, "education, and specifically the academic training that German universities could provide, were perceived as a tool for social change. The catalyst for each generation's response to Germany was systematic American racism that threatened individual and group survival."[30] As, however, my examples below also suggest, "these intellectuals visualized a Germany of poets and thinkers without perceiving the darker forces that would lead to war and genocide."[31] Still, by the time of the Cold War, African American activists and intellectuals were putting pressure on the U.S.

government with regard to American race relations, which in turn fueled the East German propaganda machinery with potent ammunition.

Why East Germany?: African American Perspectives

While the specific contexts of each black leader's involvement with the GDR differ, their underlying driving force was identical in their overall attempt to expose and end racism in the United States. DuBois expressed the idea succinctly at the mature age of ninety-three in a letter to Robeson written in Romania, which culminated in the aside that "America is impossible and I'm fed up."[32] The statement epitomized frustrations of nearly a century of struggle to improve American race relations. Believing in American values while experiencing on a daily basis that they excluded black Americans, DuBois turned elsewhere to find solutions. The birth of a Communist world and liberated African nations, which DuBois witnessed in the course of his long life, held promise for changing American realities. Robeson certainly looked to the East for similar reasons, especially when, after the McCarthyism of the 1950s, during which time white America had attempted to silence the singer and actor, his passport was finally returned to him. Representing a vigorous, young generation of black Americans had brought Davis national and international fame, which she used to further the cause by turning to those who had been particularly supportive during her trial—such as the GDR.

Robeson, in his public expressions, can be placed somewhere between the Cold War rhetoric of both sides. He never openly admitted to being or having been a Communist, but at the same time he clearly sympathized with the East Bloc and repeatedly visited East Bloc countries.[33] On the one hand, he received and accepted awards from the Soviet Union and the GDR and gave speeches that fitted East Bloc propaganda, and he expressed his admiration for Joseph Stalin, as is evident in an April 1953 article entitled "To Our Beloved Comrade."[34] In it, Robeson unabashedly joined in the personality cult surrounding Stalin (he had received the Stalin Peace Prize just months earlier). Remembering a 1937 theater performance in the Soviet Union, Robeson reminisced, "in a box to the right—smiling and applauding . . . stood the great Stalin. I remember the tears began to quietly flow, and I too smiled and waved. Here was clearly a man who seemed to embrace all. So kindly—I can never forget that warm feeling of kindliness and also . . . of sureness. Here was one who was wise and good."[35] Of course, the article was written before Nikita Khrushchev in 1956 exposed some of the crimes that had been committed under Stalin's dictatorship.

On the other hand, if Robeson was open to a utopia, it was not primarily Communist but multicultural. The East was attractive because it claimed to have overcome racism and created a world where all peoples could peacefully coexist. Robeson actually suggested as much in the above-cited article, in which he also discussed the Soviet dictator's apparent success in improving race relations. Stalin appeared to be celebrating multiculturalism; of course, appearances and realities are two different things, but the appearances in this case worked for Robeson. He pointed out that in the development of national minorities, "Stalin had played and was playing a most decisive role . . . in the Soviet Union, Yakuts, Nenetses, Kirgiz, Tadzhiks—had respect and were helped to advance with unbelievable rapidity in this socialist land. No empty promises, such as colored folk continuously hear in these United States, but deeds."[36]

It was consequently possible for Robeson to remain an American patriot in spite of everything, dreaming of a truly multicultural America and referring to American constitutional principles in defending himself in the United States. His 1956 testimony before the House Un-American Activities Committee (HUAC) stressed his concern with decolonization of African and Asian peoples besides uplifting black Americans. He wondered, "why is [John Foster] Dulles afraid to let me have a passport, to let me travel abroad to sing, to act, to speak my mind?"[37] The question, he continued, "has been partially answered by State Department lawyers who have asserted in court that the State Department claims the right to deny me a passport because of what they called my 'recognized status as a spokesman for large sections of Negro Americans' and because I have 'been for years extremely active in behalf of independence of colonial peoples of Africa.'" Robeson then emphasized his continued devotion to that cause, "to speak out against injustices to the Negro people, and . . . to do all within my power in behalf of independence of colonial peoples of Africa." If America tried to silence him in this effort, it seemed only logical that he would turn wherever he could find a platform.

Davis's case, at its core, is very similar to Robeson's, though she was openly and actively committed to Communism. Her visibility in the world media actually exposed the virulent racism in the United States, belying American democratic ideals and playing into the hands of Communist propaganda.[38] When Davis was awarded an honorary Ph.D. degree in the GDR, East German professors in their laudation cited the opening lines of the Declaration of Independence, only to add immediately thereafter that Davis early on in her life had found out "that these humanistic ideas are in blatant contradiction to American reality."[39] They then simply listed violent incidents from the Birmingham, Alabama, civil rights movement.

But while Davis openly embraced GDR Communism, her main moti-
vation was the improvement of American race relations. On the one hand,
Davis seems to have been touched by the official East German support, which
was entangled with personal voices. In a preface Davis wrote for a 2010 biography authored by Klaus Steiniger, who during her trial had been a correspondent for the East German SED party newspaper *Neues Deutschland* (new
Germany), Davis wrote that "back in those days, I was particularly moved
by the impressive 'free Angela Davis' campaign in the GDR."[40] Her gratitude
was also expressed in contemporary East German newspaper articles.[41] On
the other hand, however, her 1974 autobiography did not simply emphasize
her commitment to Communism but, above all, her commitment to improving the situation of blacks, which was deeply rooted in her experiences as a
child growing up on Birmingham's infamous "Dynamite Hill" as well as in
her upbringing as a strong and self-confident black woman.[42] Davis's loyalties
were with black people above all, for which Communism was a vehicle that
seemed to promise improvement after other means had failed.

During her 1960s stay in West Germany, Davis made use of opportunities
to visit East Germany. In her perception, the East German establishment was
much more active and successful in rooting out racism than West Germany.[43]
For instance, in contrast to white American tourists trying to enter the GDR,
she never experienced a long wait, which led her to conclude that "this was
their way of showing their solidarity with Black people."[44] One could, however, argue that the East German establishment simply used American race
relations to their own advantage by giving black Americans a better treatment than whites. It worked with Davis in that she used the incident to
make a point against racism. While in Berlin back then, she discussed with
friends from Birmingham "the socialist transformation of the GDR and its
active campaign against the remnants of fascism and the mentality of the
people."[45] Such statements do not automatically mean that she allowed herself
unwittingly to be used. Instead, she accepted a treatment at the hands of the
East German establishment that would be viewed as a provocation in white
America.

Yet another episode from a 1981 visit to East Germany illustrates Davis's
approach. On June 29 Hermann Axen, a member of the Politburo and secretary of the SED's Central Committee, met with Davis and asked her to
share information about internal political developments in the United States
and the CPUSA's current objectives. According to Davis, "the USA was then
witnessing the onset of a mass movement against the [Ronald] Reagan
administration, which the bourgeois press was attempting to deny. The party
[CPUSA] considered it its most important task to achieve the unity of the

working class in the struggle for jobs, social improvements, and peace." After this introduction, however, Davis continued to focus on African Americans in the process: "In doing so," she argued, "the fight against racism was of particular importance, as racism continued to thrive, even among oppositional forces, and thus it had the potential of preventing unified action on the part of the coalition." She pointed out attempts to have the Ku Klux Klan prohibited, an organization that "has direct ties to the right-wing terror organizations in the FRG [Federal Republic of Germany, or West Germany]." She conceded that, "of course, the Ku-Klux-Klan is not the main enemy, but the demand to have it prohibited has now become a slogan of the masses, which would have been unthinkable just three years earlier."[46] Davis thus employed U.S. activism against the Ku Klux Klan in order to justify her Communist convictions to East German officials. She was obviously interested in the first place in overcoming the racial schism in America rather than promoting the implementation of a Communist utopia there. After all, to her—just like Robeson—it appeared that, at least in its propaganda, the East had been more aggressive and successful in rooting out racism.

America's Achilles' Heel: African American
Civil Rights in East German Propaganda

A 1957 radio broadcast based on Robeson's statement before HUAC a year earlier illustrates the workings of East German propaganda. The original script of Robeson's statement, which his wife, Eslanda, had apparently sent to Franz Loeser, the future chairman of the East German Paul-Robeson-Committee, started out observing that "it is a sad and bitter commentary on the state of civil liberties in America that the very forces . . . who have denied my access to the lecture podium, the concert hall, the opera house, and the dramatic stage, now hale me before a committee of inquisition in order to hear what I have to say." Robeson ended his statement pledging that "by continuing the struggle at home and abroad for peace and friendship with all of the world's people, for an end to colonialism, for full citizenship for Negro Americans . . . I intend to continue to win friends for the best in American life."[47]

Claiming to be authentic, Loeser's version for the East German radio audience added a few details.[48] The broadcast opened with a scene during which U.S. senators were heard talking on top of one another, "Impudence from that nigger—what are we talking here at length, get rid of him—get rid of this lousy nigger—dirty arrogance—we will stuff his mouth," which was followed by the repeated slogan, "Stuff the nigger's mouth—stuff his mouth, mouth,

mouth!" into which Robeson was eventually blended singing the song *"Die Peitsche des Sklaventreibers"* (likely "No More Auction Block for Me"—the German translates literally as "the slave master's whip"). After two stanzas, the narrator demanded to let Paul Robeson sing. Only then did an actor begin to speak as Robeson, uttering in a German translation the first lines of his HUAC testimony, whereby the interjection "Impudence! Inquisition!" was added after Robeson's reference to inquisition.[49] After this opening, Loeser himself took over, claiming, "You just heard a scene that *really* happened like this in Washington on June 12, 1956."[50]

Mostly in such "adapted" form did African Americans play a noteworthy role in East German propaganda since the early days of the GDR,[51] illustrating that "the race question was a definite part of the struggle against American imperialism."[52] As the above episode suggests, however, not the facts themselves mattered but how they were presented. Already Victor Klemperer had observed with regard to the Third Reich that dictatorships create their own linguistic codes; in his post-1945 diaries, he also referred to the GDR.[53] Hence GDR newspaper articles on black Americans tended to be similar in content. Catchy to read, they could nonetheless be quite incoherent and illogical.[54] Moreover the dictatorship carefully selected and promoted the works of proclaimed "progressive" American working-class authors (such as representatives of realism), who were studied in East German American studies departments during the next few decades.[55] The East German film *Hotelboy Ed Martin* focused on American race relations as early as in 1955. It was based on the 1932 screenplay *Afraid to Talk* by Albert Maltz, one of the future Hollywood Ten.[56]

East German propaganda stressed the idea of a revolutionary *fighting* for something, such as "fighting for peace." African American leaders who appeared ready to violently overthrow a racist American establishment were particularly interesting to GDR propaganda—especially when they also happened to be Communists. Davis is likely the most prominent case in point. While in West Germany in the 1960s, she became convinced that her place to be was the United States, where "a new Black *militancy* was being born."[57] Explaining her academic interests back then with hindsight in 1998, she pointed out, "I was most interested in ways in which philosophy could serve as a basis for developing a critique of society and how that critique of society could figure into the development of practical strategies for the *radical* transformation of society."[58] It was a language East German Communists appreciated.

Racial consciousness in official GDR correspondence thus served to point out its usefulness for propaganda purposes rather than a Marxist concern to assist in the African American freedom fight. Letters by Albert Norden, a member of the SED's Politburo who was in charge of propaganda, provide examples. For instance, when encouraging head of state Ulbricht to send Robeson a telegram on the occasion of the latter's seventieth birthday on April 7, 1968, Norden did not fail to point out that he was talking about the "*American Negro* singer and peace *fighter*," thus highlighting a few key propaganda terms. Norden continued, "I suggest that as the state council chairman [*Staatsratvorsitzender*], you send him a birthday telegram, whi*ch should also be published in our press*."[59] Norden even added a draft telegram. The felicitations would consequently serve as a desirable news event above all to boost the GDR's image.

In interacting with African American civil rights activists, the main objective was to control what kind of message they sent. For instance, Robeson visited the GDR repeatedly, and a few of his East German associates took advantage of his prolonged 1963 stay at an East Berlin hospital to propose to Norden in early 1964 the creation of what was to become the first Paul Robeson archives, still extant.[60] Headed by the Paul-Robeson-Committee, the archives eventually found a home at the GDR's Academy of Arts. In spring 1971 the Robeson-Committee organized a high-level symposium to celebrate African American activism and specifically Robeson. The symposium was supported on the top GDR level as an opportunity to gain in international prestige at a time when Communist Germany was struggling to be recognized officially in the Western world. Norden had his staff inform the Robeson-Committee that "the intended press releases about the symposium should not only be sent to the communist press in the USA but to all relevant newspapers of white and black Americans."[61] He then mused, "by the way, why only send the press releases to the USA-media? England etc. should be covered as well . . . it would certainly increase the GDR's prestige." This led him to an even bolder suggestion: "Why have only communists present at the symposium? A bourgeois musicologist might be very useful," to which he immediately added—for propaganda purposes—the necessary requirement, "as long as he has an adequate reputation beyond the borders of his country." And, of course, "no anti-communist may lecture." Besides pointing out the desirability of widely advertising the GDR's civil rights symposium in the Western world, the letter makes it obvious that an open debate with potential opponents of Communism would have to be prevented.

The GDR's Robeson-Committee fulfilled a primarily political task. It was actually rooted in older British connections. Central to both were the Loesers (sometimes spelled Loesser). There were three of them—Ernst in London[62] as well as Franz (also Frank) and Diana in East Germany. Franz and Diana had spent time in Great Britain during the 1950s, where Franz had been busy in Salford with the National Paul Robeson Committee as its general secretary to support Robeson in his passport affair.[63] According to letters between Eslanda Robeson and London County Council member from Greenwich, Peggy Middleton,[64] the Loesers seemed to be personally close with the Robesons. They grew even closer when the Robesons resided in Great Britain (1958–1963) and began visiting the GDR. While in an East Berlin hospital for several months in 1963, Robeson received nearly daily visits from Franz, which prompted the general secretary of the GDR Peace Council, Heinz Willmann, to write to Loeser's employer at Humboldt University pointing out that Loeser was engaged in a "responsible political task," for which he asked the university's understanding in light of the fact that Loeser would for the next eight to ten weeks be forced to neglect his academic duties.[65] Middleton, in turn, was the first choice of the GDR's Robeson-Committee to gather archival materials.[66] In early 1968 the Academy of Arts in Berlin, seat of the East German Robeson-Committee, gave "full authorization to Councilor Peggy Middleton to collect, on its behalf, material relating to Paul Robeson and his wife Eslanda Robeson. To make as full and complete a Paul Robeson Archive as possible, we respectfully request all possible assistance and support for her in this endeavour."[67]

East German propaganda experienced a full blossom with the early 1970s Davis trial, which was as much a mobilization of protest in the United States on the part of Davis's supporters there as it was one in East Germany that culminated in the slogan of "One Million Roses for Angela Davis."[68] Besides her avowed Communism and connections with radical, militant circles, Davis, of course, was an intelligent *and* beautiful young woman who was imprisoned for her convictions and even threatened with the death penalty. In short, she could ideally be styled a martyr in the face of what East German propaganda denounced as American imperialism. Best of all, Davis obviously was open to communicating with and even visiting and certainly accepting honors from the GDR. It is not surprising, then, that Davis would, after her release, travel to the GDR, where, among other things, on September 11, 1972, the honorary citizenship of the city of Magdeburg and, two days later, an honorary Ph.D. degree from the University of Leipzig (then Karl-Marx-University) were bestowed upon her. In either case, it is not clear why the venue was chosen.

Before Davis, DuBois and Robeson had already been awarded honorary Ph.D. degrees from Humboldt University in East Berlin—DuBois in 1958 in economics and Robeson in 1960 from the department of musicology. It was one way to exploit African American civil rights activism for East German propaganda purposes, whereby—as Robeson's case reveals—it was carefully checked beforehand whether the iconic black leader would actually be willing to visit the GDR in order to pick up the prize. DuBois's case, in turn, illustrates that a prominent black leader was, nonetheless, silenced in the GDR to make sure that the dictatorship stayed in control of the African American message to the East German people.

Honorary doctoral degrees for prominent African Americans were treated as propaganda highlights, though DuBois was eventually censored. Officially—that is, according to the GDR constitution—there did not exist any censorship.[69] But of course there are many examples of how censorship was nonetheless exercised, such as in the form of self-censorship when publishers—to avoid possible conflicts with the authorities—refused publishing certain items. An example would be the attempted publication of DuBois's speech after he had been awarded the honorary Ph.D. degree.[70] The dean of the Humboldt University business school, Heinz Mohrmann, had contacted the editor-in-chief, Hans W. Aust, of the East German publishing house Rütten & Loening in Berlin, which published a journal on German foreign policy. Aust was at first quite open to the idea of including a German-language version of the speech.[71]

Censorship in this case happened as an internal discourse that never reached the public. The opinions of African American civil rights activists were only allowed in the East German media as long as they fit with the expectations of the Communist leadership. On December 19 Aust informed Mohrmann that it did not seem advisable to publish the speech.[72] He cautiously proceeded to point out DuBois's importance as "without any doubt a deserving personality, and his speech, also without any doubt, is very interesting." But publishing the speech "would be more detrimental than it would be useful." He explained, "besides the many correct observations, which it contains, it would create confusion and ambiguity in a number of questions." That is to say that DuBois was not in step with the "correct," or rather official, SED party line, which of course meant that being connected with the publication of his speech could backfire. One example concerned the "question of the Garvey movement, which is described here in a way for which we cannot take responsibility." The idea of "taking responsibility" thus served as an internal code to suggest that the message did not conform to party ideology. To stress the implicit threat, Aust immediately continued, "and we definitely cannot take the responsibility for the question of the connections between the socialist movement and the national liberation movements." All of this culminated in Aust's announcement that "it appears that DuBois defines socialism differently than we do, he accords it characteristics that seem to be contrary to communism, and, in any case, he denies our convictions in this question." It would be intriguing to analyze the differences in DuBois's and the GDR Communists' ideas of socialism, but the cautious Aust did not go into that. Apparently already the threat of a concept of socialism that potentially differed from what the East German Communists expected sufficed to quietly shelve the speech and thereby silence DuBois.

Robeson, by contrast, was a celebrity known around the globe. To get him to East Germany would mean a considerable boost in prestige—his public refusal to come could be disastrous for the small Communist dictatorship. GDR officials thus proceeded with great caution. They went so far as to consider conferring an honorary Ph.D. degree on his wife, Eslanda, simply to test whether the Robesons would be open to publicly sympathize with East Germany. The fact that Eslanda was considered and rejected as a candidate for the honorary degree exposes the pragmatic underlying motives. The GDR's main objective was not to honor both Robesons' commitment to the African American freedom fight but instead to benefit from Paul's international standing, his willingness to openly communicate with Communist governments, and his resulting usefulness for the GDR's striving for recognition.[73]

Finally, the laudation prepared for Davis at the University of Leipzig reveals a desire to use references to African American contexts in order to promote Communist goals and, in doing so, impart the message on East German youth by force if need be. The speech contains similar passages as a speech that Rev. Ralph Abernathy had delivered in Davis's support on February 2, 1971, to a New York mass meeting, and which had duly made its way to the GDR.[74] In the Davis laudation, though, statements were turned more Communist by adding references to Karl Marx, such as "to say it with Karl Marx . . . true philosophy does not stop with interpreting the world. Its slogan is 'to change it,'"[75] after which Davis was addressed directly as a case in point. Moreover, correspondence between Gerhard Winkler, then head of the University of Leipzig, and the directors of the various university departments in preparation for the event reveals an obsession with having many young people turn up clad in the *Blauhemd* (blue shirt), the uniform of the East German youth organization.[76] It is the very uniform that Davis herself is wearing in the photograph to which I initially referred. Even more interesting is a statement in Winkler's memo ordering the department heads "to ensure attendance resorting to *appropriate means*."[77] It was left open what those "*appropriate means*" were. More explicit attention was given to the meals to be served in the course of the day, which were all but frugal proletarian foods.[78]

The Communists' Dilemma:
Martin Luther King Jr. and Nonviolent Protest

The East German dictatorship also faced limits when exploiting the African American freedom fight for its own purposes—the dilemma was how to point out the oppression of African Americans to the East German public (thus making the United States look bad) *without* inspiring them to draw parallels between African Americans and their own situation. Martin Luther King Jr. personified the idea especially as—in contrast to the other three black leaders—he was not a Communist supporter while being particularly visible as an African American civil rights icon. For both reasons, he actually greatly appealed to the East German opposition, which embraced the idea of nonviolent protest to attain freedom. In other words, King's reception in the GDR occurred on different levels and reveals that East German propaganda and African American civil rights goals did not match even when both resorted to similar language.

King's attraction to the East German dictatorship was rooted in the fact that with the Southern Christian Leadership Conference (SCLC), he headed an effective and, for the U.S. government, highly uncomfortable movement. "And whatever proved uncomfortable for the US government was of interest to the GDR media,"[79] which of course constructed a rather selective public image of King, with his concept of "nonviolence" presenting a crucial hurdle. Even though it could have been discussed in the context of Friedrich Engels's theory of violence,[80] GDR officials labeled it "weak pacifism."[81] King's nonviolent protest was thus depicted as implicitly unsuccessful, especially since he died a *violent* death. A recent King biography calls for a more complex picture of the civil rights leader, one that does not box him up exclusively as the personification of nonviolent resistance in U.S. contexts.[82] But as insinuated earlier, Communist propaganda had no use for subtle differentiations.

The East German Communists actually patronized King, which reflects underlying, long-standing European traditions of hierarchic, racist thinking—belying the East German dictatorship's assumed commitment to the African American cause. East German propaganda deprived King of mature intellectual insight when it condescendingly presented him as someone who, toward the end of his life, *almost* succeeded in finding the light (that is, Communism) and applauded him for having made an effort. For instance, Greta Kuckhoff, vice president of the GDR Peace Council, stated in a polemic article published after King's assassination that "his honest striving to understand reality freed Martin Luther King from the vicious circle with which the imperialist minority of his country sought to isolate their own, repressed people from the peoples in the Soviet Union and in the new socialist coun-tries."[83] She continued, "Dr. King did not become a Marxist; but he now made an effort to understand the role of the USA in Vietnam."[84] Finally, she claimed that King had realized that "Anticommunism led us into too many dumps."[85] Such statements contradict the claim that the GDR was more successful in rooting out racism.

As King was a Christian rather than a Communist, when still alive he had already become a symbolic figure for East Germans in oppositional circles, which typically found shelter in churches. This does not mean that East Ger-man churches were automatically oppositional. To the contrary, the story is complicated, with churches also being forced to find ways of accommodat-ing secular Communist demands.[86] As David Steele observed, "the church struggled extensively with its political identity, its relation to the state. Yet it still represented the primary ideological alternative to the SED, simply by vir-tue of its existence as the only major institution that the state was never able to control completely. Consequently, the values and theology, as well as the symbols and ritual, of the church had impact beyond their immediate reaches within society." Steele continued that the "church's strategic commitment to nonviolence had a direct impact on the peaceful nature of the protest" in the 1980s. Moreover, "at the same time, the church's strategic commitment to non-violence influenced the independent groups and the crowds that gathered for the demonstrations."[87] As a result, churches became places of refuge for oppositional groups ranging from representatives of the peace movement to environment protection and youth groups, all of which would carry the 1989 Peaceful Revolution (rather: nonviolent revolution) that brought down the Berlin Wall.

Against this background, King served as a source of inspiration for the East German peace movement. After his assassination, East Germans (explic-itly not the establishment) openly displayed their sympathies with him.[88] In the little town of Hoyerswerda, a Martin Luther King House was established in 1969; King's widow, Coretta, was asked permission to do so.[89] Also after King's assassination, Georg Meusel corresponded with Coretta King, such as in preparation of a stamp collection that honored King's commitment to nonviolence.[90] In 1998 Meusel became the director of the new Martin Luther King Jr. Center of Nonviolence and Civil Courage Germany (Martin-Luther-King-Zentrum für Gewaltfreiheit und Zivilcourage e.V.). This King Center was founded by, among others, representatives of the former GDR peace movement. It is located in Werdau in the East German countryside, where active resistance against the SED dictatorship can be traced to the early days of the GDR.[91]

East German oppositional groups turned to wherever they found means to express their frustrations with the lack of freedom and the oppression of those who did not fit the East German Communist concept. Yet apart from those in the King centers and houses, the activists were not necessarily aware of the origin of their songs and nonviolent forms of protest. They simply adopted what reflected their feelings. It proved effective in 1989.[92] Unfortunately, by 2012 German public history continues to be unaware of the connections between the African American and the East German civil rights movements. For instance, a comparison of the English- and the German-language Wikipedia entries on King reveals a few striking differences. The English entry points out that his nonviolent commitment was also rooted in Mohandas Karamchand Gandhi's teachings. The German Wikipedia omits any such references. King is simply introduced as a figure of significance for the United States. The movement's larger implications and its perception, not just in East Germany, are missing.

Conclusion

The Cold War context allowed for the racial schism in the United States to attract worldwide attention and thus put pressure on the U.S. government especially as Communist propaganda did not fail to exploit the facts. But there is more to it. In supporting African American civil rights activism, the East German dictatorship acted out its own scheme to obtain recognition in the West, especially since the early 1970s. African American civil rights leaders, in turn, did not merely become tools in the Communists' quest. While some of them more or less idealistically perceived of the Communist bloc as a world that seemed to have made much progress in destroying racism, they actively utilized the GDR's ideology to strategically promote civil rights for African Americans (and Africans).

The political activism of African American leaders was also derived from various philosophical concepts that had inspired black visitors to Germany since at least the nineteenth century. The Cold War setting thus proved fertile transatlantic grounds for black intellectuals in their fight for civil liberties and equality. That the East German Communists could not control the expressions of the black freedom struggle reveals just how powerful and focused the black freedom struggle was despite attempts to manipulate it on the part of the GDR dictatorship. The progress of the civil rights struggle in the United States is thus also reflected in the fact that, eventually, East German activists nonviolently brought down the GDR dictatorship in 1989 demanding "no violence."

Notes

1. Balbier and Rösch, *Umworbener Klassenfeind.*
2. There are many individual case studies. See Beck, "Censoring Your Ally." Sophie Lorenz is preparing a Ph.D. dissertation, "'Freiheit für Angela Davis': The German Democratic Republic and Angela Davis, 1965–1989" (working title), at the University of Heidelberg. Aspects of the relationship of African Americans and the GDR are discussed in Greene and Ortlepp, *Germans and African Americans.* More general studies on the relations between the United States and the GDR are available: Grosse, *Amerikapolitik und Amerikabild der DDR;* Hühnerfuß, *Diplomatische Beziehungen.*
3. Concept of Paul-Robeson-Archives, 6, enclosed in Büro Norden to Heinz Willmann, February 1, 1964, Bundesarchiv Berlin, DZ 9/1858. See also Duberman, *Paul Robeson*, 518.
4. Press release, May 4, 1972, Bundesarchiv Berlin, DZ 7 /17.
5. Press release, ADN November 18, 1971, Bundesarchiv Berlin, DZ/7/16. Also *Berliner Zeitung*, November 19, 1971, Bundesarchiv Berlin, DZ 9/1830.
6. Schroeder, "Ollie Harrington."
7. For example, Engels, *Role of Force in History.*
8. Conversation with Tobias Hollitzer, director of the Stasi-Museum Leipzig, February 13, 2012.
9. See Fikes, "African Americans Who Teach German Language and Culture"; Hopkins, "Expanding the Canon"; Hopkins, *Who Is a German?*; Hopkins, "'Black Prussians.'"
10. Hopkins, "'Black Prussians'"; Walker, "'Of the Coming of John [and Jane].'"
11. Amo and Nwala, *Anton William Amo's Treatise;* Mabe, *Anton Wilhelm Amo;* Glötzner, *Anton Wilhelm Amo;* Brentjes, *Anton Wilhelm Amo;* Heyden, *Unbekannte Biographien.*
12. Hopkins, "'Black Prussians,'" 67.
13. Edgcomb, *From Swastika to Jim Crow;* Grill and Jenkins, "Nazis and the American South."
14. Wandert et al., "Black German Identities."
15. I find an estimated number of ca. 500,000 Afro-Germans today, but it is not clear on which data this number is based. The German census *Statistisches Bundesamt* does not collect information on ethnicity, only on nationality.
16. Nejar and Carstensen, *Mach nicht so traurige Augen;* Massaquoi, *Destined to Witness.*
17. Pommerin, *Sterilisierung der Rheinlandbastarde.*
18. Fehrenbach, *Race after Hitler;* Faria, *Zwischen Fürsorge und Ausgrenzung;* Frankenstein, *Soldatenkinder.*
19. Krüger-Potratz, Hansen, and Jasper, *Anderssein gab es nicht;* Elsner and Elsner, *Ausländer und Ausländerpolitik.*
20. Kenna, *Homecoming;* Aukongo, *Kalungas Kind;* Engombe, *Kind Nr. 95.*
21. Höhn and Klimke, *Breath of Freedom.*
22. For example, Lankowski, "Social Movements."
23. Schmieding, "Jugendkultur HipHop in der DDR."
24. For example, Barkin, "W. E. B. DuBois' Love Affair."
25. African Americans who studied in Germany before World War I included Solomon Carter Fuller (1872–1953), Richard Robert Wright Jr. (1878–1967), and Charles C. Cook.

Ernest Everett Just (1883–1941) was invited to pursue advanced research at the Kaiser-Wilhlem-Institut-für-Biologie in Berlin in 1930. Hopkins, "'Black Prussians,'" 74–75.

26. Solbrig, "American Slavery."

27. Barkin, "'Berlin Days'"; Barkin, "W. E. B. DuBois' Love Affair"; DuBois, *Autobiography*.

28. Aptheker, *Correspondence of W. E. B. DuBois*.

29. "Angela Y. Davis," in Yancy, *African-American Philosophers*, 21–22.

30. Hopkins, "'Black Prussians,'" 78.

31. Ibid.

32. W. E. B. DuBois to Paul Robeson, July 25, 1961, Paul-Robeson-Archiv Berlin, 273, typed copy. In an earlier letter, DuBois had suggested that if the new Kennedy administration would not renew his passport, Robeson should simply "take out citizenship in a European or, African country." DuBois to Paul Robeson, January 5, 1961, Paul-Robeson-Archiv Berlin.

33. *Ebony*, October 1957, 31–42, Paul-Robeson-Archiv Berlin, 772. Eslanda replied to *Ebony*, September 16, 1957, Paul-Robeson-Archiv Berlin, 322. See also Duberman, *Paul Robeson*.

34. Robeson, "To Our Beloved Comrade," *New World Review* (April 1953): 11–13, Paul-Robeson-Archiv Berlin, 211. An East German publication reproduced selected passages about a half a year later. See *Der Amerikanische Imperialismus*, Herausgegeben vom Presseamt beim Ministerpräsidenten der Regierung der Deutschen Demokratischen Republik, Freitag, October 2, 1953, 36, Paul-Robeson-Archiv Berlin, 220.

35. Robeson, "To Our Beloved Comrade."

36. Ibid.

37. Paul Robeson, Statement to House of Representatives Committee on Un-American Activities, Paul-Robeson-Archiv Berlin, 227. Following quotes in ibid.

38. Dudziak, *Cold War Civil Rights*.

39. LAUDATIO anläßlich der Ehrenpromotion der mutigen amerikanischen Kommunistin und Bürgerrechtskämpferin ANGELA DAVIS an der Karl-Marx-Universität Leipzig am 13 Sep. 1972, Bundesarchiv Berlin, DZ 9/246. My translation. Original: "Daß diese humanistische Idee im krassen Gegensatz zur amerikanischen Wirklichkeit steht, müssen Sie früh genug erfahren."

40. Angela Davis, "Vorwort," 10, in Steiniger, *Angela Davis*. My translation. Original: "Die beeindruckende Aktion «Freiheit für Angela Davis» in der DDR hat mich in jenen Tagen besonders tief bewegt."

41. For example, *Neuer Tag*, June 6, 1972, Bundesarchiv Berlin, DZ 7 /17.

42. Davis, *Angela Davis*, 199.

43. Ibid., 138.

44. Ibid., 140.

45. Ibid., 141.

46. Vermerk über ein Gespräch des Genossen Hermann Axen, Mitglied des Politbüros und Sekretär des ZK der SED, mit Angela Davis, Mitglied des Zentralkomitees der KP der USA, und Hilton Btaithwaite am 29 June 1981, Bundesarchiv Berlin, DY 30/IV 2/2.035 112.

47. Robeson, Statement to House of Representatives Committee on Un-American Activities.

48. Franz Loeser, script of East German radio broadcast based on Robeson's HUAC testimony, 1957, Paul-Robeson-Archiv Berlin, 720. Following quotes in ibid. My translation. Original: "Frechheit von dem Nigger—Was reden wir hier viel, weg mit dem—mit diesem lausigen Nigger—dreckige Arroganz—wir werden ihm den Mund stopfen." "Stopft dem Nigger den Mund—stopft ihm den Mund, den Mund, den Mund!"

49. Robeson, Statement to House of Representatives Committee on Un-American Activities.

50. Loeser, script of East German radio broadcast, 1957, 720. My translation. Original: "Eben hörten Sie eine Szene, und die hat sich am 12. Juni 1956 in Washington wirklich so zugetragen."

51. Propaganda was not only directed at East Germans. See open letter, Friedrich Karl Kaul, attorney in the German Democratic Republic, to Richard E. Arnason, judge in the Angela Davis case, February 14, 1972. Reprinted in *World Magazine*, March 25, 1972, Bundesarchiv Berlin, DZ 7 /17.

52. Wirth, "Martin Luther King," 938. My translation. Original: "So oder so war jedenfalls die Rassenfrage integraler Bestandteil des Kampfes gegen den amerikanischen Imperialismus."

53. Recent English editions are Klemperer and Brady, *Language of the Third Reich*; Klemperer and Chalmers, *Lesser Evil*.

54. For example, Greta Kuckhoff, "Martin Luther King," *Die Weltbühne* 23.16 (April 16, 1968): 490–492, Nachlass Greta Kuckhoff, Bundesarchiv Berlin, N 2506 /65.

55. Schnoor, *Amerikanistik in der DDR*; Becker, "Amerikanistik."

56. See Brüning, *Albert Maltz*; Brüning, *Das amerikanische Drama der dreissiger Jahre*; Haas, "African American Civil Rights Drama."

57. Davis, *Angela Davis*, 144. My emphasis.

58. Yancy, *African-American Philosophers*, 21. My emphasis.

59. Albert Norden to Walter Ulbricht, March 29, 1968, Bundesarchiv Berlin, DY 30/ IV A 2/2028/124, Bl. 60. My translation and emphasis. Original: "der amerikanische Negersänger und Friedenskämpfer" and "Ich schlage vor, daß Du ihm zu seinem 70. Geburtstag als Staatsratvorsitzender ein kurzes Glückwunschtelegramm übermittelst, *das auch unsere Presse veröffentlichen sollte*."

60. E. H. Meyer, G. Knepler, F. Loeser, and A. Katzenstein to Norden, January 6, 1964; Norden to Loeser, January 17, 1964, both in Bundesarchiv Berlin, DY 30/ IV A 2/2028/124, Bl. 1–11.

61. H. Stadtler to Franz Loeser and Prof. Katzenstein, November 17, 1970, Bundesarchiv Berlin, DY 30/ IV A 2/2028/124, Bl. 93–94. Following quotes in ibid. My translation. Original: "2. Die vorgesehene Meldung über das Stattfinden des Symposiums sollte nicht nur an die kommunistische Presse der USA geschickt werden, sondern an alle in Frage kommenden Blätter der Amerikaner weisser und schwarzer Farbe. 3. Warum übrigens eine solche Pressemitteilung nur für die USA-Presse? Auch England usw. sollte berücksichtigt werden. Das ... hebt ... das Prestige der DDR. 4. Warum sollen bei dem Symposium nur Kommunisten auftreten? Ein bürgerlicher Musikwissenschaftler, wenn er entsprechenden Ruf auch über die Grenzen seines Landes hinaus geniesst, würde sehr nützlich sein. Einzige Bedingung: Kein Antikommunist darf auftreten."

62. Ernst Loeser (London) to Paul Robeson, July 19, 1968, Paul-Robeson-Archiv Berlin, 295. E. Loeser informed Robeson that "as you may know Frank helped to produce a programme on the German Radio abaut [sic] you and they also held a festival programme to honor you on your sixtieth birthday in one of the biggest halls in Berlin. At the end of the festival they showed 'Bridge across the Ocean.' I can assure you that they look very much forward to seeing you. (Only last night did the Deutschlandsender re-broadcast part of Frank's programme)."

63. Aubrey Pankey (Deutsche Konzert und Gastspiel Direktion Berlin, DDR) to Frank Loesser [sic] (General Secretary National Paul Robeson Committee, Salford), November 23, 1956, Paul-Robeson-Archiv Berlin, 696.

64. Duberman, *Paul Robeson*, 461. Eslanda's letters to Middleton were quite formal in 1957, but they grew more intimate in the following years. See letter and documents relating to passport for Robeson, 1958, Paul-Robeson-Archiv Berlin, 673 and 335.

65. Heinz Willmann to Herrn Prof. Dr. H. Ley (Humboldt Universität, Institut für Philosophie), September 10, 1963, Bundesarchiv Berlin, DZ 9/1761.

66. Protocols, Sitzung Paul Robeson Komitees, February 8, April 24, May 29, and July 20, 1967, Bundesarchiv Berlin, DY 30/ IV A 2/2028/124, Bl. 30, 34, 38, 48.

67. Dr. K. Hossinger (Direktor, Deutsche Akademie der Künste zu Berlin, Sektion Bildende Kunst Darstellende Kunst Dichtkunst und Sprachpflege Musik, DDR) to whom it may concern, January 5, 1968, Paul-Robeson-Archiv Berlin, 693.

68. For example, *Junge Welt*, January 26, 1971, Bundesarchiv Berlin, DZ 9/246. *Junge Welt*, the Communist propaganda newspaper for young East Germans, was particularly active in campaigning for Davis in the early 1970s. Also "'A Million Roses for Angela Davis': A Selected Bibliography of Media Coverage of East German Solidarity Campaigns with Angela Davis" (online).

69. Article 9 (2) of the GDR constitution from 1949 (valid through 1968) stated that there would not be any censorship of the press. See "DDR im Unterricht—DDR-Verfassungen im Original," http://www.ddr-im-unterricht.de/die_ddr_verfassung.html.

70. For example, Beck, "Censoring Your Ally," 213.

71. Mohrmann to Aust, November 8, 1958; Aust to Mohrmann, November 13, 1958, both in Humboldt University Archives, Berlin (HUA), Ehrenpromotion, Wi.-Fakultät, W. E. B. DuBois.

72. Aust to Mohrmann, December 19, 1958, HUA, Ehrenpromotion, Wi.-Fakultät, W. E. B. DuBois. Following quotes in ibid. My translation. Original: "Er würde neben dem Richtigen, das in ihm enthalten ist in einer Reihe von Fragen Verwirrung und Unklarheit schaffen. . . . Oder in der Frage der Garvey-Bewegung, die hier so dargelegt wird, wie wir es nicht verantworten können. Und schon gar nicht in der Frage des Verhältnisses von sozialistischer Bewegung und nationaler Befreiungsbewegung. DuBois definiert im übrigen Sozialismus offenbar anders als wir, er gibt ihm einen dem Kommunismus irgendwie entgegengesetzten Charakter, jedenfalls leugnet er unsere Anschauungen in dieser Frage."

73. Sekretär des Rektors, Humboldt Universität, an Staatssekretariat für das Hochund Fachschulwesen, Sektor Ausland, September 1, 1959, Bundesarchiv Berlin, DR 3/1. Schicht/2779. Marked "*Eilt sehr*" (very urgent).

74. Ralph Abernathy, "On Trial: Angela Davis or America?," Bundesarchiv Berlin, DZ 9/246. Indeed, Abernathy's speeches were known in the GDR: for example, Protokoll der Sitzung des Paul-Robeson-Komitees, March 17, 1971, Bundesarchiv Berlin, DY 30/ IV A 2/2028/124, Bl. 127–129. Abernathy's 1989 autobiography contains a Cold War reference in its title: *And the Walls Came Tumbling Down.*

75. LAUDATIO, Bundesarchiv Berlin, DZ 9/246. My translation. Original: "um mit den Worten von Karl Marx zu sprechen. . . . Wahre Philosophie bleibt bei der Interpretation der Welt nicht stehen. 'Sie zu verändern!'—ist ihr Losungswort. Es ist auch die Losung Ihres kämpferischen Lebens."

76. Rektor der Karl-Marx-Universität Leipzig an die Direktoren der Sektionen und Institute, Direktor des Bereichs Medizin, Universitätsdirektoren, Hauptabteilungsleiter, September 7, 1972, Leipzig University Archives (LUA), Rektorat, Ehrungen von Persönlichkeiten, June–November 1972, R 0531, Bd. 3, Bl. 51. An earlier draft with corrections is in LUA, Rektorat, Empfang in- und ausländischer Gäste des Rektors, 1970–1980, R 0720, Bl. 52.

77. Rektor an die Direktoren, September 7, 1972, LUA, R 0531, Bd. 3, Bl. 51. My emphasis and translation. Original: "Ich bitte Sie, durch geeignete Maßnahmen die Teilnahme zu sichern und zu veranlassen."

78. Karl-Marx-Universität, Direktorat für Ökonomie, Abt. Mensen/gastr. Einrichtungen (Petzold, Abteilungsleiter), "Entwurf Organisationsplan für Sonderversorgungsaufgaben anläßlich des Besuchs von Frau Prof. Angela Davis an der Karl-Marx-Universität durch die Abteilung Mensen und gastr. Einrichtungen," September 6, 1972, LUA, R 0720, Bl. 55–58.

79. Wirth, "Martin Luther King," 938. My translation. Original: "Und was den herrschenden Kreisen in den USA zu schaffen machte, mußte die Medien in der DDR interessieren."

80. Engels, *Role of Force in History.*

81. Wirth, "Martin Luther King," 939.

82. Jackson, *From Civil Rights to Human Rights.*

83. Kuckhoff, "Martin Luther King," Bundesarchiv N 2506 /65. My translation. Original: "Sein ehrliches Streben, die Wirklichkeit zu verstehen, hatte Martin Luther King aus dem Verteufelungskreis befreit, mit dem die herrschende imperialistische Minderheit seines Landes die eigene unterdrückte Bevölkerung von der Sowjetunion und den neuen sozialistischen Ländern zu isolieren suchte."

84. Ibid. My translation. Original: "Dr. King wurde kein Marxist; aber er bemühte sich jetzt um Klarheit über die Rolle der USA in Vietnam."

85. Ibid. My translation. Original: "Der Antikommunismus hat uns in zu viele Sümpfe geführt."

86. Neubert, *Geschichte der Opposition.*

87. Steele, "At the Front Lines," 139.

88. Wirth, "Martin Luther King."

89. Bundesarchiv Berlin, DO 4 / 83819, Bd. 1140; also Martin-Luther-King-Haus Hoyerswerda-Neustadt, http://www.woiteweb.de/guests/kinghaus/frame/haus.htm.

90. For example, Georg Meusel to Coretta King, January 30, 1970, December 28, 1971, January 7, 1979; C. King to Meusel, August 17, 1971. Supplied by Georg Meusel.

91. Martin-Luther-King Center Werdau, http://www.king-zentrum.de/zentrum/index
.php?option=com_content&task=view&id=77&Itemid=77.

92. Conversation with Tobias Hollitzer, director of the Stasi-Museum Leipzig, February
13, 2012.

Bibliography

Archival Sources

Bundesarchiv Berlin: DO 4/8381, DR 3/1.Schicht/2779, DY 30/IV 2/2.035 112, DY 30/ IV
A 2/2028/124, DZ/7/16, DZ 7/17, DZ 9/1858, DZ 9/1761, DZ 9/1830, DZ 9/246, Nachlass
Greta Kuckhoff N 2506 /65.
Humboldt University Archives, Berlin: Ehrenpromotion, Wi.-Fakultät, W. E. B. DuBois.
King Center Werdau: Georg Meusel correspondence.
Leipzig University Archives (LUA): R 0531, R 0720.
Paul-Robeson-Archiv Berlin: Nos. 220, 227, 273, 322, 335, 673, 693, 720.

Internet Resources

"DDR im Unterricht—DDR-Verfassungen im Original." http://www.ddr-im-unterricht.de/
die_ddr_verfassung.html.
Hopkins, Leroy T. *Who Is a German? Historical and Modern Perspectives on Africans in Germany* (American Institute for Contemporary German Studies, 1999). http://www.peuple
sawa.com/downloads/19.pdf.
Martin-Luther-King Center Werdau. http://www.king-zentrum.de/zentrum/index.
php?option=com_content&task=view&id=77&Itemid=77.
Martin-Luther-King-Haus Hoyerswerda-Neustadt. http://www.woiteweb.de/guests/king
haus/frame/haus.htm.
"'A Million Roses for Angela Davis': A Selected Bibliography of Media Coverage of East
German Solidarity Campaigns with Angela Davis." www.aacvr-germany.org/davis.

Secondary Sources

Abernathy, Ralph. *And the Walls Came Tumbling Down: An Autobiography.* New York:
Harper & Row, 1989.
Amo, Anton Wilhelm, and T. Uzodinma Nwala. *Anton William Amo's Treatise on the Art of
Philosophising Soberly and Accurately (with Commentaries).* Nsukka: William Amo Centre for African Philosophy, University of Nigeria, 1990.
Aptheker, Herbert, ed. *The Correspondence of W. E. B. DuBois.* Vol. 1, *Selections 1877–1934.*
Amherst: University of Massachusetts Press, 1973–1978.
Aukongo, Stefanie-Lahya. *Kalungas Kind: Wie die DDR mein Leben rettete.* Reinbek bei
Hamburg: Rowohlt, 2009.

Balbier, Uta A., and Christiane Rösch. *Umworbener Klassenfeind: Das Verhältnis der DDR zu den USA*. Berlin: Links, 2006.

Barkin, Kenneth D. "'Berlin Days,' 1892–1894: W. E. B. DuBois and German Political Economy." *Boundary 2* 27.3 (Fall 2000): 79–101.

———. "W. E. B. DuBois' Love Affair with Imperial Germany." *German Studies Review* 28.2 (May 2005): 284–301.

Beck, Hamilton H. "Censoring Your Ally: W. E. B. DuBois in the German Democratic Republic." In *Crosscurrents: African Americans, Africa, and Germany in the Modern World*, ed. David McBride, Leroy Hopkins, and C. Aisha Blackshire-Belay, 197–232. Columbia, S.C.: Camden House, 1998.

Becker, Anja. "Amerikanistik [American Studies]." In *Geschichte der Universität Leipzig. Band IV: Fakultäten, Institute, Zentrale Einrichtungen (1. Halbband)*, ed. Ulrich von Hehl, Uwe John, and Manfred Rudersdorf, 12–31. Leipzig: Universitätsverlag, 2009.

Brentjes, Burchard. *Anton Wilhelm Amo: Der schwarze Philosoph in Halle*. Leipzig: Koehler & Amelang, 1976.

Brüning, Eberhard. *Albert Maltz, ein amerikanischer Arbeiterschriftsteller*. Halle (Saale): M. Niemeyer, 1957.

———. *Das amerikanische Drama der dreissiger Jahre*. Berlin: Rütten & Loening, 1966.

Davis, Angela Y. *Angela Davis: An Autobiography*. 1974. Reprint, New York: International Publishers, 2008.

Duberman, Martin Bauml. *Paul Robeson*. New York: Alfred A. Knopf, 1988.

DuBois, W. E. B. *The Autobiography of W. E. B. DuBois: A Soliloquy on Viewing My Life from the Last Decade of Its First Century*. 1968. Reprint, New York: International Publishers, 2007.

Dudziak, Mary L. *Cold War Civil Rights: Race and the Image of American Democracy*. 2002. Reprint, Princeton, N.J.: Princeton University Press, 2011.

Edgcomb, Gabrielle Simon. *From Swastika to Jim Crow: Refugee Scholars at Black Colleges*. Malabar, Fla.: Krieger, 1993.

Elsner, Eva-Maria, and Lothar Elsner. *Ausländer und Ausländerpolitik in der DDR*. Berlin: Gesellschaftswiss. Forum, 1992.

Engels, Friedrich. *The Role of Force in History* [Die Rolle der Gewalt in der Geschichte]. N.p.: 1887/1888.

Engombe, Lucia. *Kind Nr. 95: Meine deutsch-afrikanische Odyssee*. Berlin: Ullstein, 2004.

Fehrenbach, Heide. *Race after Hitler: Black Occupation Children in Postwar Germany and America*. Princeton, N.J.: Princeton University Press, 2005.

Fikes Robert, Jr. "African Americans Who Teach German Language and Culture." *Journal of Blacks in Higher Education* 30 (Winter 2000–2001): 108–113.

Frankenstein, Luise. *Soldatenkinder: Die unehelichen Kinder ausländischer Soldaten mit besonderer Berücksichtigung der Mischlinge*. Munich: Steinebach, 1954.

Glötzner, Johannes. *Anton Wilhelm Amo: Ein Philosoph aus Afrika im Deutschland des 18. Jahrhunderts*. Munich: Ed. Enhuber, 2002.

Greene, Larry A., and Anke Ortlepp, eds. *Germans and African Americans: Two Centuries of Exchange*. Jackson: University Press of Mississippi, 2011.

Grill, Johnpeter Horst, and Robert L. Jenkins. "The Nazis and the American South in the 1930s: A Mirror Image?" *Journal of Southern History* 58.4 (November 1992): 667–693.

Grosse, Jürgen. *Amerikapolitik und Amerikabild der DDR, 1974–1989.* Bonn: Bouvier, 1999.

Haas, Astrid. "African American Civil Rights Drama in GDR Scholarship and Theater Practice." In *Germans and African Americans: Two Centuries of Exchange*, ed. Larry A. Greene and Anke Ortlepp, 166–184. Jackson: University Press of Mississippi, 2011.

Heyden, Ulrich van der. *Unbekannte Biographien: Afrikaner im deutschsprachigen Europa vom 18. Jahrhundert bis zum Ende des Zweiten Weltkrieges.* Berlin: Kai Homilius, 2008.

Höhn, Maria, and Martin Klimke. *A Breath of Freedom: The Civil Rights Struggle, African American GIs, and Germany.* New York: Palgrave Macmillan, 2010.

Hopkins, Leroy T. "'Black Prussians': Germany and African American Education from James W. C. Pennington to Angela Davis." In *Crosscurrents: African Americans, Africa, and Germany in the Modern World*, ed. David McBride, Leroy Hopkins, and C. Aisha Blackshire-Belay, 65–81. Columbia, S.C.: Camden House, 1998.

———. "Expanding the Canon: Afro-German Studies." *Die Unterrichtspraxis—Teaching German* 25.2 (1992): 121–126.

Hühnerfuß, Bianca. *Diplomatische Beziehungen zwischen der DDR und den USA.* Munich: Grin Verlag, 2007.

Jackson, Thomas F. *From Civil Rights to Human Rights: Martin Luther King and the Struggle for Economic Justice.* Philadelphia: University of Pennsylvania Press, 2006.

Kenna, Constance. *Homecoming: The GDR Kids of Namibia.* Windhoek, Namibia: New Namibia Books, 1999.

Klemperer, Victor, and Martin Brady. *The Language of the Third Reich: LTI, Lingua Tertii Imperii: A Philologist's Notebook.* London: Continuum, 2006.

Klemperer, Victor, and Martin Chalmers. *The Lesser Evil: The Diaries of Victor Klemperer 1945–59.* London: Phoenix, 2004.

Krüger-Potratz, Marianne, Georg Hansen, and Dirk Jasper. *Anderssein gab es nicht: Ausländer und Minderheiten in der DDR.* Münster: Waxmann, 1991.

Lankowski, Carl. "Social Movements in Germany and the United States: The Peace Movement and the Environmental Movement." In *The United States and Germany in the Era of the Cold War, 1945–1990: A Handbook*, ed. Detlef Junker et al., 2:430–436. Cambridge: University Press, 2004. Originally published in German in 2001.

Lemke Muniz de Faria, Yara-Colette. *Zwischen Fürsorge und Ausgrenzung: Afrodeutsche "Besatzungskinder" im Nachkriegsdeutschland.* Berlin: Metropol, 2002.

Lorenz, Sophie. "'Freiheit für Angela Davis': The German Democratic Republic and Angela Davis, 1965–1989." Ph.D. diss., University of Heidelberg, in progress.

Mabe, Jacob Emmanuel. *Anton Wilhelm Amo interkulturell gelesen.* Nordhausen: Traugott Bautz, 2007.

Massaquoi, Hans J. *Destined to Witness: Growing up Black in Nazi Germany.* New York: W. Morrow, 1999.

McBride, David, Leroy Hopkins, and C. Aisha Blackshire-Belay, eds. *Crosscurrents: African Americans, Africa, and Germany in the Modern World.* Columbia, S.C.: Camden House, 1998.

Nejar, Marie, and Regina Carstensen. *Mach nicht so traurige Augen, weil du ein Negerlein bist: Meine Jugend im Dritten Reich.* Reinbek bei Hamburg: Rowohlt, 2007.

Neubert, Ehrhart. *Geschichte der Opposition in der DDR, 1949–1989.* Berlin: C. Links, 1998.

Pommerin, Reiner. *Sterilisierung der Rheinlandbastarde: Das Schicksal einer farbigen deutschen Minderheit 1918–1937.* Düsseldorf: Droste Verlag, 1979.

Schmieding, Leonard. "Jugendkultur HipHop in der DDR: 1983—1990." Ph.D. diss., Universität Leipzig, 2011.

Schnoor, Rainer. *Amerikanistik in der DDR: Geschichte-Analysen-Zeitzeugenberichte.* Berlin: Trafo Verlag Dr. W. Weist, 1999.

Schroeder, Aribert. "Ollie Harrington: His Portrait Drawn on the Basis of East German (GDR) Secret Service Files." In *Germans and African Americans: Two Centuries of Exchange,* ed. Larry A. Greene and Anke Ortlepp, 185–200. Jackson: University Press of Mississippi, 2011.

Solbrig, Ingeborg H. "American Slavery in Eighteenth-Century German Literature: The Case of Herder's 'Neger-Idyllen.'" *Monatshefte* 82.1 (Spring 1990): 38–49.

Steele, David. "At the Front Lines of the Revolution: East Germany's Churches Give Sanctuary and Succor to the Purveyors of Change." In *Religion: The Missing Dimension of Statecraft,* ed. Douglas Johnston and Cynthia Sampson, 119–152. New York: Oxford University Press, 1994.

Steiniger, Klaus. *Angela Davis: Eine Frau schreibt Geschichte.* Berlin: Neues Leben, 2010.

Walker, Corey D. B. "'Of the Coming of John [and Jane]': African American Intellectuals in Europe, 1888–1938." *American Studies Quarterly* 47.1 (2002): 7–22.

Wandert, Timo, Randolph Ochsmann, Peary Brug, Anna Chybicka, Marie-Françoise Lacassagne, and Maykel Verkuyten. "Black German Identities: Validating the Multidimensional Inventory of Black Identity." *Journal of Black Psychology* 35.4 (2009): 456–484.

We Saw the German Democratic Republic. Dresden: Verl. Zeit im Bild, 1967.

Wirth, Günther. "Martin Luther King: Erinnerungen und Reflexionen." *UTOPIE kreativ* 132 (October 2001): 938–945.

Yancy, George, ed. *African-American Philosophers: 17 Conversations.* New York: Routledge, 1998.

III. CULTURAL MASTERY IN FOREIGN SPACES

Evolving Visions of Home and Identity

Abdias Nascimento

Afro-Brazilian Painting Connections Across the Diaspora

Kimberly Cleveland

Until his death in 2011 at the age of ninety-seven, Abdias Nascimento was one of the most important individuals of the organized black movement in Brazil. He embodied the spirit and goals of the fight for racial equality that grew over the course of the twentieth century. A political nuisance for more than one administration, and jailed more than once for his oppositional views, by the start of this century, however, he had become an internationally lauded figure. In 2005 the Brazilian government was one of several sponsors that honored the nonagenarian with an exhibition at the National Archives in Rio de Janeiro. Many Brazilians and U.S. Americans are familiar with Nascimento's work as an actor, activist, writer, and politician. A smaller number of people know that, a self-taught painter, he also produced a significant body of acrylic on canvas paintings.

From the late 1930s onward, Nascimento's cultural production was intrinsically linked to his wider involvement in national and international black movements and ideologies. When American artists and art historians were studying connections between African and Diasporic arts in the late 1960s and early 1970s, exhibitions of Nascimento's paintings in the United States provided tangible evidence of African influences in Brazilian art. Over time, Nascimento even took on the role of cultural ambassador, educating blacks in the United States and Brazil about each other's respective situations.

Through an examination of Nascimento's artwork from the late 1960s to the mid-1990s, one underscores not only how Nascimento chose to represent Afro-Brazilian culture to the international community at different points in his career but also how he shed light on the political side of painting Afro-Brazilian art at home and in the United States. In focusing on an individual who used his paintings to demonstrate cultural resistance in relation to national

and international black movements, we may further our understanding of
Afro-Brazilian art and its connections to African art and culture. Through
the prism of art, Nascimento illuminated intellectual, in addition to artistic,
connections that cut across the Diaspora. The growth of his incorporation of
African and Diasporic references (as a result of his increased political and
cultural contact with African and African-descendent communities) reveals
that these connections are not static, but that they are forever shifting in the
mind of the individual artist.

Nascimento in Brazil: Early Endeavors

Nascimento discovered the challenges inherent in fighting for racial equality in
Brazil at a young age. Just sixteen in 1930, he left his small hometown of Franca,
in São Paulo state, for the capital, Rio de Janeiro. There, he became active in
Brazil's first organized black movement, the Frente Negra Brasileira (FNB), or
Brazilian Black Front. The group's interest in Brazil's African heritage countered the government's promotion of a unified cultural nationalism. Intolerant
of political opposition, the *Estado Novo* (New State) government (1937–1945)
jailed Nascimento and other university students for distributing pamphlets
against President Getúlio Vargas. As the FNB had gone on to declare itself a
political party, the administration shut the FNB down in 1937 to dissuade the
organization from any further such type of dissident action and competition.

Despite the end of the FNB, its members refused to forego their cause and
remained undeterred by the *Estado Novo*'s repressive tactics. Nascimento realized that he could circumvent the administration's aversion to other political
parties by creating a cultural group. In 1944 he founded the Teatro Experimental do Negro (TEN), or Black Experimental Theater. Not only did TEN offer its
Afro-Brazilian members—the majority of whom were unschooled domestic
servants, laborers, and the unemployed—the opportunity to participate in the
theater, but it also provided services such as literacy classes. Through their
work in the theater and contact with Senegalese writer Alioune Diop's journal
Présence Africaine, Nascimento and the other group leaders learned about the
philosophy of Négritude introduced by Léopold Senghor, Aimé Césaire, and
Léon Damas in the 1930s. TEN actors and activists looked to Négritude as
a means for Afro-Brazilian social liberation in tandem with valorization of
African culture; they became the principal disseminators of this philosophy
in Brazil in the 1940s and 1950s.[1] However, given the country's conservative
political climate, their hopes and efforts generated few concrete results.

In 1968 Nascimento focused on a second major cultural endeavor in his attempt to end racial inequality in Brazil. In an open letter published in *Présence Africaine*, he expressed dissatisfaction with the way the Brazilian Ministry of Culture had excluded Afro-Brazilians from participating in various preparatory aspects for the first World Black and African Festival of Arts and Culture held in Dakar in 1966, including the production of materials and the selection of national representatives.[2] This festival was, after all, an unprecedented opportunity for Afro-Brazilians to highlight both their African heritage and their place within artistic and cultural production in the Diaspora to the international community.

In an effort to counter marginalization on the part of the Brazilian establishment, since the 1950s Nascimento had been working on creating a Museu de Arte Negra (MAN), or Museum of Black Art, that would give Afro-Brazilians an active role in educating the Brazilian public about art from Africa and the African Diaspora.[3] Unlike the National Fine Arts Museum in Rio de Janeiro, with its Yoruba-heavy collection of art from West Africa, Nascimento's museum would include artwork produced by Brazilian artists of African descent. Numerous public figures recognized the possible benefits that could result from such an institution and supported the plans for MAN despite Nascimento's somewhat controversial reputation and prior run-ins with the government. Various intellectuals, diplomats, and even some political officials publicly endorsed the idea for the museum, which, as scholar Eduardo Portela asserted, would "help promote understanding of African participation in the formation of Brazilian society" and "increase cultural relations with African countries."[4] In 1968 Nascimento managed to organize in Rio de Janeiro an exhibition of the pieces he had gathered for the collection thus far, although he was never able to fully realize his museum.

The political and social situation in Brazil deteriorated in the 1960s, causing many Brazilians to seek refuge abroad. In 1964 General Humberto Castelo Branco became president following a military coup and instituted a racist and tyrannical dictatorship. When Nascimento received an invitation from the Fairfield Foundation (New York) to visit several black theatrical groups in the United States, he therefore eagerly accepted. In 1968 he joined numerous intellectuals, artists, and other individuals who left Brazil due to the repressive social conditions. Nascimento's initial plans for a temporary stay outside Brazil eventually developed into an extended period of self-imposed exile. He spent most of the period 1968–1981 in the United States, where he exhibited his artwork and lectured at institutions of higher education.

Painting Afro-Brazilian Religion in the United States

Although Nascimento had begun to paint just months before going into exile, reputable American museums and galleries demonstrated interest in his work soon after he came to the United States. In 1969 the Harlem Art Gallery, Yale University's Malcolm X House, and Columbia University's Crypt Gallery held exhibitions of his work. By the mid-1970s some of the museums and institutions with the strongest focus on black art in the country—including the Museum of the National Center for Afro-American Artists (1971), the Studio Museum of Harlem (1973), and Howard University (1975)—organized exhibitions of his paintings. By his own account, at the time he left Brazil in late 1968 he was fifty-four years old and had been marginalized his entire life.[5] However, in the United States he was met with respect and admiration for his artistic work and perspective.

From 1968 to 1981 Nascimento divided his time between painting and scholarly activities. He taught at the Yale School of Dramatic Arts in 1969 and participated in Wesleyan University's Seminar on Humanity in Revolt the following year. From 1971 to 1981 he taught at the State University of New York at Buffalo. In his first year there he founded the chair of African Culture in the New World at the school's Puerto Rican Studies and Research Center. While on leave in 1976–1977, he taught in the University of Ife's Department of African Languages and Literatures in Nigeria.

From the late 1960s to the mid-1990s Nascimento based the majority of his paintings on themes taken from the Afro-Brazilian religion of Candomblé, which draws its primary influence from the sacred beliefs and practices of the Yoruba people of West Africa.[6] Candomblé forms a deep spiritual and cultural bond between followers of Yoruba religion on both sides of the Atlantic, and is evidence of how enslaved Yoruba maintained their religious beliefs after arriving in Brazil. For Nascimento, this religion's various *orixás* (deities) provided a wealth of subject matter with their corresponding symbols, colors, and characteristics. He had explained already in 1969 why he chose to focus on religious themes in his paintings:

> I am not solely preoccupied with aesthetic forms, but of primary importance to me are the spiritual events of the Afro-Brazilian. The myths, the religious history, the fables, the ritualistic signs, the dance, the songs, the poetry, the colors, the rhythm, the worship. The spiritual vitality of the black race in my country, in spite of adverse conditions, in spite of political persecution, has always asserted itself in an astounding way.[7]

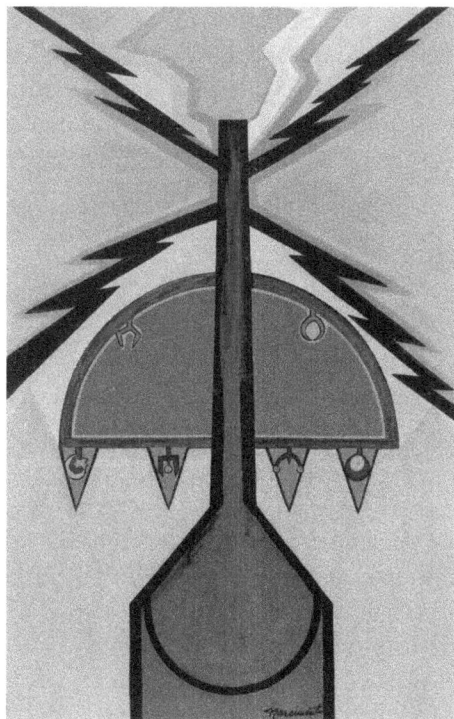

Fig. 8.1. Abdias Nascimento, *The Donors of Technology: Ogun and Shango*, 1975, acrylic on canvas, 60 x 40 in. (152 x 102 cm). IPEAFRO Collection, Rio de Janeiro.

The artist's exploration of Afro-Brazilian religious subjects was his way to counter what he saw as both the government's and the Catholic Church's dismissal of African-influenced culture and religion in Brazil.[8] His depictions of such subjects spoke to Afro-Brazilians' religious resistance in the face of centuries of repressive economic, political, and social conditions. His was a public testimony in the form of artworks that were made outside the spaces of the Afro-Brazilian religious communities. They were meant for secular viewing.

In the 1970s the vast majority of audiences in the United States would not have been familiar with the shapes and concepts found in Candomblé, although they would have been able to recognize—and perhaps identify with—the more universal forms in some of Nascimento's works. The 1975 painting *The Donors of Technology: Ogun and Shango* is a good example (fig. 8.1). As the god of war in the Candomblé pantheon of deities, Ogun is associated with metal and especially iron. By extension, humans who work with metal, including blacksmiths, are connected to Ogun. Nascimento references the deity's association with metal and those who work with metal in the small, upside-down wrenches and other tools in the center of the painting. Along with Ogun, the artist features Shango, the *orixá* of thunder and lightning. This temperamental deity punishes mortals by striking them down with his thunderbolts during storms.[9] These thunderbolts take the form of a double-headed ax, which is also Shango's liturgical instrument. Nascimento's use of the double-headed ax, thunderbolts, and "fiery" red color are all references to the deity of thunder and lightning. Both Ogun and Shango are strong gods whose powers have a profound effect on what happens in the secular realm. According to art historian Robin Poyner, Ogun is the "founder and champion of civilization" and, because of the association with metal, affects "every facet of civilization."[10] Blacksmiths and others who work with metal use fire's heat and flames to shape their materials. Nascimento pairs Ogun and Shango to create a visual explosion of bright, glowing color in this work. When these two deities' strengths combine, they create a powerful force for society. It is not humans who invent technology, but the gods who extend their abilities to humans and propel civilization forward.

Nascimento's decision to focus on Afro-Brazilian religious subjects in his artwork while he lived and exhibited abroad reveals his preoccupation with long-standing social issues in his home country rather than reaction to his immediate reality in the United States. In Brazil, in the decade after he left, academics began to pay greater attention to Candomblé. It was not necessarily an indication of increased respect or understanding, but rather intellectuals' folklorization of Afro-Brazilian religion that blossomed in the 1970s, a time when the region of Bahia was undergoing a process of cultural "re-Africanization."[11] This grassroots movement inspired broader interest in Candomblé regionally as well as a greater mixing of both whites and blacks participating in Afro-Brazilian religions.

Nascimento resented such folklorization of Afro-Brazilian religion, which he believed was part of a long-standing paternalistic attitude toward Afro-Brazilian culture that dated back to the early twentieth century.[12] He sought to slice through any romanticized airs in his own work by associating Candomblé's deities with living individuals. Already in 1969 he had explained why he took this approach:

> My Orixás aren't immobilized in time and space. They are dynamic; they inhabit Africa as well as Brazil and the United States. The Orixás, the spiritual and creative life of the black man, are not petrified in the dead centuries. They are forces of the present. They emerge in daily life and secular affairs; they are bequeathed

to us from history and the ancestors. The Orixás receive the names of living persons; they undertake the defense of heroes and martyrs, who are offered even today by the black race, as sacrifices in the holocaust of their search for liberty.[13]

In his own attempt at reverence and preservation, Nascimento combined the sacred with the secular, the past and the present, and, in the painting *The Donors of Technology: Ogun and Shango*, symbols that spoke of both the gods and the blue-collar laborer.

Nascimento, a Bird of a Different Feather?

As African Americans were gaining greater equality in the United States in the 1960s and 1970s, scholars, activists, and artists focused on Africa. Many African American artists and academics emphasized Africa as the cultural and artistic root of the majority of artwork created by black artists. Some African American artists, including Ben Jones and members of AfriCobra (African Commune of Bad Relevant Artists), a group cofounded in 1969 by Jeff Donaldson and Wadsworth Jarrell, used African or African-influenced themes and motifs in the creation of political or protest art associated with the Black Arts Movement, an approach called "Neo-Africanism" or "Afrocentricity."[14] African American artists and intellectuals looked outside the United States to nations within Africa and also countries with large African-descendent populations for aesthetic inspiration and information that would support their own social and political objectives. Nascimento's arrival in late 1968 was thus timely given these Americans' artistic and scholarly interests.

Although Nascimento's paintings provided black institutions and individuals with immediate tangible evidence of African influences in Afro-Brazilian art, his work did not fit the canon of African American political art as it was popular at that time. He did not respond to the history of social inequality and repression of African-influenced culture in Brazil by directly exposing and exploring social realities. Instead, he chose to depict African-influenced themes through abstract religious representations, which is not surprising considering Nascimento's previous cultural endeavors and lack of formal artistic training.

Unlike the United States, Brazil did not have a strong tradition of protest or political art. Nascimento's paintings from the 1970s indeed fell at the other end of the visual spectrum from overtly political works by African American artists such as David Hammons's *Injustice Case* (1970) or Betye Saar's *The Liberation of Aunt Jemima* (1972). Disjuncture in national politics between the two countries further fostered the divide. For example, Humberto Castelo Branco's repressive dictatorship (1964–1967) censored the television and press and hampered the country's cultural production.[15] Considering the possibility of repercussions, Brazilian artists had to be subtler with their criticism than artists from the United States. But despite the fact that Nascimento was living and painting outside Brazil and thus no longer subject to an unfavorable cultural climate, he did not become more direct in his artwork. His style of artistic expression during this decade consequently requires deeper consideration of his continued links to international black movements and philosophies that could be used in the fight against racial inequality in his homeland.

Nascimento's work from the 1970s was ideologically and, to some extent, also visually closer to artwork of the Ecole de Dakar (Dakar School) artists in Senegal in the 1960s and 1970s than it was to much African American artwork from the same decades. As president of Senegal, Léopold Senghor had instituted a national arts curriculum that was strongly guided by Négritude.[16] Art historian Elizabeth Harney has clarified that, artistically speaking, Négritude was, in fact, more of a philosophy or theme than a set of aesthetics or definitive style for the Senegalese artists; it therefore allowed for individual expression.[17] However, it did have the overarching goal of emphasizing African traditions and subjects over European ones. Nascimento shared this aim, a connection that can be traced to his previous involvement with Négritude in Brazil and the fact that he was an activist for Afro-Brazilian people and culture long before he began producing artwork.

In spite of Nascimento's familiarity with the beliefs and some of the key figures of Candomblé, his works were, to an extent, attempts at aesthetic preservation or historical reference made from the viewpoint of an outsider, as he never underwent religious initiation. Painting Afro-Brazilian sacred subjects as a person familiar with, albeit not initiated into, the religion in question, he was not altogether different from the Senegalese artists whom art historian Sidney Kasfir perceived culturally distanced from the subjects that they depicted under the Négritudist aesthetic program.[18] For the Senegalese artists working under Senghor as well as for Nascimento, celebrating the "tradition" of African and African-influenced aesthetics trumped independent realities. Moreover, both Nascimento and the Senegalese artists chose "foreign" art forms as their bases to represent African-related themes and subject matter, for easel painting is not an art form intrinsic to Candomblé—just as the monumental wall tapestries and paintings on canvas, two art forms associated with the Dakar School, were not indigenous to Senegalese artistic production.[19]

Despite the iconographic and aesthetic differences between Nascimento's production and that of African American artists, the Brazilian's self-association with African artistic expression and production was similar to that of many black artists in the United States in the 1970s. There were, of course, exceptions. In 1974 Nascimento participated in *Kindred Spirits: An African Diaspora*, an exhibition and seminar organized by the Museum of the National Center of Afro-American Artists and the Department of Afro-American Studies at Harvard University. Among the well-known African American artists whose work was included in the show were Romare Bearden, Ernest Chichlow, Charles Searles, and Charles White.

Nascimento, White, and Nigerian artist Z. K. Olorumtoba spoke in a panel discussion about points that the artists believed to be important for the vitality of the visual arts relative to black cultures. Charles White indicated that he did not believe in an umbrella category of "black art" that extended beyond the work of black Africans on the African continent to also encompass production by black artists across the African Diaspora. Four years earlier, he had already explained why he believed the label "black art" did not apply to work by African-descendent individuals living outside Africa. Speaking about "black art" from across the Diaspora, he stated, "There is no such thing. There is a black artist. There is African art, which is a style, a certain way of doing. It has an identity and is indigenous to a continent and its peoples."[20] Nascimento disagreed with White's views on black art and did not hesitate to refute his ideas during the panel discussion. More than thirty years later, Nascimento still believed that White was wrong and recalled about the incident, "I had to fight him to show that he was mistaken."[21] At the time of the panel, it was difficult for Nascimento to accept that a fellow African-descendent artist construed black art as exclusively produced by artists from the African continent and not also by artists from across the African Diaspora. After all, Nascimento knew that the Afro-Brazilian religious subject matter that he and other Brazilian artists depicted could be viewed as an extension of black art produced by Africans and, as was clear in Brazil, was quite distinct from Brazilian mainstream (read white, "European-influenced") art.

While Nascimento may have been firm about his position with regard to black art, in private he struggled over how to reconcile his artistic production with the diversity of the audiences he reached. For example, after a decade in the United States, Nascimento not only enjoyed exhibiting his paintings in the "ghettos" of the United States in the spirit of "brotherhood" and "sisterhood" but also showed his works in "the ultra white universities of Yale, Harvard, and Tulane," among others.[22] Back in Brazil, he himself had called attention to the ambiguous nature of his Museum of Black Art's collection because it also included works by white artists; moreover, he had criticized the TEN members for directing themselves toward the traditional theater audience—the white upper class. Nascimento thought that it was contradictory to employ the "language" and financial support of the same part of the population that had traditionally "exploited the blacks economically."[23] Once he had arrived in the United States, however, the white elite segment of the population also formed a good part of his audience.

A Cultural Ambassador Gone Bad

Nascimento's experiences in the United States added another dimension to the way in which he viewed the black Brazilian struggle within the wider international movements for racial equality. He met a variety of people while abroad, from the poet Amiri Baraka (formerly LeRoi Jones) to the militants in the Black Panthers.[24] Whereas Nascimento had once simply quoted international figures involved in black liberation movements, he now found himself face-to-face with key individuals who were making change happen. As a result, Nascimento developed a more refined perspective from which to contrast the social status of African descendants in the United States and Brazil.

In order to make people more aware of the social discrepancies between blacks in the United States and Brazil and to turn indifference into action, Nascimento often highlighted incongruities for his respective audiences. When he returned to Brazil briefly in 1975 to promote an exhibition of his paintings, he used the Brazilian press as a platform to point out the differences between the types of jobs that black Americans and black Brazilians held in the workforce.[25] While in the United States, in turn, he tried to educate African Americans about the comparatively greater repression and racism Afro-Brazilians faced in the 1970s. He published several articles in American scholarly journals and, together with his wife, Elisa Larkin Nascimento, served as guest editor for a special issue of the *Journal of Black Studies* focusing on the Afro-Brazilian experience.[26] Nascimento also introduced the American public to Candomblé and emphasized the vitality of African-influenced culture in Brazil.[27] His focus on differences in addition to similarities between populations of African descent in the United States and Brazil was part of his underlying objective to turn into action what he believed was Americans' and Brazilians' apathy and lack of awareness of each other. Nascimento embraced the idea of a more cohesive, international African-descendent brotherhood and sisterhood joined by racial and political awareness.

Foreshadowing his later work in politics, Nascimento became somewhat of an unofficial ambassador for Afro-Brazilian culture to the United States. He realized that by living in the United States, he could foster cultural exchange between black populations in both countries. In several articles, Brazilian newspaper journalists indeed recognized his role as an educator and disseminator of cultural information abroad.[28] For Nascimento, it was the beginning of what would become long-term connections and fruitful exchange with African and African American artists and intellectuals in the United States, including Jeff Donaldson, Anani Dzidzienyo, Edmund Barry Gaither, Molefi K. Asante, Maulana Ron Karenga, and James Early.

Some Brazilian officials and intellectuals believed Nascimento's contact with African Americans could only have negative results because Nascimento's social views were more in keeping with the American approach toward recognizing social diversity than with the Brazilian policy of promoting a unified cultural nationalism. Much to the Brazilian government's chagrin, at the second World Black and African Festival of Arts and Culture (FESTAC II) in Lagos, Nigeria, in 1977, Nascimento publicly declared that Brazil was not a country characterized by harmonious racial relations, as the Brazilian government wanted the world to believe, but that it was a country plagued by racism. Despite the fact that Nascimento had firmly established his political views well before going to the United States, Brazilian officials pinpointed American society and certain African Americans as the negative source of influence behind what they perceived to be Nascimento's ill-mannered behavior at FESTAC II. In a report to the Ministry of Education and Culture, Gumercindo Rocha Dorea, one of the official Brazilian delegates to the festival, claimed that African American activist Maulana Ron Karenga had instructed Nascimento to criticize the Brazilian government.[29] Dorea believed that Nascimento had adopted American racial politics, evidenced by what he called Nascimento's use of a "characteristically radical leftist North-American language . . . that of 'the whites cannot hold the black Brazilians back from developing and living with dignity, [and] respecting their African roots.'"[30] Dorea specifically associated this type of public protest with African Americans even though Nascimento was a visiting scholar in Nigeria at the time of FESTAC II (rather than coming over from the United States for this purpose). Back in 1968, when Nascimento arrived in the United States, blacks had gained some measure of social equality through the civil rights movement. In Brazil, greater acceptance of Afro-Brazilian society and culture was just beginning to develop in the 1970s. It was consequently easy to associate Nascimento's actions with American so-called liberal politics.

After nearly a decade of concentrating on his artistic and academic work in the United States, from the late 1970s onward Nascimento increasingly focused on the organized black movement in Brazil and its place in the wider movement of Pan-Africanism. As the Brazilian government, the Catholic

Church, and the majority of white Brazilians continued to marginalize the Afro-Brazilian population and culture, Nascimento grew gradually more frustrated with Brazil's racial inequality and became more pointed in his criticism. Hence, while still based in the United States, the artist and activist made a brief visit to Brazil in July 1978 to help found the Movimento Negro Unificado (MNU), or Unified Black Movement.[31] In his book *O Quilombismo* (1980), Nascimento outlined his political and social beliefs, which he linked to Pan-Africanism.[32] He became more militant in his work with this latest organized black movement in Brazil than he had been with the earlier Brazilian Black Front or TEN.

Although Nascimento employed various means to educate the international community about Afro-Brazilian art, culture, and society during the time he spent in exile, his dedication to the fight for better social and economic conditions for Brazil's African descendants ultimately led him back there in 1981. Upon his return, the artist, together with his wife, Elisa, created the Instituto de Pesquisas e Estudos Afro-Brasileiros (IPEAFRO), or the Afro-Brazilian Studies and Research Institute. He also acted upon his discontent over racial inequality in Brazil by entering into national politics with the specific aim of representing the Afro-Brazilian population's interests. In 1983 he became Brazil's first Afro-Brazilian congressman. A decade after he returned to his home country, Nascimento was appointed Rio de Janeiro's state secretary for the new State Secretariat for the Defense and Promotion of Afro-Brazilian Peoples.[33] It was an apt position for the activist and gave him an official title for work that he had been performing for decades.

Eshu: A Brazilian Politician at the Crossroads

Nascimento's artistic production tapered after the late 1970s, when he began to devote himself to a greater variety of projects. After returning to Brazil, his involvement in IPEAFRO and political responsibilities left less time for painting. Nascimento was also occupied with participating in numerous international gatherings as a part of his agenda to protect and promote awareness of Afro-Brazilian history and culture, and he increased his contact with groups and institutions that focused on Africa and African descendants. Besides his trips to Africa, he returned to the United States in 1990 to spend a year as a visiting scholar in the Department of African-American Studies at Temple University in Philadelphia.

Immediately prior to Nascimento's involvement in politics and again between his terms as a congressman (1983–1986) and senator (1991,1997–1999),

Fig. 8.2. Abdias Nascimento, *Pade for Eshu*, 1988,
acrylic on canvas, 59 x 39 in. (150 x 100 cm).
IPEAFRO Collection, Rio de Janeiro.

there was a brief rise in his artistic production that, although still centered on Candomblé subject matter, had a more intimate focus. In comparison with his previous production, this small body of paintings reflected the greater personal significance that his artwork held for him in relation to his own life's journey. From the time he had begun to paint in the late 1960s through the 1970s, the artist had depicted various deities and symbols from the pantheon of *orixás*. By contrast, in the 1980s Nascimento focused on Eshu, the deity of the crossroads between the mortal and immortal spheres.

Eshu plays a fundamental role in communication between humans and gods. In the painting *Padê for Eshu* (1988), Nascimento introduced the theme of communication through references to Eshu and *jogo de búzios* (cowrie divination) (fig. 8.2). In this type of divination, which links Candomblé practices with Yoruba religion in West Africa, a diviner tosses cowrie shells onto a wooden divination tray and then interprets the pattern in which the shells fall.[34] Through this interpretation, an answer to the particular question or problem becomes identifiable. The circular shape in the middle of

Nascimento's painting is visually similar to the round tray used in the divination practice. However, Nascimento breaks with the standard position of a representation of Eshu along the edge of the tray, and instead moves Eshu to the middle. In so doing, he brings the viewer face-to-face with this religious being. Nascimento completes the composition by juxtaposing the circular form with a patterned red and black background, the colors associated with this deity. Although the Afro-Brazilian religious theme is predominant in this painting, Nascimento has also included non-Candomblé elements in the work. The "face" of Eshu consists of two Egyptian eyes and an ankh, the ancient Egyptian hieroglyph meaning life, for the mouth. With such human features, the deity appears to be ready and able to communicate its message to the audience.

Nascimento's *Padê for Eshu* is one of several paintings he did of this subject, and is one form of artistic offering he made to the deity of the crossroads. He not only turned his attention to Eshu in his painting but also sought protection and strength in return for his devotion in his written *Padê for Freedomfighter Eshu*.[35] Because Eshu holds such an important position in the pantheon of *orixás*, all ceremonies must begin with a *padê* (offering or salute) to Eshu.[36] The paintings of the god of the crossroads from the 1980s can be understood as part of Nascimento's larger oeuvre, which he created to honor the various *orixás* of Candomblé through representation of their forms and colors. Different from the majority of his artworks, however, these pieces can also be understood as individual offerings made specifically to Eshu—much as religious initiates are required to make offerings of food and animals to the various *orixás*.

Abdias Nascimento: Pan-Africanist

While Nascimento, who had been active in the Pan-Africanist movement since the 1970s, linked his own political and social ideology, *quilombismo*, to Pan-Africanist objectives, he did not take what can be considered a Pan-Africanist artistic approach to his painting until the 1990s. Reminiscent of some African American artwork from the 1970s that included a panoply of African artistic forms, Nascimento mixed Afro-Brazilian with African elements as an artistic approach toward a universal African cultural or symbol bank from which he could draw in his final phase of production.

In *Obatalá Apis Veve* (1993), Nascimento created a visual pastiche of symbols and forms taken from diverse cultures from the African continent and Diaspora (fig. 8.3) and juxtaposes elements from three African and

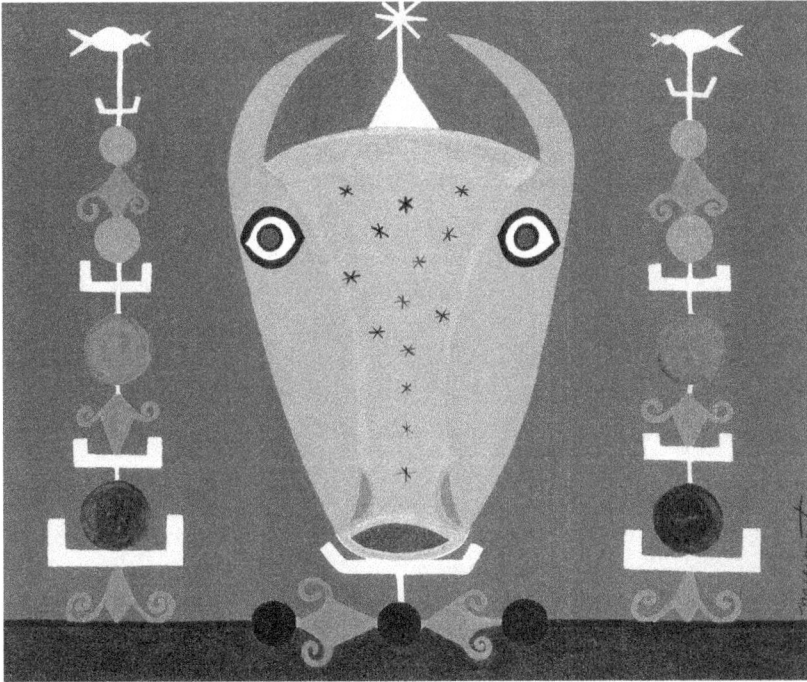

Fig. 8.3. Abdias Nascimento, *Obatala Apis Veve*, 1993, acrylic on canvas, 16 x 20 in. (40 x 50 cm). IPEAFRO Collection, Rio de Janeiro.

African-influenced religions. In the Afro-Brazilian religion Candomblé, Obatalá is a hermaphrodite god associated with creation and procreation.[37] Apis is the sacred bull or bull deity from Egyptian mythology. In Haiti, in turn, members of the Vodou religion create *veve* (sacred drawings) on the floor in chalk, which are used in association and communication with each deity in the Vodou religious pantheon.[38] The same graphic *veve* forms are used in the *drapo* (sacred flags) that are created for the various deities.[39]

Nascimento's painting resembles such sacred flags in its composition. He also decorates the animal's face with small, star-shaped Vodou *pwen* (power points). Along the sides and below the bull deity, Nascimento included just the tips of crosses. This type of tip or arrow that curls back is a common element in Haitian artwork, particularly metal crosses.[40] The intersection of two lines or the cross motif is associated with the idea of the four moments of the sun and the cyclical nature of life, a set of beliefs associated with the Kongo peoples of West-Central Africa.[41] All of these diverse elements from different cultures highlight the connection between religion and the cycle of life. Just as he did in *Padê for Eshu*, Nascimento once again positioned the deity face-to-face with the viewer (figs. 8.2 and 8.3). Humans and god contemplate each other, forming a connection across the line that delineates the sacred and the secular realms.

By the time Nascimento entered into his final phase of production, he was free from having to prove that Afro-Brazilian art indeed existed, and he could therefore shift his focus to demonstrating its place within the larger universe of African and Diasporic cultures. His incorporation of a wider range of African and Diasporic references and symbols in his artwork from the 1990s mirrors the growth of his political and cultural involvement and contact with a greater number of African peoples and countries than earlier in his artistic career, including the year he spent back in the United States working alongside his friend Molefi K. Asante, a scholar of Afrocentrism at Temple University, shortly before he painted *Obatalá Apis Veve*. In juxtaposing African symbols from a variety of cultures in a single painting, Nascimento aligned himself and his work with other African peoples and forms of expression.

Nascimento's use of African elements in his works from the 1990s further highlights how his production reflected his links to national and international black movements and ideologies. Similarly, some African American artists incorporated African, and specifically Egyptian, signs in their works in the 1960s and 1970s as a display of Pan-Africanist solidarity. Curator Edmund Barry Gaither in particular notes the frequent use of "African or nationalist symbols, such as the 'ankh'" in the works by the AfriCobra artists from the late 1960s onward.[42] Artists such as Ben Jones and Jeff Donaldson demonstrated their affiliation with Africa in their work from the 1970s when the Pan-Africanist movement experienced renewed international interest. Although Nascimento was in the United States during that decade, he continued to focus on Afro-Brazilian religious themes and forms. By the time Nascimento linked himself with Pan-Africanism artistically and adopted an "Afro-centric" artistic approach in the 1990s, it was no longer a contemporary tendency for African Americans. Many black American artists had meanwhile moved on to participate in other international artistic trends and movements such as post-modernism and performance art. Though Nascimento's production was not reflective of avant-garde expression, it remained significant for its symbolic plastic language based on African-influenced forms, colors, and subjects.

Conclusion

Following his return to Brazil in the early 1980s, Nascimento's work as a politician and activist overshadowed his earlier theatrical and artistic career.

Whether as an actor, politician, or artist, however, he was an ardent spokesman and advocate for Afro-Brazilians through his words and art. In 2001 he participated in the third World Conference against Racism in Durban, South Africa, and in 2004 UNESCO honored him with the Toussaint L'Ouverture prize. After leaving his post as a senator, Nascimento remained involved in Brazilian politics and was known nationally and internationally foremost for his lifelong dedication to the protection and preservation of Afro-Brazilian culture and heritage.

While Nascimento contributed to the advancement of the Afro-Brazilian population in several areas, there is still much to learn about the role that he and his work played in increasing awareness and understanding of twentieth-century (Afro-)artistic production from Brazil and across the African Diaspora. His encounter with Charles White and his contact with African American artists and institutions in the 1970s and 1980s exemplified his participation in international discussions and awareness of arts from the African Diaspora. Both Nascimento's words and paintings attest to his efforts to use his art as a demonstration of cultural resistance not only for black movements in Brazil but across the globe. His artwork was a reflection of his involvement in national and international movements, besides being a visual record of his own journey through life in paint.

Notes

1. Nascimento, *O Sortilégio da cor*, 311.

2. Nascimento, "Open Letter," 208–218.

3. Nascimento, "Abdias do Nascimento," 42; Nascimento and Nascimento, *Africans in Brazil*, 40–41.

4. Correio da Manhã, "Museu Negro recebido com entusiasmo."

5. Nascimento, "Abdias do Nascimento," 49.

6. See Omari-Tunkara, *Manipulating the Sacred*.

7. Nascimento, *Orixás*, 6.

8. Nascimento, "Persecuted Persistence of African Culture," 93–100; Nascimento, "Syncretism or Folklorization?," 101–107.

9. Poyner, "Yoruba and the Fon," 253.

10. Ibid., 251.

11. Sansone, *From Africa to Afro*, 9–10; Sansone, *Negritude sem etnicidade*, 94.

12. Nascimento, "Bastardization of Afro-Brazilian Culture," 109–118.

13. Nascimento, *Orixás*, 6.

14. Gaither, *Afro-American Artists*; Patton, *African-American Art*; Donaldson, "AfriCobra and TransAtlantic Connections," 249–251.

15. Skidmore, *Brazil*, 157.

16. Harney, "Ecole de Dakar," 12–31, 88.

17. Harney, *In Senghor's Shadow*, 10.

18. Kasfir, *Contemporary African Art*, 168.

19. Though tapestry weaving was not a Senegalese tradition, Senghor publicly linked the origins of tapestry production to ancient Egypt, thereby providing it with "an African pedigree." Ibid., 170.

20. Charles White, interview by James Hatch and Camille Billops, December 21, 1970, Altadena, Calif., quoted in Bearden and Henderson, *History of African-American Artists*, 417.

21. Abdias Nascimento, interview by author, November 29, 2005, Rio de Janeiro.

22. Nascimento, "Abdias do Nascimento," 51.

23. Ibid., 43.

24. Nascimento and Nascimento, "Reflexões sobre o Movimento Negro no Brasil," 217.

25. "Na pintura a busca de suas raízes," *Jornal do Brasil*, June 5, 1975.

26. Nascimento, "Quilombismo," 141–178.

27. Nascimento, "African Culture in Brazilian Art," 389–422.

28. "Abdias do Nascimento—a visita de um artista afro-brasileiro ao seu país"; "Mostra de Abdias do Nascimento."

29. Olinto, *Brasileiros na África*, 302. Ron Everett, later known as Maulana Ron Karenga, is a well-known African American author and activist who, among other things, created a black nationalist organization called the U.S. in the 1960s and the African American holiday Kwanzaa.

30. Ibid.

31. Nascimento and Nascimento, "Reflexões sobre o Movimento Negro," 219.

32. Nascimento's choice of the term "*quilombismo*" linked contemporary racial inequality with the country's history of slavery and resistance. The *quilombos* were maroon slave societies, and, according to Nascimento, he extracted the "basic social principles upon which the quilombos operated" and modernized them for use in the twentieth-century fight against inequality in Brazil. Nascimento, *O Quilombismo documentos*, 16.

33. Nascimento, *Orixás*, 169; Nascimento and Nascimento, *Exposição Abdias Nascimento*, 44.

34. Thompson, *Flash of the Spirit*, 18–33, 37–40; Thompson, *Face of the Gods*, 174–180.

35. Nascimento, *Orixás*, 13, 15, 17–18.

36. Omari-Tunkara, *Manipulating the Sacred*, 102; Verger, *Orixás*, 79.

37. Thompson, *Flash of the Spirit*, 11.

38. Ibid., 188–191.

39. Polk, "Sacred Banners," 325–347.

40. Morris, "Style of His Hand," 383–395.

41. Thompson, *Flash of the Spirit*, 108–116.

42. Gaither, "Heritage Reclaimed," 27.

Bibliography

"Abdias do Nascimento—a visita de um artista afro-brasileiro ao seu país." *O Globo*, June 9, 1975.

Bearden, Romare, and Harry Henderson. *A History of African-American Artists: From 1792 to the Present*. New York: Pantheon Books, 1993.

Correio da Manhã. "Museu Negro recebido com entusiasmo." February 3, 1968.

Donaldson, Jeff. "AfriCobra and TransAtlantic Connections." In *Seven Stories about Modern Art in Africa*, ed. Clementine Deliss and Jane Havell, 249–251. London: Whitechapel Art Gallery, 1995.

Gaither, Edmund Barry. *Afro-American Artists: New York and Boston*. Boston: Museum School, 1970.

———. "Heritage Reclaimed: An Historical Perspective and Chronology." In *Black Art: Ancestral Legacy: The African Impulse in African American Art*, ed. Dallas Museum of Art, 17–34. Dallas: Dallas Museum of Art; distributed by Abrams, New York, 1989.

Harney, Elizabeth. "The Ecole de Dakar: Pan-Africanism in Paint and Textile." *African Arts* 35.3 (2002): 12–31, 88.

———. *In Senghor's Shadow: Art, Politics, and the Avant-Garde in Senegal, 1960–1995*. Durham, N.C.: Duke University Press, 2004.

Kasfir, Sidney. *Contemporary African Art*. London: Thames & Hudson, 2000.

Morris, Randall. "The Style of His Hand: The Iron Art of Georges Liautaud." In *Sacred Arts of Haitian Vodou*, ed. Donald J. Cosentino, 383–395. Los Angeles: UCLA Fowler Museum of Cultural History, 1995.

"Mostra de Abdias do Nascimento." *A Gazeta*, July 7, 1975.

"Na pintura a busca de suas raízes." *Jornal do Brasil*, June 5, 1975.

Nascimento, Abdias. "Abdias do Nascimento." In *Memórias do exílio, Brasil, 1964–19??: Obra coletiva*, ed. Pedro Celso Uchôa Cavalcanti and Jovelino Ramos, 23–52. São Paulo: Editorae Livraria Livramento, 1978.

———. "African Culture in Brazilian Art." *Journal of Black Studies* 8.4 (1978): 389–422.

———. "An Open Letter to the 1st World Festival of Negro Arts." *Présence Africaine* 30.58 (1966): 208–218.

———. *O Quilombismo documentos de uma militância Pan-Africanista*. Petrópolis, Brazil: Vozes, 1980.

———. *The Orixás: Afro-Brazilian Paintings and Text*. Middleton, Conn.: Malcolm X House (Afro American Institute), Wesleyan University, 1969.

———. *Orixás: Os deuses vivos da África Orishas: The Living Gods of Africa in Brazil*. Rio de Janeiro: Instituto de Pesquisas e Estudos Afro Brasileiro (IPEAFRO)/Afrodiaspora, 1995.

———. "Quilombismo: An Afro-Brazilian Political Alternative." *Journal of Black Studies* 11.2 (1980): 141–178.

———. "Racial Democracy." In *Brazil: Myth or Reality?* 2nd ed. Trans. Elisa Larkin Nascimento. Ibaden: Sketch Publishing, 1977.

Nascimento, Abdias, and Elisa Larkin Nascimento. *Africans in Brazil: A Pan-African Perspective*. Trenton, N.J.: Africa World Press, 1992.

———. *Exposição Abdias Nascimento: 90 anos memória viva: Arquivo Nacional, 16 de novembro de 2004 a 30 de janeiro de 2005*. Rio de Janeiro: IPEAFRO, 2004.

———. "Reflexões sobre o Movimento Negro no Brasil, 1938–1997." In *Tirando a máscara: Ensaios sobre o racismo no Brasil*, ed. Antônio Sérgio Guimarães and Lynn Huntley, 203–235. São Paulo: Paz e Terra, 2000.

Nascimento, Elisa Larkin. *O Sortilégio da cor: Identidade, raça e gênero no Brasil*. São Paulo: Selo Negro Edições, 2003.

Olinto, Antônio. *Brasileiros na África*. 2nd ed. São Paulo: Edições GRD, 1980.

Omari-Tunkara, Mikelle Smith. *Manipulating the Sacred: Yoruba Art, Ritual, and Resistance in Brazilian Candomblé*. Detroit: Wayne State University Press, 2005.

Patton, Sharon F. *African-American Art*. New York: Oxford University Press, 1998.

Polk, Patrick. "Sacred Banners and the Divine Cavalry Charge." In *Sacred Arts of Haitian Vodou*, ed. Donald J. Cosentino, 325–347. Los Angeles: UCLA Fowler Museum of Cultural History, 1995.

Poyner, Robin. "The Yoruba and the Fon." In *A History of Art in Africa*, ed. by Monica Blackmun Visonà, 228–273, 532–533. Upper Saddle River, N.J.: Pearson/Prentice Hall, 2001.

Sansone, Livio. *From Africa to Afro: Use and Abuse of Africa in Brazil*. Amsterdam, Dakar: SEPHIS; Codesria, 1999.

———. *Negritude sem etnicidade: O local e o global nas relações raciais e na produção cultural negra do Brasil*. Trans. Vera Ribeiro. Salvador, Brazil: Pallas, 2003.

Skidmore, Thomas E. *Brazil: Five Centuries of Change*. 2nd ed. New York: Oxford University Press, 2010.

Thompson, Robert Farris. *Face of the Gods: Art and Altars of Africa and the African Americas*. New York: Museum for African Art, 1993.

———. *Flash of the Spirit: African and Afro-American Art and Philosophy*. New York: Random House, 1983.

Verger, Pierre. *Orixás: Deuses iorubás na África e no Novo Mundo*. Salvador, Brazil: Editora Corrupio Comércio, 1981.

"Of Remarkable Omens in My Favour"

Olaudah Equiano, Two Identities, and the
Cultivation of a Literary Economic Exchange

Edward L. Robinson Jr.

Writing the Emerging Black Atlantic

For an aspiring writer of African descent, the end of the eighteenth century marked a favorable period of remarkable literary opportunity, sociopolitical craftiness, and religious collaboration.[1] *The Interesting Narrative of the Life of Olaudah Equiano, or Gustavus Vassa, The African, Written by Himself* (1789) was part of a growing genre of black autobiographies designed to write people of African descent into the existing world order emerging in the modern Atlantic communities of the Western Hemisphere.[2] Equiano was at the top of this burgeoning group of black writers, whose experiences and awareness of Europe and America marked the flowering of a black literary tradition that stretched across the Atlantic seaboard. His Middle Passage experience at an early age and upbringing on merchant boats and warships provided him a prime position as witness, victim, and participator of an emerging Euro-American capitalist class responsible for the displacement of millions of poor Europeans and Africans to the many shores of North and South America.[3]

It is little wonder, then, that Equiano's *Interesting Narrative* represented a keen awareness of the sociopolitical and economic landscapes of the Atlantic. On the coast of Africa, he witnessed the market exchange of African bodies as he was disconnected from his African origins and turned into a slave. On the coasts of North and South America, he witnessed social revolutions and market exchanges that did not extend to him or his fellow Africans. Although Equiano adapted to the refinements of English society, such as religious piety and restraint, he continued to respond to the injustices and social plights of his fellow Afro-British and espoused economic opportunities for his ancestral Africa. At first glance, *The Interesting Narrative* appears as an African roadmap to modern civility and progress as told through an African, himself. However, *The Interesting Narrative* also reveals a careful cultivation of two communities, African and European, in which he experiences a degree of alienation from both.

Within the emerging Black Atlantic, people of African descent were converging around principles of religious piety, universal freedom of all humankind, and a revision of an African identity. Historian James Sidbury writes, "During the second half of the eighteenth century a group of African-descended authors and activists living in England and America began to present themselves as 'African' despite the negative connotations that term carried in many whites' minds."[4] Black communities across the seaboard sought to rewrite an ancestral past out of the denigration and absence constructed by Enlightenment philosophers.[5] Equiano, who came of age on the Atlantic seas, would have had to reconfigure his own image within the popular notions espoused by fellow emerging Africans of the period.

Colonial Africans in America and Europe had built social organizations and benevolent societies focused on the welfare and issues of black people, using Africa as a central tenet of self-identification.[6] Along with the institutionalization of African-titled organizations, there was a flowering of black poets and writers at the end of the eighteenth century who were also reconstructing Africa in their texts.[7] Often overlooked in the critique of *The Interesting Narrative* is Equiano's displacement from his African community and his careful cultivation of African issues on both sides of the Atlantic. In metropolitan London, a few exceptional West Africans had already experienced notoriety as respected and renowned lawyers, linguists, and musicians.[8] In contrast, at a time when name recognition garnered prestige and social capital, Equiano was not a visitor from a royal African family but a traveler who had spent his formative years at sea.

Therefore *The Interesting Narrative* is an ingenious cultivation of African and European communities. For Equiano, the narrative stands as a careful negotiation of the complexities that were critical in cultivating sociopolitical and economic capital in the commercial Atlantic. Africa had a major source of labor, and Europe held valuable resources needed in developing modern Africa. In cultivating his authenticity as both Equiano and Vassa, the narrator authorizes an African past needed in developing the support of a growing international black community whose poetry, reflections, and religious writings were gaining notoriety while simultaneously authorizing the cultural capital found in his European name and Christian values (referencing a celebrated Swedish noble who would later become King Gustav I). Situated between conflicting cultures, he could represent the ideals and values of both communities and act as an essential guide and speaker of both worlds.

Creating the African

Although Peter Linebaugh and Marcus Rediker argue that seamen were more integrated and promoted individual talents rather than racial differences, Equiano rarely spoke of any camaraderie with fellow Africans on his sea adventures.[9] In his narrative, however, he did speak randomly of his experiences as an overseer and his ability to choose Africans amenable to his missionary hopes of creating a benevolent plantation.[10] Thus Equiano would have had a social and political need to reconnect himself to the Afro-Atlantic community ethnically and emotionally as he developed his narrative. The colonial historian, John W. Sweet, writes that Africans were "constantly vulnerable to social dislocation and to being cut off from community ties that defined African conceptions of 'selfhood' and freedom, conceptions that stood in sharp contrast to emerging European ideas of enlightened individualism."[11] Sea travelers, such as Equiano, disseminated information across the Atlantic seaboard, including happenings within black communities. Nevertheless, his narrative shows that he considered his early experiences as "favored" over most of the experiences and fortunes of fellow Africans.

Beginning his narrative with his village-based kinship ties and familial relationships with his mother and sister, Equiano, from the onset, was forging a Diasporic connection to a greater African community. He identified the Igbo as his ancestral home and birthplace by discussing the ethnic community's cultivation methods, labor, and religious practices. Equiano contended that his native kingdom of Benin and his birthplace of Eboe and community of Essaka were a great distance from the capital and the seacoast, which he also argued was largely untouched by Europeans and slave traders. He wrote, "for I had never heard of white men or Europeans, nor of the sea; and our subjection to the king of Benin was little more than nominal; for every transaction of the government, as far as my slender observation extended, was conducted by the chiefs or elders of the place."[12] In Equiano's rendering of his birthplace as free from European control, he could suggest that his ancestral community's smooth and logical governance made him the logical candidate to act as a liaison and prophet between two continents' issues that he critiques throughout the narrative.

For example, Equiano laid claim to his father's high social position as Embrenche in the Igbo community as his natural birthright. He noted, "I had

seen it conferred on one of my brothers, and I was also *destined* to receive it
by my parents. Those Embrenche, or chief men, decided disputes and pun-
ished crimes, for which purpose they always assembled together."[13] Not only
did Equiano assert an African identity, but he also claimed ancestral rights
and traditional ascendancy of family occupations as his legitimate nomination as representative and titleholder of African aristocracy. Literary scholar
Katalin Orban argues that Equiano visualized an ancestral past that comple-
mented his desired authority in the present. She contends:

> Equiano's narrative creatively reconstructs the past. He projects a potential for
> his present accomplishments back into the past, thereby making the past accept-
> able for the present on the present's terms. This he needs to do in order to be able
> to incorporate his African past into his present self and in order to speak for his
> African brethren as a public spokesman.[14]

Brandishing an African past would elevate him along with his fellow Africans.
Recalling an authentic Ibo past made Equiano one of them.

   Writing Africa into his autobiographical past meant that he was also connecting himself to his generation of black writers who were following the
social and literary imperatives of African communities in North America and
London. Afro-Atlantic writers such as Ignatius Sancho, James Albert Ukaw-
saw, Phillis Wheatley, and Quobna Ottobah Cugoano were building a consensus around the themes of religious discovery and freedom, a Middle Passage
memory, and antislavery sentiment. Literary critic Henry Louis Gates Jr.
writes, "Whereas black writers most certainly revise texts in the Western tradition, they often seek to do so 'authentically,' with a black difference, a compelling sense of difference based on the black vernacular."[15] Early black writers
wrote within the literary confines of a white public sphere but also wrote to
revise each other's text with cultural and religious imperatives critical to their
own personal Atlantic experiences. Equiano was revising the existing Black
Atlantic texts with his own version and vision of an ancestral Africa.

   Writing Africa into the black literary tradition had a genesis traced to
London. One of the first prominent Afro-British writers, Ignatius Sancho
(1729–1780) was a successful grocery store owner in Westminster—the heart
of enterprising London. He was a lover of literature, music, and theater, and
his writings in *Letters of the Late Ignatius Sancho, An African* (1782), published
posthumously, reveal the trajectory of Africa as a social identifier of black
identity. Sancho was a rare English citizen with rights as a voter. His letters
show him to have been a critical commentator on social and political events
in England and the plight of Africans.[16] Whenever he cited the struggles and

concerns of Africans, he always claimed a shared identity and identification to Africa. In a letter to the Reverend Sterne (July 1766), Sancho made a plea for the acknowledgment of his fellow Africans. He wrote, "Dear Sir think in me you behold the uplifted hands of thousands of my brother Moors."[17] Also, in an attempt to compare the similarities of Irishmen being unfairly conscripted as seamen, Sancho used irony to signify to the readers of the *General Advertiser* that his ancestral history shared a similar fate to that of the Irishmen. He asserted "that the honoured name of England may be rescued from the scandalous censure of man-stealing, and from the ingratitude also of letting their preservers perish in the time of peace!"[18] Sancho signs his name as "AFRICANUS," expressing a shared plight with the Irish by signifying on his own African history as scandalous behavior at the hands of his residing country. Similar to Sancho and the arrival of Phillis Wheatley to London, Equiano followed this pattern in his letter to the queen with the signature of "The Oppressed Ethiopian."[19]

Phillis Wheatley, the American poet who arrived in London to oversee the publication of her collection of poetry titled *Poems on Various Subjects, Religious and Moral* (1773), highlighted a transnational movement of early black writers coalescing around similar literary strategies. An enslaved African American before her arrival in London, Wheatley had gained prominence with her selection of American poetic eulogies of famous clergymen and generals. Her arrival in London foresaw a change in literary strategies that included the fall and redemption of Africa through the Exodus biblical story, Ethiopia as African ethnic identification, and Middle Passage subjectivity within her revised edition of poems.

For example, Wheatley trumpeted her newfound subjectivity and Middle Passage memory in her poem "To the University of Cambridge in New England." In her poem, she commissioned the muses to assist her and authorize her literary presence through her Middle Passage memory:

> WHILE an intrinsic ardor prompts to write,
> The muses promise to assist my pen;
> 'Twas not long since I left my native shore
> The land of errors, and Egyptian gloom:
> Father of mercy, 'twas thy gracious hand
> Brought me in safety from those dark abodes.

Claiming God's adornment of a safe passage from darkness, Wheatley reorders the social hierarchy present in her addressing the Ivy League students. Although the students are socially, economically, and politically above her,

Wheatley claimed moral authority through God's grace and redemption from what she calls her land of errors and gloom. Hence she claims a privileged position through her Middle Passage, suggesting that God held sway on the religious elected and should be feared by the socially elected. She ends her poem with a warning from the spiritual elected position of Ethiopia:

> Improve your privileges while they stay,
> Ye pupils, and each hour redeem, that bears
> Or good or bad report of you to heav'n.
> Let sin, that baneful evil to the soul,
> By you be shun'd, nor once remit your guard;
> Suppress the deadly serpent in its egg.
> Ye blooming plants of human race divine,
> An Ethiop tells you 'tis your greatest foe;
> Its transient sweetness turns to endless pain,
> And in immense perdition sinks the soul.[20]

Wheatley distinguished herself as one who was "elected" by the "Father" who brought her out of darkness, which in turn authorized her to speak of the "intrinsic ardor" on issues she felt prompt to address publicly to the students.

Similar to Phillis Wheatley and Ignatius Sancho, Equiano would have been compelled to write Africa back into his freedom story in order to represent himself to the greater Afro-British and European public.[21] The self-identified African, as seen through the writings of Africans in the Atlantic, sought to elevate Africa on par with European society through cultural civility, familial relationships, and the inclusion of Africans into the Christian narrative.[22] Although Equiano's accuracy regarding his African Middle Passage has been challenged over the last decade, Africans in America and Britain were establishing communities to which writers like Equiano would have had important ties.[23] Scholar Hakim Adi writes, "West Africans' political identities and their political consciousness have changed over time and according to specific historical conditions. A Pan-African consciousness, for example, can be seen in the writing and activities of Equiano, Cugoano, and other 'Sons of Africa' in the eighteenth century."[24]

Equiano's elevation of his African name, especially in his public signatures, suggests a sociopolitical recognition with the late struggles of Africans in Britain. Although there was not a large African middle-class community in Britain, historian Douglas Lorimer notes that there was a working-class African community that looked to the courts for legal standing and inclusion as British citizens. He argues that court cases, such as the famous Somerset case, created pathways to freedom for black servants within the British Commonwealth.[25] As Orban observed, the writer used his European name when addressing England's elite and royalty in personal correspondence; yet he followed with the signature "The oppressed Ethiopian" in petitions addressing aristocrats on behalf of his African brethren.[26] Becoming African provided Equiano with an established Black Atlantic community with organizational titles such as "Sons of Africa." These were critical influences on the emerging slave narrator missing from the discussion of black Nationalism in early Black Atlantic texts.

Becoming Gustavus Vassa

If creating an ancestral African identity benefited Equiano in the Afro-Atlantic community, becoming Gustavus Vassa allowed the Afro-Atlantic writer the opportunity to appeal to his Euro-American audiences through a shared Christian faith and heroic status associated with his new name. Equiano now had the opportunity to serve as cultural insider as well as cultural critic. He could speak authoritatively within the language of religious morality, and he could also promote his benevolent commercialism and Christian conversion to Native Americans and Africans.

In the narrative, Equiano's recollection of how he attained his European name was wrapped in a symbolic confrontation between social interaction and exchange. He informed his readers that he first preferred the biblical name of Jacob but was superseded by his master's choosing. He writes:

> While I was on board this ship, my captain and master named me Gustavus Vassa. I at the time began to understand him a little, and refused to be called so, and told him as well as I could that I would be called Jacob; but he said I should not, and still called me Gustavus; and when I refused to answer to my new name, which at first I did, it gained me many a cuff; so at length I submitted, and by which I have been known ever since.[27]

Equiano constructs a binary between religious piety and the commercial Atlantic. His enslavement meant that he could not orchestrate his own will and that he would have to submit to the laws of commercial exchange that rendered him under the charge of his owner, who could superimpose his will through persuasive actions, including violence.

Interestingly, Equiano ended his naming episode by stating that his new identity had endurance. In fact, Gustavus Vassa provided the author with name recognition and association to higher claims in the Euro-American world. Vincent Carretta notes, "British audiences associated the name Gustavus Vasa with eighteenth century arguments over political freedom in Britain."[28] Apparently Equiano was named in part after Gustav I of Sweden (1523–1529), heralded as a liberator and founder of modern-day Sweden.[29] Since his owner would have been more aware of the popular play *Gustavus Vasa, the Deliverer of His Country*, which was published in 1739 and enjoyed many reprintings until the first theater version in 1805, Equiano's new name most likely derived from the literary version since slaves were subjected to inappropriate names of historical figures.[30] Nevertheless, the origins of the narrator's European identity had considerable benefits, including a famous connection to someone heralded as a defender of rights.

Becoming Gustavus Vassa represented Equiano's evolution and accumulation of social and political values associated with the developing Atlantic World. In *The Interesting Narrative*, the author immediately begins with his discovery of the printed word. Similar to early Black Atlantic writers, Equiano used the trope of the "Talking Book" to signify his entrance into enlightened subjectivity as advocated throughout the Atlantic by Western philosophers of the Enlightenment.[31] With his new identity and knowledge of the Christian Bible, Equiano could refute claims that Africans did not have the capacity of intellectual thought and ability.[32] As the literate Vassa, he could also indicate his connection to Euro-American institutions through naming and literacy, both of which were social propelling forces into Western society.

Moreover, Equiano's new identity afforded him the opportunity to highlight the institutions, laws, and personal freedoms as a new cultural insider. As Vassa, the author could present himself as a fellow countryman with the ability to survey the actions and demeanor of his fellow subjects. In chapters 3 and 4 of the narrative, Equiano spoke of the wonders to behold as a witness to Euro-American culture:

> I now not only felt myself quite easy with these new countrymen, but relished their society and manners. I no longer looked upon them as spirits, but as men superior to us; therefore I had the stronger desire to resemble them; to imbibe their spirit, and imitate their manners; I therefore embraced every occasion of improvement; and every new thing that I observed I treasured up in my memory.[33]

Equiano acknowledged what he believed to have been the superiority of European culture. Yet he also informs his readers that he still claimed outsider status as well. Thus Equiano could acknowledge European culture for its advances, including his enlightened and shared position, but he could also keep his outsider position in recognition of the racial dynamics he knew complicated relations out in the commercial Atlantic as well as in London.

Using both his African and European names, Equiano could move easily between two identities. More important, he could capitalize on the ancestral and historical ties his names referenced. In instituting his African name, Equiano laid claim to ancestral destiny and what he termed "fancied foreboding." In comparing the Igbo's naming practices to those of Jews, he stated, "Like them also, our children were named from some event, some circumstance, or fancied foreboding at the time of their birth. I was named Olaudah, which in our language, signifies vicissitude, or fortunate also; one favoured, and having a loud voice and well spoken"[34] Equiano could imply a relationship between his past as well as compel his readers that he was a natural leader destined by ancestral fortitude.

Becoming Gustavus Vassa, Equiano must have truly believed that he was most favored. His European name, which signified natural leadership, fortitude, and great respect in European circles, had similar attributes to his African name. Becoming European, Equiano, in *The Interesting Narrative*, chronicled the collaborative efforts that individuals such as the Guerins facilitated in his religious training and baptism at St. Margaret's Church at Westminster.[35] Also in many passages about his fortunes and misfortunes out at sea, the author described favorable relations with his masters, shipmates, and fellow slaves. Upon sitting down to craft his narrative, Equiano had many social and literary confluences reaching him in London: Afro-Atlantic organizations and communities, a developing black literary tradition, and a flourishing commercial Atlantic. The narrator took the best of each of these and the favorable disposition located in his names to create the ultimate cultural representative and warrior.

The African European Warrior

The uniqueness of *The Interesting Narrative* lies in Equiano's ability to move between each identity as cultural defender. As an African outsider in a Euro-American community, he could relate African injustices and authenticate these issues through his own experiences. Writing within the Euro-American public sphere as an Afro-British citizen, the narrator could also appeal to the prevailing discourses of religious piety and benevolent commercialism. The power of the pen during the late eighteenth century was heightened after the French and American Revolutions succeeded in moving the control of public discourse away from the aristocracy and into public and private domains.[36] Equiano's mastering of public print culture allowed him a degree of control over issues regarding Africans and abolitionist issues.

Furthermore, he had been a free man for almost twenty years at the publication of his narrative. Equiano informed his readers that he had a relative amount of economic successes as well as troubles out at sea, and his return to London signaled his resignation that slavery and Atlantic commerce could not evolve into a benevolent pairing of mutual need for spiritual attainment through labor. With his subscribers delineating the upper echelon of the white British aristocracy and gentry, such as Granville Sharp, the Prince of Wales, and the Duke of York, Equiano had the ear of many influential people of the city.[37] Thus he had built social, political, and economic capital in London before the publication of *The Interesting Narrative*, and he used his clout to market his autobiography. It is at this juncture of his life that Equiano becomes the official representative warrior for his brethren in London and across the Atlantic.

As African historian Mtubani suggests, *The Interesting Narrative* was published at the height of Equiano's role as the leading African man of letters in London.[38] The author had built a literary reputation in London with publications in popular newspapers and magazines.[39] Wilfred D. Samuels writes, "From what I have suggested thus far, it is possible to conclude that Equiano's narrative is the 'intentional act' through which he becomes aware of his intentional object: slavery."[40] Originally concerned with the natural exchange of African labor for European modern civility, the narrator had to reconstruct his commercial exchange. Instead of an exchange between labor and culture, Equiano brokered a literary exchange between communities as an abolitionist and social defender of Africans and European friends.

Outlining his intimate connections to both communities, he propelled himself as cultural warrior defending Africans against the horrors and dehumanization of slavery and reminding Africans and Europeans of their role in the elevation of each community. In his literary role in London, Equiano created the honorable commercial exchange that he sought at sea. He could elevate Africa through his writings as well as admonish his European countrymen and women when they failed to live up to Christian values. Also, becoming the ultimate insider of both communities allowed him to create comparisons and contrasts that spoke to popular notions of his period, including the late eighteenth-century propensity to take a warlike disposition. Delineating the similarities between Africa's and European's warlike structures, Equiano observed, "Of these the most considerable is the kingdom of Benin, both as to extent and wealth, the richness and cultivation of soil, the power of its king, and the number and warlike disposition."[41] As noted by Samuels, Equiano was influenced by his experiences at war during his servitude on a British warship and sought to equate his native land to the warlike structure of England.[42]

For example, Equiano's rise as cultural defender and African spokesman coincided with his appointment and dismissal as a superintendent of the Commissary of Provisions and Stores for the Afro-Atlantic Poor to Sierra Leone. The colonization experiment developed out of renowned abolitionist and lawyer Granville Sharp's attempts to organize the removal of poor Africans out of Britain. In hopes of creating an Afro-British settlement in Africa with economic and religious ties to London, Equiano agreed to oversee the care and provisions for the migrating Africans.[43] He uncovered corruption and mistreatment of Africans in the preparations for the trip and reported it, leading to his dismissal. When backers of the expedition sought to damage Equiano's reputation during the aftermath, he scored a public victory through public media. The writer found his sociopolitical voice in advocating for his fellow brethren. It provided him with a welcome opportunity to take a more significant role in Afro-British politics. Mtubani notes, "The fact that he was dismissed because of his outspoken defense of the black people against the high-handed actions of Joseph Irwin, the Agent, is particularly significant, for it shows his unwillingness to be an instrument of his own people's exploitation."[44]

Equiano's public recognition in the above African colonization affair also coincided with his rise as a reporter of international travesties on the Atlantic. According to Glanville Sharpe's journal, Equiano had alerted the abolitionist about the 130 Africans being thrown into the sea by the slave-ship *Zong* for insurance purposes.[45] Equiano's reporting of the massacre spurred the 1783 Zong court case in which the crew of the slave-ship had been charged with murdering their human cargo. The proprietors of the slave-ship never faced justice for the murder of the African slaves. However, Sharp's bringing the case before a court elicited much-needed abolitionist publicity.

As an African and European warrior, Equiano actively responded to attacks on the part of white proslavery critics who questioned the character of Africans and his abolitionist friends in public. Defending British philanthropist Mr. Ramsay against a proslavery advocate's public attack, he wrote in the *Public Advertiser* in 1788, "But we trust that in spite of your *hissing* zeal and impotent malevolence against Mr. Ramsay, his noble purpose of philanthropy will be productive of much good to many, and in the end through the blessing of God, be a means of bringing about the abolition of slavery."[46] Equiano transcended identities and racial lines to defend friends of the abolitionist cause. In addition, he warned his opponents that providence for slaves would come as a blessing of a higher calling. Thus he reaffirmed his public authority through the use of Christianity, a signifier above repute in the late eighteenth century.

Furthermore, Equiano responded to the question of race more emphatically in the narrative. Although he would not comment directly on the racial genealogy of skin color, he made sure to alert his audiences that he would be the defender against demeaning racial interpretations of Afro-Atlantic people. Equiano wrote, "These instances, and a great many more which might be adduced, while they shew how the complexions of the same persons vary in different climates, it is hoped may tend also to remove the prejudice that some conceive against the natives of Africa on account of their colour."[47] He was intent on defending Africans against character assassination on the basis of their skin color. What is more apparent is his effort to speak back to Euro-American philosophers and thinkers, such as a Thomas Jefferson, who advocated racial inferiority based on skin color and the regional climate of non-Europeans.

Equiano also spoke directly to Euro-Americans' failures to live up to religious standards mediated through Christianity. He amplified these failed relationships especially in the Atlantic slave trade as impediments to the natural redemption of the African spiritual body. For Equiano, his initial discussions of African slavery revolved around the natural redemption of Africa spiritually and culturally through the benevolent exchange often espoused by proslavery advocates.[48] For instance, he displayed the benevolent exchanges between him and his owner, Dr. King. Equiano wrote, "I had good fortune to please my master in every department in which he employed me; and there was scarcely any part of his business, or household affairs, in which I was not occasionally engaged."[49] The author depicted these human relations as his good fortune. Although enslaved, he thus found value in Euro-American commerce and human exchanges. What is more important is that Equiano envisioned a market exchange where his services could prove beneficial for owner and enslaved with hopes of better returns for each entity.

By contrast, Equiano also emphasized the failure of these exchanges when slaveowners abused their privileges. In describing the harsh treatment that slaves often received from their masters, he also indicated the failure of benevolent exchange on the commercial Atlantic:

> Many times I seen these unfortunate wretches beaten for asking for their pay; and
> often severely flogged by their owners if they did not bring them their daily or

weekly money exactly to the time; though the poor creatures were obliged to wait on the gentlemen they had worked for, sometimes more than half the day, before they could get their pay; and this generally on Sundays, when they wanted the time for themselves.[50]

Unlike the kind treatment that Equiano received from some of his masters, he highlighted the abusive practice that many slave owners committed in the exchange of commerce that slaves fulfilled as laborers. Displaying the virtue of good exchanges between owners and slaves on the Atlantic and the failures exemplified by abusive masters showcased the narrator's attempt to plead for more Christian piety and fair play. He questioned a slaveowner about his abusive practice of cutting off runaway slaves' ears and the fear of God's anger. In response to his question, Equiano noted the slave master's response: "And he told me, answering was a thing of another world; but what he thought and did were policy. I told him that the Christian doctrine taught us to do unto others as we would that others should do unto us."[51] The slave master's response confirmed Equiano's dismay throughout *The Interesting Narrative* that Africans would not find an honorable exchange of labor and Christian benevolence on the Atlantic.

He skillfully used injustices against fellow Africans to brandish his own warrior-style literary justice upon slave masters who mistreated his African brethren. He narrated the experience of a fellow slave who, thanks to an industrious spirit, had a white man buy him a boat without his master's knowledge. The governor presiding over the West Indies took the slave's boat to transport sugar and thus to advance economically. Equiano argued that the slave did not receive any reimbursements from either the governor or the slave master. In recalling the eventual fortunes of the governor and slave, Equiano resorted to an explanation of biblical cause and effect:

> If the justly-merited ruin of the governor's fortune could be any gratification to the poor man he had thus robbed, he was not without consolation. Extortion and rapine are poor providers; and sometime after this, the governor died in the King's Bench in England, as I was told, in great poverty. *The last war* favoured this poor negro-man, and he found some means to escape from his Christian master, he came to England, where I saw him afterwards several times.[52]

Equating the story of the slave's final victory to "the last war," Equiano viewed the failure of these social exchanges as an act against Providence itself. In doing so, he was able to claim a literary victory in the reversal of fortune of the governor and the industrious former slave.

The failure of economic social exchanges and Christian benevolence even extended to Equiano's acquiring freedom. He noted that his freedom was predicated on the honor that his master connected to his reputation in the eyes of other white men. Thus Equiano tells his readers that he brought another white man with him as he completed the transaction agreed upon for his freedom.[53] Once again he indicated the failure of honor in the Atlantic World. He could not free himself by way of his own honest and virtuous exchange of human commerce as he envisioned it. He had to resort to the power of social capital and virtuous relationships on the part of the captain's white body. Clearly Equiano understood that he could not complete honorable commercial exchanges on the Atlantic as a free African. More critically, the elevation of the African meant that he would have to administer to Euro-Americans inherent in his European name as liberator and reformer Gustavus Vassa.

In other words, the narrative expounds the realization that enterprising Africans in the Atlantic Diaspora would not benefit from the revolutionary ideals of individual freedom and labor. This revelation marked the end of Equiano's sea adventures and eventually led him back to London. He stated, "I had suffered so many impositions in my commercial transactions in different parts of the world, that I became heartily disgusted with the seafaring life, and was determined not to return to it, as least for some time."[54] Equiano saw the manifestation of the color line that W. E. B. DuBois would make famous in *The Souls of Black Folk* (1903). At the dawn of the twentieth century, DuBois wrote, "He simply wishes to make it possible for a man to be both a Negro and an American, without being cursed and spit upon by his fellows, without having the doors of Opportunity closed roughly in his face."[55] For Equiano, in the eighteenth century, race was becoming a bigger divider between moral and ethical behavior. This is evident in his autobiography and emphatic in his efforts to realize beneficial commerce for his African brethren.

Conclusion

In the end, *The Interesting Narrative* is a remarkable text. For over 200 years Equiano has held scholars' interest, ranging from arguments over the narrative's value as a spiritual biography, slave narrative, and/or antislavery text.[56] Over the last decade, scholars have even argued over whether Equiano fabricated his African origins for self-representation and economic gain.[57] Nevertheless, the narrative was written during a period of great social upheaval and change. People of African descent were adjusting to their reality as slaves and free people in the Atlantic Diaspora and were identifying themselves according to the cultural values they brought from Africa along with the ideologies and values of wherever they lived. Equiano's *The Interest Narrative* exemplifies the changing values that the writer attempted to acculturate for Africans' fuller participation in the market economy.

Perhaps of greater significance is Equiano's use of print culture to formulate Atlantic identities. According to James Sidbury, *The Interesting Narrative*, along with other Black Atlantic texts, helped reshape the African ideological landscape. He writes, "They understood this projected social conversion in religious terms, and they expected twinned revolutionary changes on the coast of Africa through which 'pagan' Igbos, Kongos, and Temne would be converted to Christianity while also learning to produce nonhuman commodities for exchange in the Atlantic market."[58] Equiano loved Euro-American culture, social institutions, and religion. He also believed that Africa had something of value to exchange in the modern world. But, for the narrator, it was lost in the translation.

In the narrative, Equiano describes the horror he endured as he moved farther away from the ability to communicate with his fellow Igbo countrymen and women. It was through language that Equiano would mourn the loss of his African Igbo community. He explained to his reading audience that he constantly searched for kinship ties through language: "From the time I left my own nation I always found somebody that understood me till I came to the sea coast."[59] Equiano marked his passage from childhood to market exchange through his separation from the linguistic shores of Africa, lamenting, "I was now exceedingly miserable, and thought myself worse off than any of the rest of my companions; for they could talk to each other, but I had no person to speak to that could understand. In this state I was constantly grieving and pining, and wishing for death, rather than anything else."[60] In other words, Equiano's African self had to experience a metaphoric death in order to be resurrected as an Anglo-British self marked by a forced acceptance of the name Gustavus Vassa.

The narrative also suggest the narrator's acknowledgment and move from the oral tradition of Africa to the written and material world of the modern Atlantic marked by signifiers, such as the "Talking Book," time clocks, and glaring pictures.[61] Equiano was highlighting his ability to speak in the values and traditions of both audiences. As Gustavus Vassa, he informed his readers that his path from misfortune (that is, the inability to converse with his fellow Africans) and his fortune (that is, the acquisition of virtues and values of Euro-American Christian culture) during his enslavement gave him the ability to speak forthrightly to both communities.

In the end, *The Interesting Narrative* marked Equiano's realization that economic exchanges between Africans and Europeans were void of mutual respect, Christian charity, and the rule of law on the Atlantic.[62]

Equiano's realization of the failed moral standards of Europeans is emblematic of his stance to defend Africans in the Euro-American public sphere and highlighted the struggle of people of African descent, including black writers in the Atlantic, who increasingly equated slavery and racism as two pressing issues. Thus free enterprising Africans could not operate outside a social system that sought to denigrate and enslave Africans of all status and stations.[63] For example, there is an obscure moment in his narrative that reflects the struggle that both the emerging Afro-Atlantic elite and the narrator could not invert. The story comes early in his transatlantic removal from Africa and serves as a critical moment in exposing the incompatibility of slavery and African freedom:

> I was one day in a field belonging to a gentleman who had a black boy about my size; this boy having observed me from his master's house, was transported at the sight of one of his own countrymen, and ran to meet me with the utmost haste. I not knowing what he was about, turned a little out of his way at first, but to no purpose; he soon came close to me, and caught hold of me in his arms as if I had been his brother, though we had never seen each other before.[64]

One the one hand, Equiano mentioned it as a trifling event from which he wanted to turn away. On the other hand, the slave narrator could have been reflecting his metaphysical good-bye to the child he could be no more as, in the end, their fates were intertwined on the Atlantic, enslaved and free. Equiano could not merge into a capitalist community without ignoring the separation that slavery and servitude inflicted on fellow Africans. After all, their fates depended on holding each other in solidarity in the emerging modern world.

Notes

1. See Nash, *Urban Crucible*; Warner, *Letters of the Republic*; and Doyle, *Freedom's Empire*, on the development of Western print culture and revolutions.

2. See Gates, *Signifying Monkey*; and Andrews, *To Tell a Free Story*.

3. Linebaugh and Rediker, *Many-Headed Hydra*, 3–4.

4. Sidbury, *Becoming African*, 6.

5. For an example of the condemnation and vilification of Africa by Enlightenment philosophers, see David Hume, "Of National Characters" (1754), in Eze, *Race and the Enlightenment*, 33.

6. See Bethel, *Roots of African-American Identity*; White, "It Was a Proud Day"; and Carretta's discussion of the Afro-British organization called the Sons of Africa at the end of the eighteenth century in *Equiano the African*.

7. Bethel, *Roots of African-American Identity*, discusses in detail the efforts made by early African Americans after the American Revolution in order to reconstruct their past complete with an ancient beginning and local and religious heroes.

8. Mtubani, "Afro-Atlantic Voice," 87. Also Mtubani documents "Black Princes" in Europe as early as the 1749, especially Ansah Sesarakoo.

9. See Linebaugh and Rediker, *Many-Headed Hydra*, on the camaraderie of African and European sailors during the eighteenth and nineteenth centuries.

10. In the narrative, Equiano states that his main reason for accepting a position as overseer from his friend Dr. Irving was in hope of bringing sinners to Jesus Christ. He wrote, "I hoped to be an instrument, under God, of bringing some poor sinner to my well-beloved master, Jesus Christ" (202). In addition, Equiano discusses his choosing of fellow countrymen on a slave boat. He stated, "I went with the Doctor on board a Guinea-man, to purchase some slaves to carry with us, and cultivate a plantation; and I chose them all of my own countrymen, some of whom came from Lybia" (205).

11. Sweet, "Mistaken Identities?," 284–285.

12. Equiano, *Interesting Narrative*, 32.

13. Ibid.

14. Orban, "Dominant and Submerged Discourses," 657.

15. Gates, *Signifying Monkey*, xxii.

16. Sidbury, *Becoming African*, 18.

17. Ignatius Sancho, *Letter XXXV. To Mr. Sterne July 1766*, in Carretta, *Unchained Voices*, 79–80.

18. Sancho, *General Advertiser*, 80–81.

19. Equiano's letter "To the Queen's Most Excellent Majesty," 231–232.

20. Wheatly, *Collected Works*, 15–16.

21. Phillis Wheatley begins to claim Ethiopia in her poems during her visit to England. This is quite suggestive, as Afro-British involvement with the Methodist Church was evident during the period.

22. See Potkay and Burr, *Black Atlantic Writers*, on the characteristics of early Black Atlantic writers.

23. See Carretta, *Equiano the African*. Sweet, "Mistaken Identities?," offers an eloquent discussion of Equiano's birthplace controversy.

24. Adi, "Pan-Africanism and West African Nationalism," 71.

25. Lorimer, "Black Slaves and English Liberty," 121–150.

26. Orban, "Dominant and Submerged Discourses," 657.

27. Equiano, *Interesting Narrative*, 64.

28. Carretta, *Equiano the African*, 41.

29. See Roberts, *Early Vasas.*

30. See Franklin, *From Slavery to Freedom*; and Painter, *Creating Black Americans.*

31. On Enlightenment scholars' distinction between Europeans and Africans, see Hume, "Of National Characters," 33.

32. In *The Signifying Monkey*, Gates writes, "The urge toward the systematization of all human knowledge, by which we characterize the Enlightenment, in other words led directly to the relegation of black people to a lower rung on the Great Chain of Being, an eighteenth century metaphor that arranged all of creation on the vertical scale from animals and plants and insects through man to the angels and God Himself" (130).

33. Equiano, *Interesting Narrative*, 77–78.

34. Ibid., 41.

35. Ibid., 78.

36. See Habermas, *Structural Transformation of the Public Sphere.*

37. In Vincent Carretta's edited edition of *The Interesting Narrative*, he includes Equiano's list of English subscribers taken from his 1794 reprinting.

38. Mtubani, "Afro-Atlantic Voice," 90.

39. Carretta, introduction to *The Interesting Narrative*, xiii.

40. Samuels, "Disguised Voice," 66.

41. Equiano, *Interesting Narrative*, 32.

42. Samuels, "Disguised Voice," 67.

43. Sidbury, *Becoming African*, 53–54

44. Mtubani, "Afro-Atlantic Voice," 91.

45. Carretta, *Equiano the African*, 237–238.

46. "To Mr. Gordon Turnbull, Author of an 'Apology for NEGRO SLAVERY,'" *Public Advertiser*, February 5, 1788, Appendix E in Equiano, *Interesting Narrative*, 330–331.

47. Equiano, *Interesting Narrative*, 45.

48. See Morgan, *American Freedom American Slavery.*

49. Equiano, *Interesting Narrative*, 103.

50. Ibid., 101.

51. Ibid., 104–105.

52. Ibid., 102. My emphasis. "The last war" referred to the American Revolution.

53. Equiano wrote, "'Come, come,' said my worthy captain, clapping my master on the back, 'Come Robert, (which was his name), I think you must let him have his freedom;--you have laid your money out very well'; . . . my master then said, he would not be worse than his promise" (ibid., 135).

54. Ibid., 220.

55. DuBois, *Souls of Black Folks*, 17.

56. See Pudaloff, "No Change without Purchase"; Samuels, *Making Crooked Paths Straight*; and Earley, "Writing from the Center or the Margins?"

57. Paul Momod, personal communication, January 28, 2004, in Pudaloff, "No Change without Purchase," 522.

58. Sidbury, *Becoming African*, 8.

59. Equiano, *Interesting Narrative*, 51.

60. Ibid., 62.

61. Equiano describes these Western placards during his stop on a Virginia plantation: "the first object that engaged my attention was a watch which hung on the chimney, . . . I was quite surprised at the noise it made, and was afraid it would tell the gentleman anything I might do amiss: and when I immediately observed a picture hanging in the room, which appeared constantly to look at me, I was still more affrighted" (ibid., 63).

62. See Hinds, "Spirit of Trade."

63. See Rael, *Black Identity*.

64. Equiano, *Interesting Narrative*, 85.

Bibliography

Adi, Hakim. "Pan-Africanism and West African Nationalism in Britain." *African Studies Review* 43.1 Special Issue on the Diaspora (April 2000): 69–82.

Andrews, William L. *To Tell a Free Story: The First Century of Afro-American Autobiography, 1760–1865*. Urbana: University of Illinois Press, 1988.

Bethel, Elizabeth Rauh. *The Roots of African-American Identity: Memory and History in Antebellum Free Communities*. New York: St. Martin's Press, 1997.

Breen, T. H., and Stephen Innes. *"Myne Owne Ground": Race and Freedom on Virginia's Shore, 1640–1676*. New York: Oxford University Press, 1980.

Carretta, Vincent. *Equiano the African: Biography of a Self Made Man*. Athens: University of Georgia Press, 2005.

———, ed. *Unchained Voices: An Anthology of Black Authors in the English-Speaking World of the 18th Century*. Lexington: University Press of Kentucky, 1996.

Doyle, Laura. *Freedom's Empire: Race and the Rise of the Novel in Atlantic Modernity, 1640– 1940*. Durham, N.C.: Duke University Press, 2008.

DuBois, W. E. B. *The Souls of Black Folk*. New York: Alfred A. Knopf, 1903.

Equiano, Olaudah. *The Interesting Narrative of the Life of Olaudah Equiano, or Gustavus Vassa, The African, Written by Himself*. Ed. and intro. Vincent Carretta. 1789. Reprint, New York: Penguin Books, 1995.

Eze, Emmanuel Chuckwudi. *Race and the Enlightenment: A Reader*. Malden, Mass.: Blackwell, 1997.

Franklin, Benjamin. *The Autobiography and Other Writings*. New York: Oxford University Press, 1961.

Franklin, John Hope, and Alfred A. Moss Jr. *From Slavery to Freedom: A History of African Americans*. 8th ed. Boston: McGraw Hill, 2000.

Gates, Henry Louis, Jr. "Writing 'Race' and the Difference It Makes." In *"Race," Writing, and Difference*. Chicago: University of Chicago Press, 1985.

Gilroy, Paul. *The Black Atlantic: Modernity and Double Consciousness*. London: Verso, 1993.

Gould, Philip. "Free Carpenter, Venture Capitalist: Reading the Lives of the Early Afro-Atlantic." *Literary History* 12.4 (Winter 2000): 659–684.

Habermas, Jurgen. *The Structural Transformation of the Public Sphere: An Inquiry into a Category of Bourgeois Society*. Cambridge, Mass.: MIT Press, 1991.

Hinds, Elizabeth, and Jane Wall Hinds. "The Spirit of Trade: Olaudah Equiano's Conversion, Legalism, and the Merchant's Life." *African American Review* 32.4 (1998): 635–647.

Linebaugh, Peter, and Marcus Rediker. *The Many-Headed Hydra: The Hidden History of the Revolutionary Atlantic*. London: Verso, 2000.

Lorimer, Douglas. "Black Slaves and English Liberty: A Re-examination of Racial Slavery in England." *Immigrants & Minorities* 3.2 (1984): 121–150.

Marren, Susan M. "Between Slavery and Freedom: The Transgressive Self in Olaudah Equiano's Autobiography." *PMLA* 108.1 (January 1993): 94–105.

Morgan, Edmund. *American Slavery American Slavery: The Ordeal of Colonial Virginia*. New York: W. W. Norton, 1975.

Morrison, Toni Morrison. "From Rootedness: The Ancestor as Foundation (1984)." In *African American Literary Criticism, 1773 to 2000*, ed. Hazel Arnett Ervin. New York: Twayne, 1999.

Mtubani, Victor C. D. "The Afro-Atlantic Voice in Eighteenth-Century Britain: African Writers against Slavery and the Slave Trade." *Phylon* 45.2 (1984): 85–97.

Nash, Gary B. *The Urban Crucible: Social Change, Political Consciousness, and the Origins of the American Revolution*. Cambridge, Mass.: Harvard University Press, 1979.

Orban, Katalin. "Dominant and Submerged Discourses in the Life of Olaudah Equiano (or Gustavus Vassa?)." *African American Review* 27.4 (Winter 1993): 655–664.

Painter, Nell Irvin. *Creating Black Americans: African-American History and Its Meanings, 1619 to the Present*. Oxford: Oxford University Press, 2006.

Potkay, Adam, and Sandra Burr. *Black Atlantic Writers of the Eighteenth Century*. London: MacMillan, 1995.

Pudaloff, Ross J. "No Change without Purchase: Olaudah Equiano and the Economies of Self and Market." *Early American Literature* 40.3 (2005): 499–527.

Rael, Patrick. *Black Identity & Black Protest in the Antebellum North*. Chapel Hill: University of North Carolina Press, 2002.

Roberts, Michael. *The Early Vasas: A History of Sweden 1523–1611*. Cambridge: Cambridge University Press, 1968.

Samuels, Wilfred D. "Disguised Voice in the Interesting Narrative of Olaudah Equiano, or Gustavus Vassa, the African." *Afro-Atlantic American Literature Forum* 19.2 (Summer 1985): 64–69.

Sidbury, James. *Becoming African in America: Race and Nation in the Early Black Atlantic*. New York: Oxford University Press, 2007.

Sweet, John Wood. "Mistaken Identities? Olaudah Equiano, Domingus Alvares, and the Methodological Challenges of Studying the African Diaspora." *American Historical Review* 114.2 (April 2009): 279–306.

Warner, Michael. *The Letters of the Republic: Publication and the Public in Eighteenth-Century America*. Cambridge, Mass.: Harvard University Press, 1990.

Wheatley, Phillis. *The Collected Works of Phillis Wheatley*. In *The Schomburg Library of Nineteenth-Century Black Women Writers*, ed. John Shields. New York: Oxford University Press, 1988.

White, Shane. "'It Was a Proud Day': African Americans, Festivals, and Parades in the North, 1741–1834." *Journal of American History* 81.1 (1994): 13–50.

Wilson, Kathleen. "Citizenship, Empire, and Modernity in the English Provinces, c. 1720–1790." *Eighteenth-Century Studies* 29.1 (Fall 1995): 69–96.

Ruptures and Disrupters

The Photographic Landscapes of Ingrid Pollard and
Zarina Bhimji as Revisionist History of Great Britain

Kimberli Gant

British artists Ingrid Pollard and Zarina Bhimji are indirectly related—not in the familial sense, but as artistic colleagues. They were included in several texts[1] featuring British artists of color and/or artists with work concerned with social, political, and cultural identity. Additionally, Pollard and Bhimji have participated in at least one group exhibition together.[2] While their respective oeuvres have placed them within the broad genre of "Black British" art, encasing their work and careers with other internationally renowned British artists such as Lubiana Humid, Eddie Chambers, Sonia Boyce, Allan deSouza, and so forth, Pollard and Bhimji have yet to be examined in direct relation to each other. This essay is an initial attempt as I am exploring only one body of work from each artist, though there are additional projects that deserve comparative analysis. What links Pollard and Bhimji is a shared use of landscape photography as a way to confront Eurocentric hegemony in the constructions of national and cultural identities. Their images complicate the linear narratives created in British history and collective memory by bringing to the forefront what is absent or forgotten, the nonwhite subject in the construction of Britain's wealth, history, and social culture.

In 1987 Pollard created her celebrated body of work, *Pastoral Interludes*, a series of five hand-tinted photographs. The images feature the English countryside with a solitary female figure exploring her surroundings in three of the images, and a male fishing in the remaining two. A short text accompanies each photograph. Pollard's text is written in first person, permitting viewers into her, and presumably the figure's, private thoughts, while others are third-person statements and observations. In *Untitled #2*, "[it's] as if the Black experience is only lived within an urban environment. I thought I liked the Lake District where I wandered lonely as a Black face in a sea of white. A visit to the countryside is always accompanied by a feeling of unease, dread." Pollard's words convey feelings of physical and psychological isolation as a black person traveling alone in England's predominantly white rural-scape.

Pastoral Interludes, now over twenty-five years old, depicts black artists in England, like Pollard, claiming a place within British art history and using art as a means for exploring the sociopolitical transition occurring in England during the 1980s and 1990s. In viewing Pollard's images in the twenty-first century, one still feels "as if the Black experience is [still] only lived within an urban environment."

A decade later, in 1998, Bhimji created her impressive photographic series *Cleaning the Garden*. Commissioned for the 1998 exhibition *Continental Drift: Europe Approaching the Millennium* as a part of the Photo 98 festival, Bhimji's series on estate gardens is a metaphor for the shifting population demographics throughout Europe at the turn of the second millennium. She features the eighteenth-century Harewood House Estate and Gardens in Yorkshire, England, as well as the gardens at the Medieval Islamic Alhambra fortress in Granada, Spain. Bhimji prepared twelve sensuously colored backlit photographs with each image tightly cropped, seeming to merge the different gardens together. The images have no text and no figures, instead turning the landscape into the protagonist. Bhimji commented in the accompanying catalog that "[the] idea of a dialogue between different gardens in my work acts as a metaphor for the cultures of Europe."[3]

Bhimji's gardens speak to Europe's historical engagement with populations in Africa and Asia. The Alhambra stands as an architectural marker of Spain's Muslim population from as early as the eighth century BCE,[4] while the Harewood Estate denotes British imperialism in the Caribbean. The latter was built from money earned by the owner's sugar plantation in the West Indies.[5] The work carries a sense of irony since it discusses the millennia-long relationship between Europe and Africa, yet was made just before the twenty-first century, a period when Europeans were facing an "identity crisis" because of the racial and cultural changes affecting individual nations.[6]

Pollard's and Bhimji's references to nonwhite populations throughout Europe include the artists' own personal narratives. Both artists grew up in England, though the former was born in Guyana, previously known as British Guiana, while the latter is of Indian descent, even though she was born in Uganda, previously known as British East Africa (along with Tanzania and Kenya). Bhimji and Pollard are from communities that each experienced racial discrimination within England. Thus their commentaries on black bodies moving through space and historically absent bodies helping to create that space may be interpreted as statements of social critique.

Pastoral Interludes and *Cleaning the Garden* were produced and exhibited within a period of British history when black and Asian citizens tried to revise the official national narrative to include Britain's nonwhite populations.[7] Pollard's series examines the contemporary perception of rural England as an idyllic white landscape that continues to be situated in the past. Bhimji's series examines English countryside estates as popular heritage sites and the ignored history of black colonial figures in the construction of those estates. For both artists, Britain's history is not isolated, nor is its population homogenous, nor are its landscapes pure and uncomplicated. Instead, Britain is intimately tied to the national development and exploitation of Caribbean, Asian, and African populations at home and abroad.

Colonists in the Mother Country

Pollard and Bhimji grew up in England during the 1970s and 1980s, a generation after the first major wave of Caribbean and South Asian immigrants had arrived in the post–World War II era; Pollard was born in 1953 and Bhimji in 1963.[8] At that time, England's dire economic infrastructure needed workers to help rebuild it. The country imported them from across former British colonies to work as factory laborers.[9] The immigrants were promised higher wages, and the 1948 Nationality Act extended British passports to "Commonwealth citizens" in exchange for their employment.[10] As a result, the ship MV *Empire Windrush* arrived in Tilbury, England, on June 22, 1948, with some 400–700 (documents vary) persons from Jamaica aboard.[11]

Most workers immigrated to major cities such as London or Liverpool, and were to stay temporarily. Yet many remained and encouraged families and friends to join them abroad. The first groups initially comprised middle class men and women, with working classes immigrating later. As the numbers of Caribbean and Southeast Asian immigrants increased, they were increasingly perceived as a threat to the British way of life and treated accordingly. By 1958, ten years after the first ship arrived, over 125,000 Caribbeans had arrived in England.[12] Though their numbers accounted for less than 0.5 percent of the national population at that time,[13] the numbers of West Indians and Asians were large enough to be considered an "alien invasion to the body country" by the Tory government.[14] The conservative government believed these new communities would lead to the moral decay of English society.

In 1962 Parliament enacted the Commonwealth Immigrant Act, effectively ending immigration to the United Kingdom and limiting naturalization of Commonwealth citizens, unless they held employment vouchers issued by the Ministry of Labour, or, alternatively, were students, members of the armed forces, or entrants who could support themselves and their dependents without employment.[15]

The British/English Question

Conservative politician Enoch Powell famously stated in 1968 that "[the] West Indian or Asian does not, by being born in England, become an Englishman. In law he becomes a United Kingdom citizen, by birth; in fact he is a West Indian or an Asian still."[16] Powell's statement brings up two problematic issues for discussion: ethnic identity within Britain, and the confusing and complicated definitions of "British" and "English," and, by extension, "Britishness" and "Englishness." I begin with the second issue since the first is an outgrowth of it. Part of the complication between "British" and "English" is that the terms were long thought to be interchangeable, especially by individuals outside the United Kingdom.[17] Moreover, with internal political shifts throughout Britain, an ongoing debate and discourse concerning who and what is British/English has developed. Authors have written extensive articles and books examining this topic, so my contribution should be considered as a cursory explanation on a much wider, in-depth, and evolving project.[18]

"Britain" is, of course, shorthand for the United Kingdom of Great Britain and Northern Ireland, or the British Isles, a geopolitical entity including the island nations of Wales, England, Scotland, and Northern Ireland (the Republic of Ireland severed all political ties in 1949).[19] Britain also has a much longer history, dating back to as early as the fourth century,[20] though its ancient legacy is a separate conversation. In a modern context, to be British also means to be Welsh, English, Scottish, or Irish, and these regional and national terms are usually preferred in self-identification, though not exclusively. Sociologist Krishan Kumar argues that the British Empire did not begin in the seventeenth century as traditionally thought, but in the late twelfth to early thirteenth centuries with an "internal empire of Britain"[21] through England's absorption of Scotland, Ireland, and Wales into the "First English Empire" by Anglo-Norman kings.[22] This could be construed as a predecessor to what I call the "Second English Empire," or what is more known as "Great Britain," where England, having already conquered Wales, joined with Scotland in the Union Act of 1707 and Ireland in the Union Act of 1800.[23] The imperial beginnings of Great Britain, and its earlier iteration via Kumar's analysis, indicate contemporary British identity as an imperial, rather than national, one. It also highlights England's long-term dominance over the other three nations in political, social, religious, and economic matters, offering a reason why the terms "British" and "English" were, and often still are, considered synonymous.

Kumar elaborates that the British/English question:

> expresses a longstanding view, reflecting the real fact of the domination of the British Isles by the English language, English law, English culture and English political institutions. It also points to a longstanding problem for the English, in so far as they wish to assert an identity peculiar to themselves and different from those of other inhabitants of the British Isles. For much of the time the English-British confusion has . . . concealed the fact of English primacy behind the more benevolent and all-embracing cloak of Britishness.[24]

Kumar's ending statement about the "all-embracing cloak of Britishness" is a coded reference to Britain's seemingly forgotten islands of Wales, Scotland, and Northern Ireland. Historian Linda Colley makes a corresponding statement about the simultaneity of Britishness. "I am not suggesting for one moment that the growing sense of Britishness . . . supplanted and obliterated other loyalties. It did not. Identities are not like hats. Human beings can and do put on several at a time."[25] Thus the term "British" can be seen as relatively inclusive, by its ironic connection to the broader reaches of the conventional British Empire and its own internal multinational, multiethnic heritage.

It is the inference of Britishness as a signifier of multivalent cultures that brings the discussion back to ethnicity within Britain and to Enoch Powell's statement. Powell's argument of Asian or West Indian populations' inability to attain "English" identity despite their citizenship keeps Englishness as something exclusive. It is not a civic matter, but a racial and ethnic one. In essence, Englishness equals whiteness, "for [that was] the invisible norm against which all other ethnicities were measured and defined."[26] In opposition to this barrier of claiming an English identity because of skin color, nonwhite Britons adopted monikers such as "Black British." Communities were able to promote their racial heritage while enforcing a relationship to the British state. As former British MP Bernie Grant articulated, he considered himself "Black British" because "it include[d] other oppressed peoples, like the Welsh or the Scots. It would stick in my throat to call myself English."[27] Unfortunately, as shown below, the term would come under fire as it unfairly lumped together and minimized the multitude of ethnic groups encompassed within it.

Black and Asian Identities

National labeling was only one of the obstacles facing Caribbean and Asian immigrants in the early 1950s. These communities were all termed "black" despite their varying national and cultural origins, as their nonwhite skin blurred them together.[28] By contrast, in the United States the term denotes an African American, African, and/or Caribbean identity, not Indian or Pakistani. In the 1990s "Black British" was designated for Caribbean and African populations born in Britain, while "Asian" referred to individuals with origins from India, Pakistan, Bangladesh, China, and so forth, born and/or living in Britain.[29]

These communities underwent years of discriminatory practices, ranging from physical confrontations with police to restrictions regarding housing, education, and jobs. Numerous riots, beginning in Notting Hill in 1958 and continuing in Brixton, Bristol, and Liverpool by the 1980s, signaled that black and Asian communities would no longer tolerate police abuses or their secondary socioeconomic and political status.[30] Race, culture, and immigration now played major roles in England's political and social self-projection to the outside world. The population was not racially or ethnically indistinguishable, and the nation could not present itself as such. A generation of men and women born in England who considered themselves British, even though they were of Caribbean, African, and Asian heritage, would not be ignored.

One method of social and political resistance for Britain's black and Asian communities was through the visual arts. The Black (British) Arts Movement in the 1980s, a period deemed as such by numerous scholars, was a time of major artistic innovation and experimentation. Artists such as Keith Piper, Eddie Chambers, Sonia Boyce, and Isaac Julien actively used painting, photography, and film as methods of social critique.[31] Artist and scholar Rasheed Araeen curated exhibitions featuring black and Asian artists and began the internationally acclaimed arts and culture journal *Third Text* (originally known as *Black Phoenix*).

However, the use of the term "black" as a "means of affecting a unity between otherwise very diverse, powerless minorities . . . necessary for an effective anti-racist movement"[32] caused consternation to many Asian artists and communities. Sociologist Tariq Mohood wrote in 1988 of the need for Asians to assert a separate British identity, one of "people who believe that the Taj Mahal is an object of their history."[33] Mohood observed that

> when . . . an institution as central to public opinion formation as the BBC decides that the term "Black" or "Asian" is too cumbersome and that for the sake of editorial simplicity programme makers have the right to abbreviate the term to "Black,"

what are Asians in Britain supposed to conclude about their significance as a community in Britain? . . . As anyone involved in race equality issues knows, constantly being described as an appendix or as an afterthought erodes one's sense of one's worth so that one comes to believe that one perhaps is as secondary or inferior as the benevolent authorities and the media imply.[34]

Despite numerous cross-cultural art exhibitions such as the oft-cited *The Other Story: Afro-Asian Artists in Post-War Britain* (1989) and *The Essential Black Art* (1988), both curated by Araeen, the political and cultural dynamics between the various ethnic communities throughout England were extremely nuanced and complex.

Ingrid Pollard and Zarina Bhimji

Pollard's and Bhimji's early artworks in the 1980s were directly influenced by the marginalization of black, Asian, LGBT, and female communities in England during the mid to late twentieth century. Their artworks serve as examples of the wide breadth in visual discussions of identity and artistic production. As African American studies professor Michelle Wright realized, "while all theories of Black subjectivity directly counter those originary discourses that posited the Black as Other to the white subject, they must counter those Black Others in different ways *because not all Black Others are the same.*"[35] Wright's statement reiterates the aforementioned complexity of artists' participation in England's 1980s racial politics.

Pollard began documenting political events such as the Reclaim the Night demonstrations, conferences for the Organisation of Women of African and Asian Descent, and the 1984 protest against South African prime minister P. W. Botha.[36] In her 2004 monograph *Postcards Home*, Pollard states: "I did not imagine myself as an artist; I was documenting the community I was a part of. . . . Taking pictures was a seamless part of belonging—part of finding a home and being at home."[37] Her photographic portraits of prominent African American speakers, writers, and performers and candid shots at public demonstrations eventually veered toward documenting the physical landscape surrounding her. She began photographing excursions to New York and the English countryside, which initiated the *Pastoral Interludes* series. This body of work won her local and international acclaim as a major contemporary art figure.

Since then Pollard has developed several other landscape series, including *Ocean's Apart* (1989), *Seaside Series* (1988), *Landscape Trauma* (2001), and *Boy Who Watches the Ships Go By* (2002), each of which examines the English countryside as intimately tied to national and cultural identities there and in the Caribbean. Pollard is also a curator, an aspect of her professional life still lacking critical scholarship.[38]

As an artist, Bhimji seemingly was not directly involved with political liberation groups. Instead, she explored an interest in immigration policies in her early photographic and installation works, most notably her work, *She Loved to Breathe—Pure Silence* (1987). In this piece, Bhimji investigated the lives of Asian women throughout Britain and incorporated her own immigrant narrative. *She Loved to Breathe* consists of four perspex (transparent plastic) panels suspended by clear wires. In three of the panels are black-and-white photographs of ornately designed shoes and small dead birds overlaid on muslin cloth, with black and red silk-screened text across the top. One of Bhimji's poetic phrases–"the anger turned inward, where could it go except to make pain? It flowed into me with her milk"–suggests a child having to digest, and thus be affected by, his or her mother's emotional pain. The fourth panel, in its design, is somewhat separated from the others. It is a silk-screened stamp on one side and latex gloves clumped together on the other. The installation references a specific historical moment for Bhimji and for thousands of other Asian women entering England between 1975 and 1986.

The stamp in the fourth panel replicates Bhimji's own visa stamp, the one that made her an official British citizen. Her family left Uganda for England in 1975. In 1972 the British government supported the military coup of general Idi Amin, who would go on to kill thousands from his own country and force Uganda's Indian population out of the country in 1973.[39] With an influx of more immigrants into Britain, the government established "virginity tests" for Asian women arriving at Heathrow airport.[40] Bhimji alludes to these tests by juxtaposing bloody red latex gloves with the stamp. Taken together, the panels are a personal and symbolic image of dislocation and belonging, bodily control and invasion, and even cultural legacies.

Bhimji brought together "East African and Indian backgrounds, as well as [her] experience of Western culture, to play in between two realities."[41] Bhimji's later work concentrated in photography with *Cleaning the Garden*, and has since shifted into film with *Out of Blue* (2002), *Waiting* (2007), and her newest work, *Yellow Patch* (2012), all of which take place in Eastern Africa (Kenya and Uganda).

Landscape and Identity

Despite their different entries into the contemporary art world and their deviations on subject matter, Pollard's *Pastoral Interludes* and Bhimji's *Cleaning the Garden* use landscape imagery to challenge national and cultural identities in England. Each artist creates multiple, complex stories, both intimate and broadly reaching.

Landscape is a powerful allegory for national identity because, as historian Stephen Daniels writes, "national identities are co-ordinated, often largely defined by heroic deeds and dramatic destinies located in ancient or promised home-lands with hallowed sites and scenery."[42] As distinct nation-states began to form, a physical border was necessary. These "landscapes . . . [provided] visible shape; they [pictured] the nation."[43]

As England moved from an agricultural nation to a mercantile one at the turn of the nineteenth century, its numerous regions and distinct populations needed to be a part of a homogeneous, unifying space with a common history. The various medieval castle and abbey ruins dotting England's countryside brought what scholar Anne Janowitz calls the "authority of antiquity"[44] into upper class estate gardens and in landscape paintings by artists such as John Constable. The ruins were historical markers of battles, human ingenuity, political uprisings, and so forth, as viewers read the half-destroyed buildings or monuments in different ways. Their main purpose was to provide a link between humans and the land on which they lived; no matter if they were from the northern region or the southern, the village or the city, the population needed to be unified as part of the island nation of "England."[45]

While there are no traditional ruins in Pollard's or Bhimji's works, both artists do speak to the tie between land and identity. They appropriate the English country garden as a visual indication of the romanticized "belief that rural communities are warm, human, secure, friendly places with a strong spirit of 'togetherness' . . . quite different from the anonymous ways of life in towns."[46] The tourist industry emphasizes this particular version by advertising visits to quaint villages and preserved heritage sites.[47] However, Pollard and Bhimji demonstrate that the history told to tourists is often not the complete picture.

Pastoral Interludes

All five photographs in Ingrid Pollard's series are untitled. In *Untitled #1* the countryside panorama is the initial focus. The landscape's enormity, beauty, and tinted color draw in the viewer, though the vista is interrupted by the center figure. She gazes outward, taking in the view, seemingly unaware of the camera, which has captured her profile. The figure is dressed casually, holding a small bouquet of yellow flowers. A rocky stone gate inhibits her movement and suggests that she is an outsider in this landscape. The accompanying text indicates the indirect relationship between the figure and her very presence in England. "Searching for sea shells, waves lap my wellington boots, carrying lost souls of brothers & sisters released over the ship side." Pollard's discussion of seashells and lost souls references the transatlantic slave trade, the brutal economic system that had brought Africans to places like Guyana and England.

In *Untitled #2* the figure's physical presence is the focal point as her foreground size is on par with the vastness of the background hills. As she gazes off into the distance, she sits in front of another fence blocking her entrance into the wide expanse of land behind her. The fence acts as both a physical and metaphorical barrier, one that suggests the figure is unwelcome into this particular landscape. The "feeling of unease, dread" in the accompanying text, along with placing one black figure per image, reiterates feelings of isolation from black communities in more urban settings and is suggestive of experiences of black travelers into rural areas.

While there were, and are, small communities of people of color in the countryside, the overwhelming majority continue to live in the urban centers of London, Liverpool, and so forth.[48] Pollard's photograph thus symbolizes the stark contrast in the population's mindsets when changing from an urban to a rural environment, despite being among the same supposedly cosmopolitan people among whom she was raised. Pollard's black figures become signifiers of an immigrant invasion into the last remaining "white space," yet are still excluded from it.

Researchers Sarah Neal and Julian Agyeman have argued that despite increased migration into rural areas on the part of nonwhites since the 1980s, the English countryside population continues to be predominantly white.[49] Rural regions are thus perceived as "signifier[s] of an exclusive and white national identity."[50] The conservative political power in rural areas, developed from white agrarian and small business elites,[51] "construct[s] images reflecting a concern with the reproduction of a mythical and nostalgic white heritage. Any other ethnic community, seen as potentially threatening to the integrity of this representation, is excluded."[52] By contrast, Pollard's visuals go even beyond mere multiculturalism. They constitute a political commentary about British nationalism, its imperial legacy, and the societal hostility faced by nonwhite British-born subjects and their immigrant parents.

The urban/rural dichotomy stems from the myth of "Little England" associated with the Lake District. This myth is tied to the British Empire and national industrialization. "The very global reach of English imperialism, into alien lands, was accompanied by a countervailing sentiment for cosy home scenery, for thatched cottages and gardens in pastoral countryside. Inside

Great Britain lurked little England."[53] The mass appeal of cinematic adaptations of popular novels like Jane Austen's *Pride and Prejudice* and the recent introduction of television period dramas such as *Downton Abbey* perpetuate the English countryside as historically situated. A person can more easily imagine Elizabeth Bennett[54] in Pollard's photograph than her figures. The Lake District region is thus transformed into a national symbol of an idyllic past without "outsiders."

However, while rural England remained framed in the past, urbanization literally moved the rest of the nation forward. "Little England" did not include Caribbean immigrants and their British-born children. *Pastoral Interlude* portrays a multicultural and multiethnic society. By adding a dose of urbanism via the figure, Pollard's series asks if these myths can be dissolved.

As a tactic, the artist uses subtlety to initially seduce the viewer before he or she realizes the societal critiques. Pollard then takes viewers on a journey through British national and cultural history, from the mythical, homogenous, patriarchal past into the colorful, challenging, and gendered present. By hand tinting the photographs, Pollard emphasizes the luscious green color of the landscape to evoke feelings of nostalgia. Ironically, it is that very nostalgia, or "excessively sentimental, and even abnormal hankering for the return of some real or romanticized period,"[55] that Pollard refutes by inserting black figures into the image.

Pollard's aesthetics should also be examined as a continuation of English landscape painting. By continuing this legacy through photography, Pollard firmly situates her work within an established art field, yet evolves the work through contemporary political commentary and the photographic medium.

Cleaning the Garden

Zarina Bhimji's *Cleaning the Garden* series examines the development of large English estate gardens as evocative of the British Empire. The series includes over a dozen photographs, the majority of which center on the eighteenth-century Harewood House Estate in Yorkshire. Lancelot "Capability" Brown, a landscaper in demand at the time, designed the estate's garden as reminiscent of untouched, wild nature.[56]

The photographs are in transparent light boxes, adding intense color and visual brilliancy. Accompanying the images are text excerpts from eighteenth-century newspaper clippings. Bhimji selected advertisements of "for sale" and "runaway" slaves, many referred to as Indians or Moors, and purchasable colonial estates in the Caribbean. The texts are etched in reflective glass and placed next to, or between, the photographs, suggesting a mutual relationship. The texts give an intimate narrative on the Harewood Estate's construction.[57]

In *Wallings*, the photograph depicts a freshly cut lawn enclosed by a vine-covered wall. The rich green color of the grass contrasts the brown vines. With no figures, the landscape is the focal point, and, similar to Pollard's photographs, serves as both a physical and metaphorical barrier of inclusion and exclusion. As the estate owners were the gentry, the wall marks a physical and social border between their lands and those of their tenants. Persons outside the wall endeavored to be a part of the monied, privileged world inside, while those inside the wall cultivated a "tamed wilderness," an oxymoronic attempt to replicate the supposed societal "freedom" of the lower classes living outside their formal space. However, the faux version can never be the original because it is an imitation, and thus not genuine. It is an ironic realization that the inhabitants on both sides of the wall naively desire the others' lives.

Bhimji does not introduce figures because she is more concerned with the landscape, which, to her, is "a physical and multi-sensory medium ... in which cultural meanings and values are encoded, whether they are *put* there by the physical transformation of a place in landscape gardening and architecture, or *found* in a place formed, as we say, 'by nature.'"[58] *Cleaning the Garden* is concerned with the public ignorance about how these great country estates came into being and what meanings are encoded within them.

Bhimji incorporates historical texts to generate an account on the formation of the English gentry's wealth through imperialistic practices in the Caribbean, Africa, and India. Her work *Friendly* was taken from a public auction in Lichfield, England. The title indicates the unknown figure as "friendly, officious, sound-healthy, fond of labour and for colour, an excellent fine black." Presumably Bhimji wants viewers to connect the name of the piece with the unnamed figure. By suggesting the figure is named "Friendly," Bhimji makes a clever citation of the renaming of newly arrived slaves by their masters (Kunta Kinte/Toby). There is no way of knowing the artist's true intention because the viewer has no access to the rest of the advertisement.

Be that as it may, the basic information about the figure in *Friendly* is obscured. Bhimji wants recognition of a relationship between this absentee laborer in the colonies and the prosperity of the Harewood Estate in England. In *Jamaica*, the enslaved worker/owner relationship is more direct. The text is an article discussing the selling of slaves and a sugar plantation, called Wallings, in the parish of St. Thomas, by a gentleman in England. The statement implies Britain's economic reliance on Jamaica, that one nation's populace is exploited for the benefit of the other.

Bhimji's revelation of an alternate history for these nostalgic estates contests the collective yearning for Britain's venerated preindustrial era. As scholar W. J. T. Mitchell states, "Empires move outward in space as a way of moving forward in time; the 'prospect' that opens up is not just a spatial scene but a projected future of 'development' and exploitation. And this movement is not confined to the external, foreign fields toward which empire directs itself; it is typically accompanied by a renewed interest in the re-presentation of the home landscape, the 'nature' of the imperial center."[59] Bhimji's photographs of English estates point to British advancement and political strength via colonial exploitation. Yet that same exploitation is ignored in the "official" narrative of those preserved estates, and instead remembered as evidence of a romantic bygone time.

Bhimji is "exploring . . . the line between what we know to be true and what we believe to be true, the border between fact and fiction. It is this space that the memory occupies . . . it is not just about the gardens, it is about the memory spaces they represent."[60] The absence of the figures in Bhimji's photographs equate with the absence of critical forgotten and/or disregarded figures in reality.

Also utilizing subtlety, Bhimji's photographs are extremely rich in color and detail, using Cibachrome color photography to engage her audience before subjecting them to political content. The back lighting heightens the colors. Bhimji's photographs can also be examined as a continuation of landscape painting, especially in *Whereas a Black Servant Boy*. The wooded area is an example of eighteenth- and nineteenth-century picturesque English landscape design. In utilizing photography to discuss a historical time period, Bhimji not only brings the genre of English landscape forward, she revises its past.

Picturesque Photography

While the English landscape genre is traditionally associated with eighteenth- and nineteenth-century painters such as J. M. W. Turner and the aforementioned John Constable, the genre was also extremely popular with early photographers. After the invention of the camera in 1839, the daguerreotype became the most popular method of photography, as the images were "strikingly clear and detailed."[61] Due to the long exposure time, the repertoire was kept to portraiture, landscapes, buildings, still life, art works, and scientific objects. Photographers considered the camera as another artistic tool, like the paintbrush, to continue Picturesque aesthetics.[62]

Both Pollard and Bhimji bring elements of the Picturesque into the contemporary period through their respective photographic series. The Picturesque celebrates English memorials and symbols as representative of social
status.[63] The artists appropriate the English country garden as a national symbol only to challenge its iconic position and its relationship with the social
classes. For Pollard, the integration of a black figure in the rural landscape
signifies England's rigid social hierarchy and the low status of the black population within that hierarchical system. Bhimji concentrates on the gentry, yet
still invokes the servile classes.

Moreover, each artist demonstrates human control over the landscape.
Their vistas and gardens are consistently punctuated with humans or are the
result of human manipulation. Land is defined as untainted by human intervention, while "landscape is ... the land viewed, imagined, conceptualized and
depicted from particular (and largely culturally-inflected) perspectives. It is
the land plus us."[64] The Sublime, as defined by eighteenth-century philosopher Edmund Burke in *A Philosophical Enquiry Into the Origin of Our Ideas
of the Sublime and the Beautiful*, was the visual portrayal of the land's natural
wildness overtaking humans, while the Beautiful was extremely smooth and
bland landscapes completely transformed by humans.[65] Pollard and Bhimji
present the Picturesque, the making of *land* into a *landscape*, where the land
retains it natural essences and is still under the dominion of humanity.[66]

Pollard's and Bhimji's contemporary revision of an art genre considered
quintessentially English[67] signifies a revision in British art history and Englishness. Landscape painting was, and is, part of an English identity influenced by a global history involving a colonial legacy in the Caribbean, Asia,
and Africa.

Conclusion

Pollard's and Bhimji's images have contributed to the artistic and sociopolitical legacy of contemporary Britain by disrupting the established myth of the
nation's domestic and prized past. While London is considered one the major
international hubs, it is its historical countryside, as continually represented
by televised adaptations of Jane Austen and Charlotte Brontë novels, that is
more readily recognized across the world. *Pastoral Interludes* and *Cleaning
the Garden* question the very notion of an isolated, pure English culture by
presenting Britain's direct involvement in a centuries-long global empire. For
Bhimji, the estates visited annually by tourists as a replication of an idyllic
past are a fallacy. Those estates were built by absent enslaved nonwhite figures

and maintained by servants living within a rigid class-based society. Pollard establishes the English countryside as a site of fear and segregation for the contemporary nonwhite British population. It is only by appropriating the political and cultural functions of a nation's physical borders that Bhimji and Pollard are able to demonstrate to what extent identities are encoded within that space. Britain cannot afford to remain rooted in a mythical past, for it means that its depiction of its past is still incomplete.

Notes

1. Texts include Jones, "In Their Own Image"; Bailey and Hall, "Critical Decade"; and Bailey, Hall, and Sealy, *Different*.

2. The only group exhibition I have come across is *Life's Little Necessities: Installations by Women in the 1990s,* curated by Kellie Jones for the second Johannesburg Biennale (1997).

3. Bhimji, "Zarina Bhimji," 25.

4. See AlhambraDeGranada website: http://www.alhambradegranada.org/en/info/his toricalintroduction.asp.

5. See Harewood House Leeds Yorkshire website: http://www.harewood.org/house.

6. McNeill, "Foreword," 9–11.

7. While this essay is speaking specifically about Black and Asian populations, this does not mean that other ethnic or marginalized groups were not fighting for similar rights, such as the Irish, Scottish, and the nomadic cultures of the Romani.

8. Though this essay focuses on the post–World War II era, there have been African populations documented in the British Isles since the Roman Empire. See Beauchamp-Byrd and Sirmans, "London Bridge."

9. Tawadros, "Other Britains, Other Britons," 44.

10. Walmsley, *Caribbean Artists Movement*, 8.

11. BBC News, "UK *Windrush*: Ticket to New Britain."

12. Walmsley, *Caribbean Artists Movement*, 7.

13. This percentage is an estimation based on the 1951 national population statistics of forty-three million. To find this number, see *The National Populations—Figure 3.1: Actual and Projected Population of the UK and Constituent Countries, 1951-2083* on the Office of National Statistics website: http://www.ons.gov.uk/ons.

14. Houston, Diawara, and Lindenborg, *Black British Cultural Studies*, 8.

15. "Moving Here: Migration Histories," http://www.movinghere.org.uk/galleries/histo ries/caribbean/journeys/legislation.htm.

16. Powell, "Speech to London Rotary Club."

17. For examples on the interchanging uses of "British" and "English," see Paxman, *The English*; Kuman, *Making of English National Identity*; and Young, *Idea of English Ethnicity*.

18. There is large discourse on the complicated and intertwined nature of "British"/"English" and "Britishness"/"Englishness" and the terms' relationship to ethnicity in post–World War II Britain. For a sample of the more recent debate, see Colley,

"Introduction"; Kumar, *Making of English National Identity*; Ward, *Britishness since 1870*; Miller, "Reflections"; Candor, Gibson, and Abell, "English Identity"; Fenton, "Indifference towards National Identity"; Young, *Idea of English Ethnicity*; Chambers, *Things Done Change*; and Kumar, "Negotiating English Identity."

19. Welsh, *Four Nations*, 353.

20. Kumar, *Making of English National Identity*, 5.

21. Ibid., 63.

22. Ibid., 82.

23. Welsh, *Four Nations*, 201, 236–237.

24. Kumar, "Negotiating English Identity," 475.

25. Colley, "Introduction," 6.

26. Young, *Idea of English Ethnicity*, 239.

27. Paxman, "True Born Englishman," 74.

28. Houston, Diawara, and Lindenborg, "Introduction," 5.

29. Mercer, "Introduction," 28–29.

30. BBC Home: "On This Day."

31. For a larger discussion on these artists, their work, and so forth, see Beauchamp-Byrd and Sirmans, "London Bridge"; Bailey, Boyce, and Baucom, *Shades of Black*; and Bailey, Powell, and Archer Straw, *Back to Black*.

32. Modhood, "'Black,' Racial Equality and Asian Identity," 397.

33. Ibid.

34. Ibid., 400–401.

35. Wright, "Introduction," 4. My emphasis.

36. Pollard, "Looking at Ways of Working," 8.

37. Ibid.

38. Pollard's most recent exhibition, entitled *LandFall*, was viewed at the Museum of London Docklands in early 2009.

39. Cherry, "Art of the Senses," 37.

40. Ibid., 43.

41. Bhimji, *I Will Always Be Here*, 2.

42. Daniels, "Introduction," 5.

43. Ibid.

44. Janowitz, "Introduction," 3.

45. Ibid.

46. Pacione, "Rural Communities," 151.

47. Bosworth, "Perceptions of Rurality," 9.

48. According to Woods's 2005 research, the percentage is 1.6 percent. See Woods, "Rurality, National Identity and Ethnicity," 282, for more specific breakdowns.

49. Neal and Agyeman, "Remaking English Ruralities," 119.

50. Agyeman and Spooner, "Ethnicity and the Rural Environment," 197.

51. Woods, "National Politics," 84.

52. Agyeman and Spooner, "Ethnicity and the Rural Environment," 197.

53. Daniels, "Introduction," 6

54. The main character in Jane Austen's *Pride and Prejudice* (1813).

55. Berberich, "This Green and Pleasant Land," 211–212.

56. Cotter, "Art in Review."

57. Interestingly, the website discusses an exhibition organized in 2007 entitled *Harewood 1807*, which was a commemoration of the bicentenary of the abolition of the slave trade and the involvement of the Lascelles family in the transatlantic slave trade. http://www.harewood.org/learn/harewood_1807.

58. Mitchell, "Imperial Landscape," 14.

59. Ibid., 17.

60. Artnet.com, "Cleaning the Garden."

61. Ackerman, "Photographic Picturesque," 75.

62. Ibid., 76.

63. Ibid., 77.

64. Andrews, "Dispossessing the Land," 57.

65. Ross, "Picturesque," 273.

66. Ibid., 273–274.

67. There was also a strong tradition of French landscape painting, so the genre is closely associated with both Britain and France.

Bibliography

Ackerman, James. "Photographic Picturesque." *Artibus et Historiae* 24.48 (2003): 73–94.

Agyeman, Julian, and Rachel Spooner. "Ethnicity and the Rural Environment." In *Contested Countryside Cultures: Otherness, Marginalisation and Rurality*, ed. Paul Cloke and Jo Little, 190–210. London: Routledge, 1997.

AlhambraDeGranada website. http://www.alhambradegranada.org/en/info/historicalintroduction.asp.

Andrews, Jorella. "Dispossessing the Land." In *Landscape Trauma in the Age of Scopophilia*, ed. Jorella Andrews, 57–63. London: Autograph, 2001.

Artnet.com: "Cleaning the Garden: An Exhibition of Works by Zarina Bhimji." http://www.artnet.com/galleries/exhibitions.asp?gid=140558&cid=116227.

Bailey, David A., and Stuart Hall. "Critical Decade: Black British Photography in the 80s." *Ten.8* 2.3 (1992).

Bailey, David A., Sonia Boyce, Ian Baucom, eds. *Shades of Black: Assembling Black Artists in 1980s Britain*. Durham, N.C.: Duke University Press, 2005.

Bailey, David A., Stuart Hall, and Mark Sealy, eds. *Different: Historical Context, Contemporary Photographers, and Black Identity*. London: Phaidon, 2001.

Bailey, David A., Richard Powell, and Petrine Archer-Straw, eds. *Back to Black: Art, Cinema & the Racial Imaginary*. London: Whitechapel Art Gallery, 2005.

BBC Home. "On This Day, 1950–2005." http://news.bbc.co.uk/onthisday/hi/dates/stories/november/25/newsid_2546000/2546233.stm.

BBC News. "UK *Windrush*: Ticket to New Britain." http://news.bbc.co.uk/2/hi/uk_news/112688.stm.

Beauchamp-Byrd, Mora J., and Franklin Sirmans, eds. "London Bridge: Late Twentieth Century British and the Routes of National Culture." In *Transforming the Crown: African, Asian & Caribbean Artists in Britain 1966-1996*, 16–45. New York: Franklin H. Williams Caribbean Cultural Center/African Diaspora Institute, 1997.

Berberich, Christine. "This Green and Pleasant Land: Cultural Constructions of Englishness." In *Landscape and Englishness*, ed. Robert Burden and Stephan Kohl, 207–244. New York: Rodopi, 2006.

Bhimji, Zarina. *I Will Always Be Here*. Birmingham: Ikon Gallery, 1991.

———. "Zarina Bhimji: Cleaning the Garden." In *Continental Drift: Europe Approaching the Millennium—10 Photographic Commissions*, ed. Michael L. Sand and Anne McNeil, 25–30. New York: Prestel, 1998.

Bosworth, Gary. "Perceptions of Rurality and Their Implications for the Experience and Impact of Immigrants: Social and Economic Perspectives from Cornwall and Northumberland." http://regional-studies-assoc.ac.uk/events/2010/may-pecs/papers/Bosworth.pdf.

Candor, Susan, Stephen Gibson, and Jackie Abell. "English Identity and Ethnic Diversity in the Context of UK Constitutional Change." *Ethnicities* 6.2 (2006): 123–158.

Chambers, Eddie. *Things Done Change: The Cultural Politics of Recent Black Artists in Britain*. New York: Rodopi, 2012.

Cherry, Deborah. "The Art of the Senses and the Making of a Diasporan Aesthetics: Zarina Bhimji's She Loved to Breathe-Pure Silence, 1987–2002." *Tessera* 32 (2003): 34–45.

Colley, Linda. "Introduction." In *Britons: Foraging the Nation, 1707-1837*, 1–10. London: Pimlico, 2003.

Cotter, Holland. "Art in Review: Zarina Bhimji—*Cleaning the Garden*." *New York Times*, October 5, 2001.

Daniels, Stephen. "Introduction." In *Fields of Vision: Landscape Imagery and National Identity in England and the United States*, 1–10. Princeton, N.J.: Princeton University Press, 1993.

Edmunds, June. "Redefining Britannia: The Role of 'Marginal Generations in Reshaping British National Consciousness." In *History, Nationhood and the Question of Britain*, ed. Helen Brocklehurst and Robert Phillips, 73–84. New York: Palgrave MacMillian, 2004.

Fenton, Steve. "Indifference towards National Identity: What Young Adults Think About Being English and British." *Nations and Nationalism* 13.2 (2007): 321–339.

Ferguson, Moira. "Breaking in Englishness: Black Beauty and the Politics of Gender, Race and Class." *Women: A Cultural Review* 5.1 (1994): 34–52.

Harewood House Leeds Yorkshire website. http://www.harewood.org/house.

Houston, Baker, Manthia Diawara, and Ruth Lindenborg, eds. "Introduction." In *Black British Cultural Studies: A Reader*, 1–15. Chicago: University of Chicago Press, 1996.

Janowitz, Anne. "Introduction." In *England's Ruins: The Poetic Purpose and the National Landscape*, 1–19. Cambridge: Basil Blackwell, 1990.

Jones, Kellie. "In Their Own Image." *Artforum* 29 (1990): 133–138.

Kumar, Krishan. *The Making of English National Identity*. Cambridge: Cambridge University Press, 2003.

———. "Negotiating English Identity: Englishness, Britishness and the future of the United Kingdom." *Nations and Nationalism* 16.3 (2010): 469–487.

McNeill, Anne. "Foreword." In *Continental Drift: European Approaching the Millennium*, ed. Anne McNeill and Michael L. Sand, 6–9. Munich: Prestel, 1998.

Mercer, Kobena. "Introduction: Black Britain and the Cultural Politics of Diaspora." In *Welcome to the Jungle*, 1–32. New York: Routledge, 1994.

Miller, Dennis. "Reflections on British National Identity." *Journal of Ethnic and Migration Studies* 21.2 (1995): 153–166.

Mitchell, W. J. T. "Imperial Landscape." In *Landscape and Power*, ed. W. J. T. Mitchell, 1–34. Chicago: University of Chicago Press, 1994.

Modhood, Tariq. "'Black,' Racial Equality and Asian Identity." *New Community* 14.3 (1988): 397–404.

"Moving Here: Migration Histories." http://www.movinghere.org.uk/galleries/histories/caribbean/journeys/legislation.htm.

Neal, Sarah, and Julian Agyeman. "Remaking English Ruralities." In *The New Countryside? Ethnicity, Nation and Exclusion in Contemporary Rural Britain*, 99–126. Bristol: Policy Press, 2006.

Pacione, Michael. "Rural Communities." In *Rural Geography*, 151–165. London: Harper & Row, 1984.

Paxman, Jeremy. "'True Born Englishmen' and Other Lies." In *The English: A Portrait of a People*, 60–76. London: Penguin Group, 1998.

Pollard, Ingrid. "Looking Back at Ways of Working." In *Postcards Home*, 1–10. London: Autograph, 2004.

Powell, Enoch. "Speech to London Rotary Club, Eastbourne." November 16, 1968. http://www.enochpowell.net/fr-83.html.

Ross, Stephanie. "The Picturesque: An Eighteenth-Century Debate." *Journal of Aesthetics and Art Criticism* 46.2 (1987): 271–279.

Tawadros, Gilane. "Other Britains, Other Britons." *Aperture: British Photography: Towards a Bigger Picture* 113 (1988): 41–46.

Walmsley, Anne. *The Caribbean Artists Movement 1966–1972: A Literary & Cultural History*. New York: New Beacon Books, 1992.

Ward, Paul. *Britishness since 1870*. London: Routledge, 2004.

Welsh, Frank. *The Four Nations: A History of the United Kingdom*. London: Harper Collins, 2002.

Woods, Michael. "National Politics and Rural Representation." In *Contesting Rurality: Politics in the British Countryside*, 84–100. Burlington, Vt.: Ashgate, 2005.

———. "Rurality, National Identity and Ethnicity." In *Rural Geography: Processes, Responses and Experience in Rural Restructuring*, 279–290. London: SAGE, 2005

Wright, Michelle. "Introduction: Being and Becoming Black in the West." In *Becoming Black: Creating Identity in the African Diaspora*, 1–26. Durham, N.C.: Duke University Press, 2003.

Young, Robert. *The Idea of English Ethnicity*. Oxford: Blackwell, 2008.

From Port-au-Prince to Kinshasa

A Haitian Journey from the Americas to Africa

Danielle Legros Georges

During the 1960s and 1970s hundreds of young Haitian professionals moved to and worked in the Republic of the Congo (later renamed the Democratic Republic of the Congo, Zaire, and again the Democratic Republic of the Congo).[1] With little opportunity to practice in their fields in Haiti, and with a number of citizens facing harassment or persecution under the regime of François Duvalier, most saw the recruitment of Francophone professionals and technicians (primarily educators, but also doctors, engineers, lawyers, and other professionals) by the United Nations (UN) and the nascent Congolese government as an opportunity to escape repression and start or resume professional lives in the Congo.

The story is significant for a number of reasons. First, very little has been documented regarding this pioneering group of Haitians. Affected by the social tempests created in the political climate of Duvalier's rule, they left for Africa rather than for other parts of the Americas or Europe. By contrast, a great deal has been written about Haiti's general history, particularly its 1804 revolution, which served as a model for women and men engaged in liberation struggles in the United States, Latin America, and Africa. Scholars have paid careful attention to the Haiti of the 1950s through 1980s, in particular to the governments of Duvalier's *père et fils* and what anthropologist Rolph-Michel Trouillot calls "the longest dictatorial sequence in the history of that country."[2]

Second, the Haiti-Congo story adds greatly to discussions in the field of Atlantic history; postcolonial studies; cross-border intellectual histories; Caribbean migration relative to development of home country (remittances on one end of the spectrum, the idea of brain drain on the other); Haitian transnationalism and identity; the negotiation of race, gender, and class by migrant workers; the role of non-governmental organizations (NGOs) and governments in complex arrangements of movement of groups of people; and the political and economic dimensions of geographic displacement in general.

Last, this story is personal: it is my own story; more precisely, it is the story of my parents and that of dear friends and colleagues. It is a story that starts for me in the 1970s, with seeing my mother and her friends in their skirts made of fabric bought in Zaire; with hearing *Lingala* terms dropped into their conversations in Creole and French at home in the Boston of my childhood.[3] It is the tale of my father, for whom Sunday afternoons entailed playing Zairois music, whereupon much shaking of the tail feather could be seen. It is the story of heated political debates, which is the Haitian way, among friends and family in my childhood living room, which took on, obliquely or directly, Pan-Africanism, a liberated Haiti, the civil rights movement in the United States, Black Power, and Latin American nationalisms.

This essay is meant as an introduction to the Haiti-Congo story. It is meant as an outline of the conditions in the Americas that precipitated the emigration of the Haiti-Congo participants as well as of the contemporary conditions of the Congo. At its heart are the voices of Haitian people as reflected in a number of the participant narratives I have gathered in informal conversations and more formal interviews since 2000. I also draw from Camille Kuyu's *Les Haitiens au Congo*, published in 2006, which contains the important narratives of six participants.[4]

A Future Questioned: The Haitian Context

To understand the Haitian situation, it is necessary to place it in larger contexts. François Duvalier had risen to the Haitian presidency in 1957 during the early Cold War period, an era marked by ideological and actual hostility between the Soviet Union and the United States. Two years later, in 1959, Fidel Castro led an armed struggle in Cuba, which, in the context of a popular struggle for social justice, resulted in a new government there. The United States initially welcomed the prospect of a democratic government in Cuba. However, it quickly perceived the new self-identified socialist state in the Caribbean—considered to be a U.S. "backyard" or sphere of influence—as a threat to its interests. The Monroe Doctrine, a foreign policy strategy introduced by U.S. president James Monroe in 1832, articulated the "American backyard" concept—the idea that the Americas were no longer to be considered a field for colonization by European powers. In the twentieth century the doctrine was used to rationalize U.S. intervention, particularly in the Caribbean and Latin America.

Castro did not help Cuba-U.S. relations when he stressed an international-ism of the Cuban revolution as a form of anti-imperialism and self-defense, and in the service of the transformation of society.[5] He also seized American-owned utilities, which within the ideological conflict between capitalism and Communism, moved Cuba closer to the Communist bloc. Then again, during his 1960 visit to New York for a UN conference, Castro went so far as to cavort with sundry "Negroes" in Harlem, including Malcolm X.[6]

The United States understood Cuba's alliance with the Soviet Union in 1961 as a potential catalyst for a Communist revolution that—unless impeded—could spread throughout the Western Hemisphere. Historians Stephen Ran-dall and Graeme Mount observe that the Castro-Cuban revolution "marked the most significant turning point in the history of the region since the Span-ish-American war [in 1898] had driven Spain from the area . . . creating for the next three decades the most significant challenge to the western national security in the hemisphere in the twentieth century."[7]

To counter the potential of the Caribbean falling to Communism, the U.S. government began to solicit regional leaders who would support, at the very least, its anti-Communist agenda. François Duvalier was among these heads of state. Duvalier also appeared to be willing to cooperate with American interests in Haiti and support U.S. policy in the international field.[8] He was thus securing his own interests. Trouillot notes that in addition to external pressure from U.S. and allied interests and connected economic dependency, Duvalier as president was encountering local struggles in the political and cultural arenas. His answer to this partly inherited crisis would be the cre-ation and consolidation of a totalitarian regime.[9] Against this larger context, the 1960s in Haiti saw university students and young professionals living through and graduating onto a terrain of state-sponsored violence and terror, and profound uncertainty. They attempted to do what university graduates and young professionals worldwide do: secure or maintain gainful employ-ment, practice in their fields, and begin adult lives with marriages, friend-ships, families, and children. For many future émigrés, however, it became clear that, given their values, jobs would be difficult to find or hold within the world of patronage and nepotism established by Duvalier. Jean Malan, a Congo participant now living in Boston, notes, "If you were a young person, whether an engineer, or a lawyer, or doctor, or dentist, you saw that you had no future in the country. Not only was there no future, but you saw that your life was in danger, completely, every day. . . . Whatever the job, if you didn't have a *macoute* connection, if you didn't agree to train at Fort Dimanche, or march along the Champs de Mars in the blue [militia] uniform, carrying a gun on your back, then you weren't with it."[10] With *macoute* connections,

Fig. 11.1. Haitian engineering students, including Rodney Georges (second from right, bottom row); Port-au-Prince, February 1960. Courtesy of Danielle Legros Georges.

Malan is referring to the paramilitary force created by Duvalier. Officially called the Volontaires de la Sécurité Nationale (VSN)—but named *tontons macoutes* by Haitians, after the mythological bogeyman uncle who kidnaps children and carries them off in his sack—this force, often operating at night, was used by Duvalier to terrorize and control the Haitian populace, and to insulate him from a possible coup d'état by the Haitian army.

Duvalier had been in office nearly three years when a student strike rocked Port-au-Prince and reverberated across the small country. Many of the future émigrés saw the strike as a marker, a signal of things to worsen. A group of students had been reported to the government on the charge that they had been studying Communism. More than a dozen of the young men among them were arrested. While the writings of Mao Tse Tung and Marxist doctrine were popular among students of the day, many participants considered themselves not part of a Communist revolution, but a nationalist movement in pursuit of change.[11] After L'Union Nationale des Etudiants Haitiens (National Union of Haitian Students) learned of the arrests, along with the rest of the nation, it spearheaded an advocacy campaign demanding the immediate release of the students. The union's letters to the Department of the Interior, which oversaw the police at this time, were ignored. The students' whereabouts were not disclosed to the public. As a result there was great concern for their safety among fellow students, their families, and those within educational and progressive communities.

While Duvalier, who had come to power as a physician and self-proclaimed intellectual, took pains to show that he had backing among intellectuals, he nonetheless perceived educational institutions and the teaching profession as possible centers of opposition. In April 1960 he had imprisoned the president of the Union Nationale des Membres de l'Enseignment Secondaire (National Union of Secondary School Teachers) on the grounds that the teachers' union had been influenced by Communist ideology and was supporting terrorism.[12] For three months, Haitian university students and allies pressed the government for the release of the young men, to no avail.[13] The student leadership then decided to temporarily shut down the university system, and in November 1960 a strike order was given.[14]

During the strike, police cracked down on students in Port-au-Prince, and Duvalier instated martial law. According to Malan, "If you were walking the streets, and looked like you were twenty, twenty-two years old, they arrested you, took you to the police station for questioning to find out exactly what you were doing, where you were going."[15] Congo participant Max Manigat, now living in Miami, underscores in his interview "the atmosphere of constant fear created by the many arrests, executions and harassment by the *tontons macoutes*."[16] Students who had begun engaging in antigovernment activity and protest were particular targets. "My older brother, Charles, was arrested and tortured in Cap-Haïtien. My younger brother, Claude, an intern at the Faculté de Médecine, and president of the Association des Étudiants en Médecine (Medical Students' Association), had to spend many months in hiding after a strike was called by the students of this school. I knew that my own name [by association] was on a short list of people to be arrested for 'subversive activities.'"[17] Congo participant Immacula Pierre-Louise Bernard, then a high school student, now living in Boston, remembers the book exchange she had established with several friends during the time (housed in a storage space outside one of the friends' houses). "The *macoutes* set it on fire. . . . We lost so many beautiful books. I had a book of poems by Guy de Maupassant burned! Duvalier didn't want people to have too much education. Once you got education, you could ask for change."[18]

In the course of the strike and another strike that followed immediately, three of the arrested students died in jail.[19] The remaining students were eventually released in the spring of 1961, and the second strike lifted with assurances on the part of the regime that the students had nothing to fear in terms of reprisals. Yet according to several Congo participants, by now the student leadership had certainly been identified within the context of a growing opposition to what was being seen as a fascist dictatorship of the country. Moreover, rumors persisted that Duvalier had bought out some of the student leaders.[20]

Shortly thereafter, Duvalier displayed his skill at manipulating institutions by centralizing the university system under the aegis of l'Université d'Etat d'Haïti (The State University of Haiti).[21] In addition to the university system, other civilian institutions, professional associations, sports clubs, churches, and schools were compromised or shuttered. The Haitian press and media were silenced by force.[22] With all national institutions under a centralized authority, it was easy for Duvalier to declare himself president for life a few years later, in 1964.[23] It was also easy, comments Trouillot, to eliminate "thousands of professionals, middle-level bureaucrats, and army officers by means of imprisonment, torture, or forced (or encouraged) emigration,"[24] thus reducing the number of political opponents from all sectors of Haitian society. Many Haitians—young and old, not connected to or supported by the Duvalier regime—sought a way out of the chokehold that was Haiti. When the newly independent Congo and the UN came looking for Francophone teachers and technicians for the Congo, those who could answered the call.

A Way Out

When Belgium formally loosened its colonial grip on the Congo in June 1960, it left some administrators and missionaries in the Congo, but also a large vacuum in the areas of public administration and formal education. The gap would be filled by a multinational corps of Francophone educators and technicians, recruited and overseen by the UN and the new Congolese government. By 1964 more than 800 foreign teachers representing twenty-nine nationalities were teaching in secondary schools in the Congo. In addition to teachers, more than 100 experts in education, science, and communication worked for the central and provincial Congolese governments.[25]

Of the multinational, multiracial United Nations Education, Scientific, and Cultural Organization (UNESCO) corps—among them Belgians, French, Lebanese, Spanish, Italians, Syrians, Greeks, Afghans, Canadians, Rwandans, Vietnamese, Americans (U.S.), Canadians, Swiss, Norwegians, Chinese, Mexicans, Colombians—Haitians comprised a large contingent, being the most numerous of the teachers during the 1962–1963 academic year.[26] In some cases the UNESCO corps members took the place of Belgian colonists in schools, universities, hospitals, and other institutions. In other instances, the UNESCO teachers and experts assumed newly developed positions. The Haitians accepted contracts as educators, within school administration, both as directors of schools and as teachers in primary school and *athenée* (secondary school) classrooms. They also worked as technicians, engineers, physicians, and judges in the Congo.

Many Haitian participants were acutely cognizant of the contemporary politics at play in Haiti, as well as in the Caribbean and the Americas. For most, the political and accompanying economic hardships born of the climate in Haiti drove them to pursue careers and lives outside of Haiti. "The cells at Fort-Dimanche were crowded with political opponents, and public executions were common," states Manigat. He adds, "The economy, stable under President Paul Magloire, had started to deteriorate with corruption and nepotism. Most of the seasoned civil servants were replaced by faithful Duvalierists without qualifications; tourism was dead; exports at a low."[27] By contrast, few future émigrés understood the nuances of the contemporary Congolese political situation or how it mirrored, on many levels, the Haitian context they were leaving—though many had followed the emergence in the Congo of Patrice Lumumba with interest because of his progressivism. "He became popular in Haiti," notes writer and historian Jean-Claude Martineau, "when he started having problems with the Belgians. His was a story of a resistance to colonization that Haitians could identify with because of our own history. Moreover, we could express our admiration of a progressive personality such as Lumumba where we couldn't of Fidel Castro, for example, given Duvalier's anti-Castro pro-American stance. Castro was too close to home."[28] While aware of Lumumba, some participants would only later grow aware of the complicated geopolitics of the Congo—and realize the myriad implications of their movement and the powerful forces at play, for better and for worse, in their displacements.

A Way In

The Haitians made their way to towns and rural areas or bush across the vast Republic of the Congo, a country with a population more than six times greater than that of Haiti. They were 6,000 miles away from home. Some would work in Léopoldville/Kinshasa,[29] others at sites in the country's interior such as Lodja and Stanleyville/Kisangani. Some found themselves on the eastern border in Butembo, Goma, Bukavu, and Albertville/Kalemi, or in the western towns of Kikwit, Tshikapa, Banningville/Bandundu, and Kenge. Haitians also traveled to and lived in the southern cities of Luluabourg/Kananga and Elisabethville/Lubumbashi, and in the eastern cities of Kitona, Matadi, and Boma, not far from the Atlantic coast. They experienced the country's

Fig. 11.2. Democratic Republic of Congo, Map No. 4007 Rev. 10, July 2011. Courtesy of the United Nations.

varying topography of rain forests, mountainous terraces, mountains, pla-
teaus, savannas, and grasslands, along with its equatorial climate: hot and
humid in the north and west, cooler and drier in the south-central area and
the east, and its wet and dry seasons.[30]

In the Congo, they encountered both familiar and new cultures, dynamics,
and phenomena. Among these was a colonialism not known to them in Haiti.
They were unaccustomed to the apartheid they saw in the major cities of the
Congo. The Congolese capital, for example, contained a "white" city center in
which the remaining Europeans lived, and a "black" periphery, or *cité*, a ghetto
created earlier for the Congolese by the colonists. Under Belgian colonial rule
and for as long as Belgians remained and wielded some power in a postcolonial Leopoldville/Kinshasa, most Congolese were discouraged or kept from
circulating in the white section after dark, forbidden from stores and from
public accommodations.

A number of Haitians were housed in hotels in the white centers of large
towns. In smaller cities, villages, and more rural areas, many lived in houses

formerly occupied by Belgians. On several occasions Haitians desegregated "white only" venues, refusing to bend to Belgian colonial apartheid codes. Their status as foreigners and blacks or mixed-race people at times complicated their relationships with their Congolese neighbors and colleagues and with the remaining Belgian population. In some cases, the Haitians were welcomed by their Congolese colleagues and neighbors; in others, they were viewed with misgivings. The reactions of Belgian administrators and missionaries also varied, falling between viewing Haitians as colleagues and as arrogant foreign nonwhites. "Most of our Congolese colleagues were warm and considered us as allies," notes Max Manigat. By contrast, he found that his Belgian coworkers "never failed to let you understand that you were occupying some space on their turf."[31] "Once in Boma," notes Jean Malan, "there was a priest who was in charge of [academic reviews]. When he asked to see the person that had these great course evaluations, he thought they belonged to a French person. Then I showed up!"[32] Here Malan illustrates the racism he and his Haitian colleagues encountered—with the unwitting comment from and presumption on the part of his Belgian evaluator that excellent course evaluations could only have been achieved by a French person.

The Haitian educators contended with varying receptions from their Congolese students, many of whom were pleased to have Haitian and nonwhite administrators and instructors, and some who questioned their authority as professionals. Malan comments,

[The Belgians] gave us a hard time, persecuted us, created major problems for us. Their power was being diminished with the Haitian presence. Here we were talking to students about Toussaint L'Ouverture. Yet, when I got to Kisangani, it was tough because I was working with students who had been brainwashed to believe that black people couldn't be doctors, lawyers. When you told them that you were a lawyer, or a doctor, they would say "that's not true." Because the whites told them that blacks can't be lawyers or doctors. It's as if the colonial system had cut the country off from the rest of the world. All the information was filtered.[33]

For the Haitians, the idea and perception of class, which governed and ordered a great deal of Haitian urban society—particularly the small black middle class from which the majority of the participants came—did not operate similarly or as pervasively with the Congolese in the Congo as an organizing social principle. Georges Nzongola-Ntalaja, a scholar of African politics, delineates the contemporary Congolese class structure as consisting of an imperialist bourgeoisie and middle bourgeoisie (both European); a petty bourgeoisie (divided along racial lines); the traditional Congolese ruling class; and the peasantry, working class, and lumpen proletariat (all

Congolese).[34] Haiti's class structure of four main strata—elite, middle class, peasant class, and poor—is deeply influenced by the French colonial model, which saw the European metropolitan bourgeoisie and white plantocracy at the top, followed by free people of color, and the large number of Africans enslaved in St. Domingue (Haiti's colonial name) at the bottom. In Congolese social realities, ethnic group affiliations also held powerful sway. A number of participants point out this difference as among the many that distinguished Congolese and Haitian social life. What could be viewed as unusual in a middle-class Haitian milieu, for example, was not so in the Congo. Malan highlights the strength of tribal affiliations among many Congolese: "You could see a minister of the government . . . sitting with a maid and a street sweeper, as if nothing were, because they were of the same tribe." He adds, "The Congolese would say, so-and-so is my brother, and we would be surprised. Someone would introduce you to ten people, all of whom would be 'his brother.' You'd think, *this person has a lot of brothers!* We'd ask ourselves 'how many brothers does this person have?' We understood later that the 'brother' was someone who came from the same tribe."[35]

In addition, poverty in the Congolese urban centers was not necessarily accompanied by the monolingualism and illiteracy emblematic of the Haitian urban poor, who, while in general highly valuing formal education as a means for achieving mobility, did not have widespread access to it. While almost all Haitians spoke Creole, a minority had access to formal education and thus also spoke French. Every Congo participant was a Francophone. Bilingualism, or, more precisely, Francophonie, broadcasted an instant class signal for Haitians. Not so for the Congolese, in a nation in which more than 200 languages were spoken.[36] Maryse Chapoteau, a Congo participant who now lives in Port-au-Prince, comments that while "the poor lived in the *cités*, like Cité Soleil, they used French and their own languages . . . and the Zairois poor were not illiterate. The *boy* had his newspaper and came to our house and would read to me from it. He would say 'Madame, there is trouble in your country.'"[37] Where French in the Haitian context served to separate Haitian classes, in the Congolese context it served as a unifying language, one that facilitated communication between the Congolese, the Haitians, the Belgians, and others. Chapoteau's statement suggests too that at least primary levels of formal education were available to many urban Congolese.

Chapoteau's reference to "*boy*," for domestic male servant, reveals a particular aspect of the contemporary Congo reality for the Haitians, and a hold-back of Belgian colonial policy. In Congolese urban areas the domestic workers who performed generalized functions, such as cooking, serving food, and gardening, were men. Participant Rigobert Carty, who now lives

Fig. 11.3. Haitian women and children, including Sabine Malan (bottom left) with her mother, Lilia Malan (left), and Edmonde Georges (center); Kinshasa, April 1969. Courtesy of Danielle Legros Georges.

in Miami, explains this particular phenomenon of male domestics as the result of a colonial fear of the implications of miscegenation, which could take place between Belgian men and Congolese women if the latter were employed in colonial households.[38] (Presumably no such miscegenation could occur between *boys* and Belgian women.) The Congolese women who were employed by the Haitians and other UNESCO corps households were, in many cases, asked to do laundry and help with babies and provided child care. These days women were called *mama*s, according to the Haitian women participants.[39]

The narratives of the Haitian women participants add texture to the Haiti-Congo story. In addition to comments on geopolitics, the women provide such details as emerging from domestic spaces, their interactions with neighbors, with traveling Congolese market-women who went door to door with produce and wares, and with their colleagues and, in some cases, students. Several women recall the challenges of traveling from the Americas to Africa, at times alone or with children, to join their husbands and men in the Congo. Haitian men were, in most cases, engaged first by UNESCO, with a number of Haitian women being hired by UNESCO and such organizations as the Salvation Army after they had arrived in the Congo. Several women who arrived in the Congo to find their men in ill health or malnourished nursed them back to health. The women speak of collaborating to procure food in markets when food was scarce, and of the popular Portuguese *pregos* sandwiches in cafés and Primus beer under more easy circumstances. They discuss supporting one another with concerns around their children, some of whom were born in the Congo. Their letters to relatives in Haiti address the details of homemaking in the Congo. The letters of both Haitian women and men reference the remittances they were sending to Haiti, the financial support provided to relatives in Haiti.

The Congolese gender relations they observed at times angered some Haitian participants, particularly women, with several commenting on what appeared to them to be the second-class citizenship of some Congolese women relative to some Congolese men. Edmonde Georges juxtaposes the arduous field work done by rural women with the work of some men.[40] Immacula Pierre-Louis Bernard adds the image of "the woman doing the planting and the growing of the food, with the baby tied on her back all day long." Bernard comments, "when there was luggage to be carried it was carried by the woman, and the man was the *bwana*, the sir of great importance, walking in front with his cane, his hat, *bwana mukubwa*, the big chief."[41] Jean Malan expresses surprise at seeing women walk behind men in certain instances.[42] Both Haitian women and men remark on the open polygyny they witnessed in some areas of the Congo, and how the practice stood in stark relief to their often Catholic notions of family, partnerships, marriage, and ideas regarding the roles of women. A number of participants also comment on the perceived libertinage and lax mores they saw among the Belgian colonists, both women and men.

The Congolese Context

When the first Haitian cohort arrived, the Congo was experiencing upheavals similar to the ones that produced an untenable domestic situation for many Haitians. The Congo too was entering a decades-long period of dictatorial rule. Joseph Désiré Mobutu, a Congolese colonel and armed forces chief of staff, had seized power from the newly and popularly elected Congolese prime minister Patrice Lumumba. As with the Caribbean, the perceived communist threat informed U.S. foreign policy in Africa, as did the desire for access to—and a degree of control over—the significant mineral wealth and raw materials of the Congo. (Indeed, the Democratic Republic of the Congo's natural resources continue to make it contested terrain. It is the site of ongoing armed conflicts and severe human rights abuses, including unlawful killings, disappearances, mass rape, and torture.[43]) Once again the Cold War superpowers and European nations appeared behind the scenes (if not on the stage) of a national liberation struggle, which in this case existed within the context of anticolonial and independence struggles waged by Africans across the African continent.[44]

Until 1960, Belgium had ruled the Congo, or the "Belgian Congo," as a colony with the help of a large and highly paternalistic bureaucracy.[45] This bureaucracy provided an organized administration, substantial infrastructure of communication and roads, and, for the Congolese, primary education—but no secondary (high school), technical, or higher education.[46] Congolese students were not admitted to high schools until 1954.[47] Belgian colonial policy, established to support the exploitation of the Congo's considerable resources, had as a side effect the undereducation and brutalization of the Congolese.

Though Congolese resistance had occurred at every stage of colonial rule, the expression of a nationalist movement became explicit when the Alliance of the Kongo People (Abako) issued a manifesto calling for "immediate independence" in 1956.[48] Georges Nzongola-Ntalaja writes that with those two words, "Abako defined the theme of revolutionary politics in the Congo for the next three-and-a-half years."[49] Political reform in 1957 led to the emergence of a number of political parties in 1958. These parties included Abako, led by Joseph Kasa-Vubu, and Mouvement National Congolais (MNC), led by Patrice Lumumba.[50] Nzongola-Ntalaja notes, "If Kasa-Vubu's Abako can be said to be the first real political party in the Congo, Lumumba's MNC was the first truly national party, and one that played a crucial role in the political agitation for independence."[51] The growing political agitation in the Congo was accompanied by popular unrest, organized civil disobedience, violent disturbances, and nationalist sentiment.[52] They resulted in the Belgian government's abrupt decision to cede the Congo in national elections. Patrice Lumumba and Joseph Kasa-Vubu emerged as prime minister and president, respectively.[53]

Within weeks of the June 30, 1960, announcement of independence, however, Lumumba was confronted with a secessionist movement in the mineral-rich southern province of Katanga and a nationwide mutiny of the *Force Publique*, the Congolese army. Nzongola-Ntulaja suggests that both revolts were "instigated by the Belgians, who also intervened militarily on 10 July, a day before the Katanga secession was announced."[54] Recognizing the real threat to Congolese sovereignty, Lumumba sought assistance from the outside. According to writer Evan Luard, feelers were put out in different directions, including to Ghana, the United States, and the Soviet Union, before the possibility of securing help from the UN was explored.[55] Lumumba eventually appealed to the UN Security Council for the provision of UN peacekeeping troops. Writer Ludo de Witte asserts that the United States supported a UN intervention to keep Lumumba from calling on friendly African armies or the Soviet Union to combat Belgian-Katangese aggression.[56] On July 14, 1960, the UN Security Council called on Belgium to withdraw its troops and authorized a large-scale military and technical assistance program for the Congo. Thus began the Opérations des Nations Unis au Congo (ONUC), the UN operations in the Congo.[57]

With Lumumba barely in office three months, UN peacekeeping troops on the ground, and UNESCO representatives already having met with Pierre Mulele, Congo's first minister of national education, Mobutu, in a stunning radio broadcast on September 14, 1960, announced that the army would take power.[58] Congo participant Rigobert Carty observes, "Mobutu was supported by the United States. Without American support, the Belgians would have overthrown him."[59] On January 17, 1961, the democratically elected Lumumba was murdered in Katanga,[60] and Mobutu began a long-term and dictatorial rule in the Congo, not unlike Duvalier's in Haiti. At this time, the first group of Haitians was already en route to the Congo.

Opérations des Nations Unis au Congo

Between Lumumba's appeal for peacekeeping support in the summer of 1960 and his murder in 1961, the UN charged UNESCO with providing technical assistance to the Congolese government. UNESCO would take charge of the country's education system from 1960 until 1965.[61] Developing education for the new republic was seen as a major part of UNESCO's "nation-building" functions in the Congo. According to writer Garry Fullerton, UNESCO would assist the Congo to "develop secondary education and improve primary education, create new institutions of higher learning and train educational administrators, adapt educational systems to the needs of the Congo and provide machinery for future development, safeguard the research activity of major scientific institutions, and develop information media to serve the new nation."[62] At the end of the 1963–1964 academic year, the Congolese government would begin sole administration of the education development program and oversee it through the 1980s.[63]

"The Belgians who had been living in the Congo," notes Malan, "who were teachers, who were in all sectors of the administration of the country turned their backs on the country. They deserted the schools, leaving them without teachers, that's because *they* had been the teachers. Many deserted public administration in the Congo."[64] Historian and writer Adam Hochschild observes that "the colony's administration had made few . . . steps towards a Congo run by its own people."[65] The Belgian Congo had produced a large Congolese working class, as well as a group of middle-class civil servants, known as évolués, from which Lumumba had emerged.[66] At the moment of formal decolonization, however, there were few Congolese high-level administrators, lawyers, doctors, agronomists, engineers, secondary school teachers, army officers, or other professional people;[67] that is, there were hardly any trained in Western traditions.[68] In 1960 the two existing universities of the Congo, l'Université Lovanium and l'Université d'État d'Élisabethville, which had been established for the education of Belgians in the Congo, had fewer than 500 African students registered and had graduated only twenty-nine Congolese students.[69] A very small number of Congolese professionals would assume high administrative positions in the new Congo.[70]

In mid-August 1960, UNESCO representatives visited Leopoldville to assess the Congo's education needs and consult with the Congolese government. René Maheu, UNESCO's deputy director-general, was accompanied by Edmond Sylvain, a Haitian who would later serve as the educational expert in the consultative group at ONUC and as UNESCO's chief representative in the Congo.[71] On this trip they convened with Pierre Mulele, the Congolese minister of national education who made an official request for support in obtaining secondary and technical school teachers, as well as for experts to help strengthen services of the Ministry of National Education.[72]

By November 1960—the month of the major student strike in Haiti—a first program of assistance was established,[73] and UNESCO was authorized to recruit 500 secondary school teachers for the Congo with the cost to be borne by the UN.[74] It should be added that the Haitian Maurice Dartigue, of the UNESCO secretariat, quickly succeeded his compatriot Sylvain as chief of the UNESCO mission in Leopoldville and remained so through 1961. He became one of the primary recruiters and supporters of Haitians for the UNESCO corps positions.[75]

Haitians' Impressions of the Congo

With the green light from the UN in November 1960, UNESCO had the task of recruiting French-speaking teachers for the Congo as quickly as possible. Missions were sent to UN member Francophone nations around the world, including Haiti. While some future émigrés met with UNESCO and Congolese government representatives when these delegations visited Haiti several times in the early 1960s, many in years to come heard about the Congo positions via networks of students or colleagues who were members of the first cohorts of Haitians recruited. "The first technical assistants had brought with them the dossiers of friends and acquaintances interested in leaving, in order to advocate on their behalf," remembers Congo participant Renel Cantave. "The people who were accepted were informed by telegram. That was my case. My brother, who was already in the Congo, had taken steps on my behalf. My telegram was signed by Bernadin Mungul Diaka, the [Congolese] Minister of Education. I left Haiti on November 23, 1967."[76] Participant Edmonde Georges "knew about this because my husband's father was already in Zaire. My father-in-law was able to recommend Rodney for a contract, and he went for a year, and then he sent for me."[77] Participant Rigobert Carty remarks that when he left in 1965, "there had been three or four contingents before I left, though I had heard about the project in 1961 from a friend, Edwin Gouthier, who had gone with the first cohort."[78] Immacula Pierre-Louis Bernard mentions her brother Grevy Pierre-Louis, who had advocated on behalf of her husband and her.[79] Likewise, "my departure had been facilitated by an elder I knew from Saut D'eau, my home town," says participant Hérold Désil. "Already in the Congo, he had taken the same steps as I had. He was called Andre Bristout. To my great surprise, I received a telegram informing me that my application as a [technical assistant] had been accepted, and I received a plane ticket."[80]

For some professionals, a Congo employment offer did not immediately represent a ticket out of Haiti. "Leaving or entering Haiti in the '60s was not easy for Haitian citizens," states Rigobert Carty. "Everything was politicized. Corruption was rampant. To travel you had to submit your name to the immigration service, which sent it to the National Palace. The names of those requesting permission to leave Haiti were placed on a list. The lower on the list one's name was, the closer to exit one was."[81] Participant Jean-Claude Michaud notes that "the Haitian government at the time had a pretty shabby politic. On the one hand, it was necessary to prevent the departure of these young people, on the grounds that the country needed this cadre. On the other hand, racketeers let these young people leave provided their parents paid heavy fees. In some cases, an exit visa was required and involved complicated formalities. . . . Every day we'd go to see the list of 'descending names.'"[82] According to Carty, "If you were an opponent of the Duvalier régime or if anyone targeted you as such, whether you were or not, your name would be blocked. Sometimes, travelers' names weren't blocked, but they got arrested at the airport." He adds that "any Haitian citizen who wanted to go *back* to Haiti needed a visa. I remember that when I had to return in 1969. I had to get a reentry visa at the Haitian Consulate in New York. As a result, I can say that I was worried before departing Haiti."[83] Some participants left Haiti by sea rather than risk harassment or arrest at the airport. Participant Rodney Marcellus took a "boat that left Port-au-Prince for Kingston, Jamaica." He met three other Haitians along the journey and en route to the Congo, and recalls, "from Kingston, we took a Pan Am flight to New York; from New York, a Sabina flight to Brussels; and from there, an Air Congo flight to the Congo."[84]

Not all Congo participants were in Haiti at the time of recruitment. Participants Maryse and Charles Chapoteau, then a young married couple, had been studying in Paris in 1968. "When I finished, I couldn't enter the country, given the trouble with Duvalier," says Maryse Chapoteau, "and there was a lot going on in Paris at the time, so Charles found a contract in the Congo. Once there, he was sent into the bush, to a place called Lodja. I entered with Stanley [their son] eight months old."[85] Évelyne Durand and her husband had also been studying in France. In need of work, they applied for and received job offers, most notably from Canada. "At the same time, we got an offer from my cousin, who was already in the Congo, to teach there. We considered quickly and decided to go Africa first, the land of our ancestors. We told ourselves that we would have time to go to Canada later."[86] Daniel Tallyrand, a young physician, then just married and with a young child, was recruited in 1969 while living in France. He observes, "I was surprised to see that my application had been accepted in record time by the *Université officielle du Congo* [which] asked me to assume my position of Associate Professor of Pediatrics as soon as possible. A plane ticket was waiting for me at Air Congo in Paris."[87] "I arrived in Leopoldville, got through customs, and had to find my way into town," reminisces Rigobert Carty. "I was dropped off at the center of town. There were three or four of us Haitians on the plane; we were glad to find each other. At the center of town, we met a Haitian who gave us some money and told us to go the administrative building. We presented our resumes, and notified the people there of our presence on the Congolese terrain." Carty states that before leaving Haiti for the Congo, "I considered myself on an adventure, to discover a new culture, a new contact. At the same time, to leave my country and to go work in another country involved something unknown, the difficulty that would be mine, how I would solve my problems, what would my situation there be. These are the concerns that rolled around in my mind."[88]

Jacqueline Romain, a participant now living in Quincy, Massachusetts, one of the first Haitian women to receive a UNESCO assignment in the Congo, flew into the airport at Leopoldville not believing that she had arrived there. She recollects her flight over skyscrapers and highways shortly before landing in the early evening in April 1961. "I had already crossed two continents, but when I landed, I said, 'this is not Africa.' I thought I was in Europe. What was showed us about Africa on TV was not what I saw."[89] Rigobert Carty, expecting "vast forests everywhere and wild animals," was "surprised to see ... Leopoldville. I was impressed by everything I came into contact with: the people, the music, the food, the highways ... the impression was fantastic."[90] Equally struck was Max Manigat: "Everything was new. It took me a certain time to realize that I was going to spend a few years in a completely different environment."[91] These comments underscore both the excitement many participants felt at arrival and the dissonance between the projected image of Africa and Africans and its peoples, cities (some colonial), technology, and modernity.

Of his first impressions of the Congo, Manigat notes, "I was absolutely thrilled to be in Africa. My sister, Huguette, her husband hired by the UN as a judge, and their two small kids, were living in Léopoldville at the time [February 1964]. My good friend, Emmanuel Lafond, who had helped me get the contract, and another very dear friend, Louis 'Loulou' Noisin, were there to greet me." He continues, "Everything was different: the environment, the people, the languages. Fortunately, there was a sizable Haitian community in the capital of the Congo, and everyone wanted to share with me his or her experience. I remember one of the first who reviewed with me the dangers posed by the venomous snakes. . . . It took me a couple of weeks to start to understand what great change had occurred in my life; but I was determined to accept the challenge and try my best to live up to the terms of my contract as a teacher."[92]

Despite the newness and surprises of the Congo, a familiar element—corruption—also met the Haitians at the airport and as they made their way into the country. Jean Malan points out that

the first people we were in contact with were the immigration agents in Kinshasa, and the first thing these agents were asking us for was bribes. Here we were full of enthusiasm, idealism, and these immigration agents grabbed our passports, and wouldn't release them without bribes for the immigration stamps on the passport. We saw that we were running from the river and fell into the ocean. Here were some corrupt functionaries who had no clue, and had no warm welcome (especially in Kinshasa) for us at all. In their minds, we had come from Haiti in order to make some money in the country. It was with this idea that they welcomed us. They didn't welcome us professionals, as professors or instructors who came to help. I say this of Kinshasa, but this wasn't true for other parts of the country, like the East of the Congo, where people had very revolutionary ideas. They also weren't the same people.[93]

Fig. 11.4. Congolese women and child; unidentified, the Democratic Republic of the Congo, 1967. Courtesy of Danielle Legros Georges.

Assignment sites made a large difference in the experience of the Haitians. Those in major cities contended with the ills of apartheid but had typically more modern amenities and living arrangements. Those in more rural areas were often welcomed by their Congolese colleagues and neighbors but were faced with challenges having to do with lack of infrastructure. Residents of the smaller cities Kisangani and Okavu, for example, supported what Malan calls "a revolutionary ideology," while major cities such as Kinshasa and Bakongo continued to operate within a colonial paradigm.[94] It should be noted that the years 1960 through 1965, a period known as the "Congo Crisis," represented a period of struggle for democracy in the Congo. The Lumumbist movement, for example, emerged in the wake of Patrice Lumumba's 1961 assassination, and its leaders and followers engaged in armed conflict with Congolese government and allied forces.[95] As a result, some locations were dangerous for both local and foreign residents. Some assignment sites and towns lacked electricity. Some participants had to learn about venomous snakes, others how to bake bread and cook local legumes. Varying degrees of culture shock and acculturation were not unusual, as the young Haitian professionals made their lives in the Congo.

Conclusion

Many participants would stay in the Congo fewer than ten years. A number would remain well into the 1980s, and some participants are still living in the Congo. Numerous participants mention the lifelong friendships developed with one another and underscore appreciation of their Congolese colleagues and students and of Congolese culture(s). Despite cultural differences, friend-ships, collaborations, and families also emerged as a result of the interaction between the Haitians and the Congolese, as well as with teachers and tech-nicians of other nations who took part in the ONUC project. Several par-ticipants point to the heightened political consciousness they developed as a result of their Congo experiences, able afterward to better connect varying and seemingly disparate democratic struggles within and beyond the global African Diaspora, and to identify interference and challenges to democratic aspirations and institutions.[96]

Among Haiti's narratives are two familiar and persistent ones that create a dialectic in the way Haiti is represented and understood beyond its bor-ders: first, Haiti, with its successful 1804 revolution, as source of inspiration for antislavery, anti-imperial, freedom-seeking peoples the world over; and second, Haiti as "the poorest nation in the Western Hemisphere," a perpetual site of need, want, and lack and of stateless citizens.[97] These tropes locate Haiti in the centuries-old past, on the one hand, and outside of time, on the other. Between these narratives runs the thread of a third unremitting one: that of an unspoken and frightening darkness, not disconnected to the first two and not unlike that attached to representations of Africa and Africans.

Not often mentioned in the discourse about Haiti are its universities, its long traditions of higher education, its preparation of students in fields of study including law, education, medicine, economics, pharmacy, engineering, urban planning, literature, agriculture, accounting and finance, management and administration, and environmental studies. Haiti's experts and its profes-sional class have received just as little attention outside of Haiti. Its specialists and pioneers have tended to be viewed as exceptional, and not emerging from (and responding to) structures extant in Haiti.

The Haiti-Congo story presents us with a large group of Haitians who articulate an awareness of themselves in time, and as exercising choice in contexts of great constraint—a group that benefited from Haitian institutions and pushed against their compromise; a group that operated through the gears of UNESCO and the Congolese government, which engaged them as experts. Most were deeply sympathetic to the cause of African and Congolese independence and to the Congolese they worked with and among, while part of an elite multinational working corps of the UN, which many argue ulti-mately supported Western interests in the Congo. They represented a human capital loss, a brain drain, for Haiti—at a time, some participants argue, Haiti needed them most; at the same time, like many diasporic Haitians, they sup-ported loved ones and relatives in Haiti economically with ongoing remit-tances. They were black and mixed-race and privileged, and in many cases cosmopolitan and deeply committed to their country of origin—and willing to write, however difficult or complicated, their individual narratives, a collective story of collaboration, and a new Haitian transatlantic narrative.

Notes

1. The majority of Haiti-Congo participants arrived in the Congo while in their twenties and thirties. On the country's names: as of June 30, 1960, the Republic of the Congo; as of August 7, 1964, the Democratic Republic of the Congo (to distinguish it from its neighbor of the same name); as of October 27, 1971, renamed Zaire by President Mobuto Sese Seko; as of 1997, reversion to the Democratic Republic of the Congo.

2. See Trouillot, *Haiti, State against Nation*.

3. A number of the Congo participants resettled in Boston in the 1970s, the Bernard, Chapoteau, Ford, François, Georges (Rene/Lourdes), Georges (Rodney/Edmonde), Malan, Marcellus, Romain, and Sylvestre families among them.

4. Kuyu, *Les Haitiens au Congo*.

5. Saney, "Homeland of Humanity," 114.

6. Joseph, *Waiting 'Til the Midnight Hour*, 36.

7. Randall and Mount, *Caribbean Basin*, 8.

8. Nicholls, *From Dessalines to Duvalier*, 219.

9. Trouillot, *Haiti, State against Nation*, 139.

10. Jean Malan, interview by author, July 17, 2006. Fort Dimanche: the barracks that served as the training center for Duvalier's militia and later became a notorious prison and torture center. Champs de Mars: Port-au-Prince's main park, which housed the National Palace, government buildings, and monuments.

11. Duvalier himself had espoused a nationalist ideology in the early part of his presidency. Note too that anticolonial, anti-U.S., and nationalist sentiments existed throughout the Caribbean as a result of European and U.S. interventions in the region.

12. Nicholls, *From Dessalines to Duvalier*, 219–222.

13. Support for the students came from members of the Haitian Roman Catholic Church in part because of the considerable role the church played in educational institutions. Tacit support also came from members of the business community.

14. Malan interview; Nicholls, *From Dessalines to Duvalier*, 219.

15. Malan interview.

16. Max Manigat, email interview by author, July 31, 2008.

17. Ibid.

18. Immacula Pierre-Louise Bernard, interview by author, June 15, 2007.

19. Nicholls, *From Dessalines to Duvalier*, 223.

20. Trouillot, *Haiti, State against Nation*, 160.

21. Ibid.

22. Ibid., 159.

23. Ibid., 160.

24. Trouillot, *Haiti, State against Nation*, 155.

25. UNESCO, "UNESCO in Sub-Saharan Africa."

26. Fullerton, *Unesco in the Congo*, 12. He mentions that there were 123 Haitians that year.

27. Manigat interview.

28. Jean-Claude Martineau, interview by author, December 15, 2011.

29. In a policy emphasizing the value of Zairian culture over Western culture, President Mobuto Sese Seko renamed the Democratic Republic of the Congo, Zaire. Leopoldville was renamed Kinshasa in 1971, and colonial city names were changed to Zairian ones. I provide both colonial and Zairois city names in cases in which cities were renamed.

30. Meditz and Merrill, *Zaire*, xxvi. See also, U.S. Department of State, "Background Note."

31. Manigat interview

32. Malan interview.

33. Ibid.

34. Nzongola-Ntalaja, *Congo from Leopold to Kabila*, 62–77.

35. Ibid.

36. Meditz and Merrill, *Zaire*, xxii.

37. Maryse Chapoteau, interview by author, August 11, 2010. Cité Soleil: an impoverished neighborhood of Port-au-Prince.

38. Rigobert Carty, interview by author and email message, July 12, 2008.

39. Chapoteau interview; Georges interview; Bernard interview.

40. Georges interview.

41. Bernard interview.

42. Malan interview.

43. U.S. Department of State, "Background Note."

44. See Nzongola-Ntalaja, *Congo from Leopold to Kabila*.

45. The Belgian Congo was established in 1908 when the Belgian Parliament annexed the Congo Free State from Belgian King Leopold II. See Hochschild, *King Leopold's Ghost*.

46. Luard, *History of the United Nations*, 2:217.

47. Fullerton, *UNESCO in the Congo*, 42.

48. In response to a 1955 pamphlet written by A. A. J. Van Bilsen, a Belgian professor at the Colonial University at Antwerp, outlining a thirty-year plan for the political emancipation of Belgian Africa. Nzongola-Ntalaja, *Congo from Leopold to Kabila*, 81.

49. Ibid., 82.

50. Ibid., 83; Meditz and Merrill, *Zaire*, xvii.

51. Nzongola-Ntalaja, *Congo from Leopold to Kabila*, 82.

52. Including the spontaneous Kinshasa (province) revolt of January 4, 1959, involving Abako members. See ibid., 85–86. See also Meditz and Merrill, *Zaire*, xvii.

53. Lumumba would serve as head of government and Kasa-Vubu as the country's ceremonial head.

54. Nzongola-Ntalaja, *Congo from Leopold to Kabila*, 94.

55. Luard, *History of the United Nations*, 2:218.

56. De Witte, *L'assassinat de Lumumba*.

57. Chamberlin, Hovet, and Hovet, *Chronology and Fact Book of the United Nations.*

58. Luard, *History of the United Nations,* 2:250. Mobutu would later formalize his ascendancy to power with a November 24, 1965, coup in which he named himself president.

59. Carty interview.

60. De Witte, *L'assassinat de Lumumba,* 213.

61. UNESCO, "UNESCO in Sub-Saharan Africa."

62. Ibid., preface.

63. Kuyu, *Les Haitiens au Congo,* 15. I have translated the original French text into English here and elsewhere.

64. Malan interview.

65. Hochschild, *King Leopold's Ghost,* 301.

66. Nzongola-Ntalaja, *Congo from Leopold to Kabila,* 5.

67. Luard, *History of the United Nations,* 217; Fullerton, *UNESCO in the Congo,* preface.

68. I say this with research to do on Congolese local, regional, and traditional organizational and administrative structures, and social and health care services.

69. Thành Khôi Lê, *L'enseignment en Afrique tropical* (Paris: Éditions de Minuit, 1971), in Kuyu, *Les Haitiens au Congo,* 40.

70. Fullerton, *UNESCO in the Congo,* 11.

71. Ibid., 50. It may be due to Sylvain's efforts, as well as that of his compatriot and successor, Maurice Dartigue, that Haitians would make up a large part of the UNESCO-Congolese teaching corps. The roles of these two men are to be further researched.

72. Fullerton, *UNESCO in the Congo,* 50.

73. Ibid. Likely building on a 1959 UNESCO inventory of needs in primary and secondary education in tropical Africa (with special emphasis on the access of women to education) prepared for submission to the 1960 Conference of Ministers and Directors of Education of Tropical African Countries in Addis Ababa, Ethiopia. See UNESCO, "UNESCO in Sub-Saharan Africa."

74. Fullerton, *UNESCO in the Congo,* 50.

75. Kuyu, *Les Haitiens au Congo,* 46. See also the Papers of Maurice Dartigue.

76. Renel Cantave, in Kuyu, *Les Haitiens au Congo,* 80.

77. Edmonde Georges, interview by author, August 12, 2006.

78. Carty interview.

79. Bernard interview.

80. Hérold Désil, in Kuyu, *Les Haitiens au Congo,* 89.

81. Carty interview.

82. Jean-Claude Michaud, in Kuyu, *Les Haitiens au Congo,* 102.

83. Carty interview.

84. Rodney Marcellus, interview by author, November 16, 2011.

85. Chapoteau interview.

86. Évelyne Durand, in Kuyu, *Les Haitiens au Congo,* 94.

87. Daniel Tallyrand, in Kuyu, *Les Haitiens au Congo,* 67–68.

88. Carty interview.

89. Jacqueline Romain, interview by author, August 17, 2011.

90. Carty interview.

91. Manigat interview.

92. Ibid.

93. Malan interview.

94. Ibid.

95. Nzongola-Ntalaja, *Congo from Leopold to Kabila*, 6–7.

96. While Haiti and the Republic of the Congo have no formal diplomatic ties, the Congo-Haiti exchange engendered projects beyond the areas of education and technical assistance, and include the documentary and feature films made by celebrated Haitian cinematographer and Congo participant Raoul Peck, who would take Patrice Lumumba's story to viewers around the world.

97. For a recent essay on Haiti's representation, see Ulysse, "Why Haiti Needs New Narratives," 240–245.

Bibliography

Abi-Saab, Georges. *The United Nations Operation in the Congo, 1960–1964*. Oxford: Oxford University Press, 1978.

Chamberlin, Waldo, Thomas Hovet Jr., and Erica Hovet. *A Chronology and Fact Book of the United Nations, 1941–1969*. Dobbs Ferry, N.Y.: Oceano Publications, 1970.

De Witte, Ludo. *L'assassinat de Lumumba*. Paris: Éditions Karthala, 2000.

Fullerton, Garry. *UNESCO in the Congo*. Paris: United Nations Educational, Scientific and Cultural Organization, 1964.

Hochschild, Adam. *King Leopold's Ghost: A Story of Greed, Terror, and Heroism in Colonial Africa*. Boston: Houghton Mifflin, 1998.

Joseph, Peniel. *Waiting 'Til the Midnight Hour: A Narrative History of Black Power in America*. New York: Holt Paperbacks, 2007.

Khôi, Lê Thành, et al. *L'Enseignment en Afrique Tropical*. Paris: Press Universitaires de France, 1971.

Kuyu, Camille. *Les Haitiens au Congo*. Paris: L'Harmattan, 2006.

Luard, Evan. *A History of the United Nations*. Vol. 2, *The Age of Decolonization, 1955–1965*. New York: St. Martin's Press, 1982.

Meditz, Sandra W., and Tim Merrill, eds. *Zaire: A Country Study*. Baton Rouge, La.: Claitors Publishing Division, 1995.

Message of President James Monroe at the commencement of the first session of the 18th Congress (The Monroe Doctrine), December 2, 1823; Presidential Messages of the 18th Congress, ca. December 2, 1823–ca. March 3, 1825; Record Group 46; Records of the United States Senate, 1789–1990; National Archives.

Nicholls, David. *From Dessalines to Duvalier: Race, Colour, and National Independence in Haiti*. Rev. ed. New Brunswick, N.J.: Rutgers University Press, 1996.

Nzongola-Ntalaja, Georges. *The Congo from Leopold to Kabila*. London: Zed Books, 2002.

O'Balance, Edgar. *The Congo-Zaire Experience, 1960–98*. New York: MacMillan, 2000.

O'Brien, Conor Cruise. *To Katanga and Back: A UN Case History*. New York: Simon & Schuster, 1962.

Papers of Maurice Dartigue. February 14, 2010, http://atom.archives.unesco.org.

Peck, Raoul. *Lumumba: La mort du prophète*. Paris: Velvet Film, 1992.

Saney, Isaac. "Homeland of Humanity: Internationalism within the Cuban Revolution." *Latin American Perspectives* 36.1 (2009): 111–123.

Struelens, Michel. *The United Nations in the Congo, or O.N.U.C., and International Politics*. Brussels: Max Arnold, 1976.

Randall, Stephen, and Graeme Mount. *The Caribbean Basin: An International History*. London: Routledge, 1998.

Trouillot, Michel-Rolph. *Haiti, State against Nation: The Origins and Legacy of Duvalierism*. New York: Monthly Review Press, 1990.

Ulysse, Gina. "Why Haiti Needs New Narratives Now More Than Ever." In *Tectonic Shifts: Haiti since the Earthquake*, ed. Mark Schuller and Pablo Morales, 240–245. Sterling, Va.: Kumarian Press, 2012.

UNESCO. "UNESCO in Sub-Saharan Africa." In *50 Years for Education*. http://www.unesco.org/education/educprog/50y/brochure.

U.S. Department of State. "Background Note: Democratic Republic of the Congo." Last modified April 30, 2012. http://www.state.gov/r/pa/ei/bgn/2823.htm,.

Interviews

Bernard, Immacula Pierre-Louis. Interview by author, recorded, Boston, June 15, 2007.

Carty, Rigobert. Email messages to author from Miami, August 2008; interview by author, recorded, Boston, July 12, 2008.

Chapoteau, Charles. Interview by author, recorded, Port-au-Prince, August 11, 2010.

Chapoteau, Maryse. Interview by author, recorded, Port-au-Prince, August 11, 2010.

Georges, Edmonde. Interview by author, recorded, Miami, August 12, 2006.

Malan, Jean. Interview by author, recorded, Boston, July 17, 2006.

Malan, Lilia. Interview by author, recorded, Boston, July 17, 2006;

Manigat, Max. Email message to author, Miami, July 31, 2008.

Marcellus, Denise. Interview by author, recorded, Boston, October 21, 2011

Marcellus, Rodney. Interview by author, recorded, Boston, October 21, 2011

Martineau, Jean-Claude. Interview by author, recorded, Montreal, December 15, 2011.

Romain, Jacqueline. Interview by author, recorded, Quincy, Mass., August 17, 2011.

Additional interviews/conversations between 2000 and 2012

Auguste, Karl. Montreal.

Braithwaite Bey, Aziza. Boston.

Dupuy, Charles. Montreal.

Élysée Auguste, Ertha. Montreal.

François, Edith. Boston.

Georges, Gerard. Boston.
Legros, Georgette. Port-au-Prince.
Martineau, Serge. Port-au-Prince.
Moise, Georges. Boston.
Plaisimond, Marcus. Cambridge, Mass.
Sylvestre, LeClerc. Atlanta.
Sylvestre, Rosette. Atlanta.

Contributors

Keiko Araki is an associate professor in the Department of International Studies at Tokai University, Japan. She received a master's degree from the University of California, Berkeley. She has been working on Marcus Garvey's and his movement's impact on Asia and Africa, and published numerous articles on the subject in Japanese journals.

Ikaweba Bunting earned his PhD from the University of Wales, United Kingdom. He taught at California State University, Long Beach and at Loyola Marymount University in Los Angeles and is currently the division chair of behavioral and social sciences at El Camino College Compton Center. He worked in humanitarian assistance sectors for the Danish Association for International Cooperation, the British NGO, Oxfam, the Mwalimu Nyerere Foundation, and the Tanzania Film Company. He was a senior consultant for the United Nations and rapporteur general for the Burundi Peace Negotiations. He has made his home in eastern and southern Africa since 1974.

Amy Caldwell de Farias, professor of history and chair of the History Department at Monmouth College, specializes in nineteenth-century Brazilian history. Her current research interests include Black Atlantic rebels during and after the independence wars in Latin America. In addition, she spent a year in Maputo, Mozambique as a Fulbright Scholar and is now finishing an article that explores the intellectual and political ties between Brazil and Mozambique from 1800-1850.

Kimberly Cleveland, an associate professor of art history at Georgia State University, primarily researches Afro-Brazilian art. She has published numerous articles, contributed essays to *Politics of Memory: Making Slavery Visible in the Public Space* (2012), *Gender, Empire and Postcolony: Luso-Afro-Brazilian Intersections* (2014), *African Heritage and Memory of Slavery in Brazil and the South Atlantic World* (2015), and is the author of *Black Art in Brazil: Expressions of Identity* (2013).

Kimberli Gant, PhD is the McKinnon Curator of Modern & Contemporary Art at the Chrysler Museum of Art in Norfolk, VA. She is the Mellon Curatorial Fellow at the Newark Museum, has held positions at the Contemporary Austin (2013) and the Museum of Contemporary African Diasporan Arts (MoCADA, 2005-2010). Her doctorate degree in art history (2017) is from the University of Texas Austin, and she also holds an MA and BA in art history from Columbia University (2009) and Pitzer College (2002).

Danielle Legros Georges is a professor in the Creative Arts and Learning Division of Lesley University. Her areas of interest include arts and education, contemporary American poetry, African-American poetry, Caribbean literature and studies, and literary translation. She is the author of two collections of poetry, *Maroon* (2001) and *The Dear Remote Nearness of You* (2016). Legros Georges has read her work across the United States and internationally. She has received a number of literary awards and honors, most recently a 2015 Brother Thomas Fellowship and a 2014 Massachusetts Cultural Council Artist Fellowship in Poetry. In 2015 she was appointed Poet Laureate of the City of Boston.

Douglas W. Leonard earned his PhD in history from Duke University. He serves as an assistant professor of history at the United States Air Force Academy in Colorado Springs, Colorado, where he primarily teaches European and African history. His research centers on the French-speaking colonial world, particularly in the nineteenth and twentieth centuries.

John Maynard is a Worimi Aboriginal man from the Port Stephens region of New South Wales. He is currently Chair of Aboriginal History at the University of Newcastle and Director of the Purai Global Indigenous and Diaspora Research Studies Centre. He has held several major positions and served on numerous prominent organizations and committees including, Deputy Chairperson of the Australian Institute of Aboriginal and Torres Strait Islander Studies (AIATSIS). He was the recipient of the Aboriginal History (ANU) Stanner Fellowship 1996, the New South Wales Premiers Indigenous History Fellow 2003, Australian Research Council Postdoctoral Fellow 2004, University of Newcastle Researcher of the Year 2008 and 2012 and Australian National University Allan Martin History Lecturer 2010. In 2014 he was elected a member of the prestigious Australian Social Sciences Academy. Professor Maynard's publications have concentrated on the intersections of Aboriginal political and social history, and the history of Australian race relations. He is the author of several books, including *Aboriginal Stars of the Turf*,

Fight for Liberty and Freedom, The Aboriginal Soccer Tribe, Aborigines and the Sport of Kings, True Light and Shade: An Aboriginal Perspective of Joseph Lycett's Art and *Living with the Locals – Early Indigenous Experience of Indigenous Life.*

Kendahl Radcliffe has served as a lecturer of African of African American, history and Women's Studies departments at the University of California, Los Angeles and is a professor of history at El Camino College, Compton Center, Compton, CA. She holds a master's in African Area studies and a PhD in history both from the University of California, Los Angeles. She has served on the faculty of the University of Arizona, Tucson and California State University, Fullerton, teaching African American, African and women's studies. Her interest in how people of African descent at the turn of the last century attempted to reconcile, negotiate, and in many instances reject European cultural, political and economic paradigms is reflected in her past and present research. Her most recent works include "We Shall Make Farmers of Them Yet: Tuskegee's Uplift Ideology in German Togoland," is featured in *Germany and the Black Diaspora: Points of Contact 12:15-1914 (Berghahn Books/ 2013).*

Edward L. Robinson, Jr. is an instructor at California State University at Fullerton & Dominguez Hills. He received his doctorate at Claremont Graduate University, Claremont California in Cultural Studies with an emphasis in African American literature, literary theory, culture, and media. His literary projects and scholarship includes work on the African American poets Lucy Terry and Phillis Wheatley, Black humanity in early American national literature, and the construction of Gay Masculinities in Black American and Diasporic Literature. Edward is presently preparing to debut his literary blog "The Baldwin Room" and website where he writes about popular culture and new diasporic literature and Black development of Superheroes. He is presently working on his novel *The Prince of Dover's Bluff.*

Jennifer Scott serves as faculty in the graduate program of Museum and Exhibition Studies at the University of Illinois at Chicago, and, since 2003, as a part-time assistant professor of anthropology at The New School for Public Engagement in New York and Parsons School of Art and Design History and Theory. She teaches courses in cultural anthropology, arts and social engagement, race and ethnic studies, cultural pluralism, museum studies, and the African diaspora. As a Fulbright Scholar, Jennifer conducted research in West Africa on women dressmakers and textiles in urban Accra, Ghana. In addition, she works closely with a number of history centers, museums and arts organizations. She served for ten years as the Vice Director and Director of Research at Weeksville Heritage Center in Brooklyn, New York, a historic house museum, where she specialized in nineteenth- and early twentieth-century history. She continues this focus as the Director of the Jane Addams Hull-House Museum at the University of Illinois at Chicago, a nationally significant historic site focused on women, immigrant and urban history during the Progressive Era. Jennifer holds degrees in philosophy, African American studies/history, and anthropology from Stanford University; the University of California, Los Angeles; and the University of Michigan, Ann Arbor, respectively. Recent publications include: "Reimagining Freedom in the Twenty-first Century at a Post-Emancipation Site," (*The Public Historian/* May 2015).

Anja Werner, née Becker, is a postdoctoral research associate at the Institute for the history and ethics of medicine at Martin Luther University Halle-Wittenberg, Germany. Her research interests include educational, medical, and scientific transatlantic transfers with a special focus on black and deaf perspectives. Currently, she is working on Black Deaf history as well as on a transnational history of Deaf people in the divided Germany. She earned her Ph.D. degree in American and French studies from the University of Leipzig, Germany, in 2006 and subsequently coordinated the International Alexander-von-Humboldt-in-English-Project at Vanderbilt University in Nashville, Tennessee (until 2009). She recently directed a German-language project about transnational pharmaceutical research during the Cold War (University of Leipzig Press, 2016). Among her major publications is *The Transatlantic World of Higher Education: Americans at German Universities, 1776–1914* (Berghahn Books, 2013).

Index

Note that this index reflects the diversity of references to Black experiences in general, in the context of which variations in spelling such as "black" and "Black" illustrate the individual choices of the contributors to this volume.

Belgian colonialism: apartheid codes, 237;
colonists, 240; policy, 236, 238, 241
Bennett, Elizabeth, 219
Bennett, Herman, 48
Berlin Wall, 153
Bernard, Immacula Pierre-Louise, 233, 240,
244, 249n
Bhabha, Homi K., 62n
Bhimji, Zarina, 6, 14, 209, 211, 215, 216, 217,
219, 220, 221, 222, 223
bilingualism, 238
Black (British) Arts Movement, 214
black Africanism, 123
black Americans, 4, 67, 68, 104, 119, 140, 143,
144, 147, 176; artists, 182; experience, 3
black and white mixing, 40
black art, 170, 175
Black Arts Movement, 14, 173
Black Atlantic, the, 3, 4, 6, 7, 8, 9, 14, 16, 48,
100, 173, 188, 190; community, 193; intellectual, 9; rebel, 47, 57; texts, 193, 201;
writers, 194
Black Atlantic World, 6, 7
Black Brazilians, 13, 177; struggles of, 176
Black Britons, 213, 214; activists and artists,
14; art of, 209
Black Diaspora, 4, 5, 14–15; experiences, 7
black Haitians, 29
black Jacobins, 10, 47
Black Liberation movements, 69, 176
black Moses, 108
black Nationalism, 193
black nationalist movement, 99, 118
Black Other, 215
Black Panther Party for Self Defense, 69,
176
black people, 7, 9, 12, 14, 33, 34, 35, 36, 39, 67,
100, 104, 118, 122, 123, 125, 127, 128, 129,
131, 132, 188, 197, 237; achievements of,
40; agency, 4; agitation, 102; and Asian
communities, 214, 223n; autobiographies, 187; bodies, 210–11; in the Caribbean, 128, 145, 176; colonial figures, 211;

communities, 189; consciousness, 66;
diversity, 4; evolution, 34; experience, 4,
7, 16, 209, 210; folks, 65; freedom fight/
struggle, 13, 140, 154; identities, 48, 190;
intellectualism, 6, 16; intellectuals, 8, 9,
11, 28, 30, 40, 48, 140, 154; leaders, 12, 112,
120, 123, 126, 131, 143, 152; literary traditions of, 190, 195; militia, 53; poets and
writers, 188; in political protests, 112;
as radicals, 123; in the rural landscape,
integration of, 222; as signifiers of an
immigrant invasion, 218; solidarity
with, 145; subversion by, 133n; troops, 52;
writers, 187, 190
Black political movements, 68
Black Power, 69, 70, 230; activists, 12; movement, 14, 68, 69, 87
Black Progressives, 106
Black Prussians, 142
black race, 37, 119, 132, 170, 173
Black Student Unions, 69
Bolívar, Símon, 50, 51, 56
border, physical, 217
Bordier, Arthur, 39
Botha, Pieter Willem, 215
Bourdieu, Pierre, 3, 42
Boyce, Sonia, 209, 214
Branco, Humberto Castelo, 169, 174
Brazil: African-influenced culture and
religion, 171, 172; black movement in,
167, 177, 183; constitution, 54; empire, 51;
independence, 51; intellectual, 56; mesti-
zos and mulattos, 10, 47, 53, 58; myth of
independence, 60n; national literature,
51; post-independent, 55; subliterature, 51
Brazilian Constituent Assembly, 54
Breton Woods, 81
Briggs, Cyril, 126
Britain: art history, 222; artists, 209; British-
ness, 212, 213, 223n; nationalism, 218
British Black Arts Movement, 6, 14
British Commonwealth, 106, 193
British Empire, 212, 213, 219

www.ingramcontent.com/pod-product-compliance
Lightning Source LLC
Chambersburg PA
CBHW031414270326
41929CB00010BA/1457